George H. Napheys

The transmission of life

counsels on the nature and hygiene of the masculine function

George H. Napheys

The transmission of life
counsels on the nature and hygiene of the masculine function

ISBN/EAN: 9783742815859

Manufactured in Europe, USA, Canada, Australia, Japa

Cover: Foto ©Thomas Meinert / pixelio.de

Manufactured and distributed by brebook publishing software
(www.brebook.com)

George H. Napheys

The transmission of life

PREFACE.

THE opportunities afforded by a professional practice in a large city, as well as information derived from many parents and educators, have led the author of this work to believe that a great amount of suffering and crime would be avoided, did young men and those who have the charge of youth more clearly understand the nature and hygiene of the function of their sex.

It is in this department of medicine more than in any other that the unscrupulous charlatan finds a congenial field, because here he is favored by the general ignorance and the natural diffidence of his victims. Absurd and exaggerated statements have been forcibly thrust upon the public, not to allay, but to excite groundless fears. These it has been the author's aim to dispel.

On the other hand, real and serious evils result both to the individual and the community from a violation of the laws of this as of any other function. They have repeatedly been adverted to by physicians and educators, but, out of a mistaken delicacy, so vaguely that the intended warnings have been of little avail. The author, therefore, has endeavored to write in terms that cannot be misunderstood, and yet that shall not offend by want of refinement. ·

Fearing that he might not have accomplished this difficult task, he has submitted the advance sheets of the work to the Rev. John Todd, D. D., the eminent author of "The Student's Manual," the "Index Rerum," and other highly prized works for students; and to other distinguished educators. Their commendations have encouraged him to believe that his efforts have been successful, and that they will prove of real value to those for whom this book is designed.

CONTENTS.

(9)

PART II.—THE CELIBATE LIFE.

PART III.—THE MARRIED LIFE.

PART IV.—NERVOUS DISORDERS ORIGINATING IN THE MALE GENERATIVE SYSTEM.

CONTENTS.

THE TRANSMISSION OF LIFE.

INTRODUCTORY.

It is time that science, renouncing a reticence which long experience has proved pernicious, should explain and apply to the public good the hygienic laws which pertain to that instinct which, beyond all others, controls the destinies of men for good or for evil; we mean the instinct of procreation, the faculty of the *transmission of life*. The physiological importance of this function alone would justify this. The unborn generations to all time are in great part moulded by ourselves, and receive from us, their progenitors, the imprints which consign them to happiness or misery, health or disease. Add to this consideration the fact that the purest joys of life, those which centre around the family circle, and also the most flagrant stains on our civilization, those which parade our streets in shameless attire, and those which poison the purity of youth with vicious narrative, alike spring from the same impulse; and there is reason enough to convince the most incredulous that this is no subject to be timorously shunned. Even yet, the half is hardly told. More vital, more immediately concerning each man, are the consequences

2 (13)

to the individual of the intelligent observation or the ignorant violation of the laws of this instinct.

No one whose avocation does not lead him within the most
secret chambers of the human heart can conceive one tithe
of the anguish which arises from a want of knowledge on
this subject. For with this want of knowledge is associated
want of power to resist the evil and to cleave to the good.

Regarding it in its multiplied and intimate relations to the
life of man here and hereafter, we do not hesitate to say that
no branch of sanitary science surpasses this in importance,
and we may also add no branch has been so much neglected
and so much misunderstood.

The matter is of course difficult to treat; it has rarely been
ventured upon except by those who batten on the wretchedness of their fellow-men, and therefore we well know there
may be a prejudice against one who undertakes the task of
discussing it with candor. Only after considerable hesitation have we concluded to encounter this prejudice, trusting
that the manner in which we shall accomplish our labor, the
value of the counsels we have to communicate, and the solid
information we hope to convey, will not leave any doubt
either as to our motives, or as to the propriety of our course.

We could adduce abundance of testimony from the writings of those most interested in the amelioration of the race,
and its progress in moral and social directions, to show the
necessity long felt of a work of this nature. But we believe
no person of intelligence can harbor a doubt upon this point,
and it only remains for us to submit to them the present treatise, and ask for it an unprejudiced examination.

PART I.

THE NATURAL HISTORY OF MANHOOD.

THE PHYSICAL TRAITS OF THE MALE.

THE distinction of sex is no after-thought, no hap-hazard accident in the formation of the individual, but commences with the very beginning of life. "Male and female *created* He them," says the inspired Word, and the patient investigator with microscope and scalpel fails to discover any other cause of sex than the imprint fixed by the Creator upon the individual at the moment of conception. There is nothing in the development of the human germ which decides whether it shall be male or female.

As it is the earliest, so sex is also the most potent of all elements in the individual life. From infancy to age it controls and modifies all other traits. Does any one imagine that boys and girls are at any time physically alike? Error; no matter how tender in years, the distinctions are numerous and marked. Even at birth itself, this is true. Physicians have carefully weighed and measured hundreds of new-born infants, and have established the following curious and interesting facts: Male children at birth weigh on an average one pound more than females, their stature is four-tenths

(15)

of an inch greater, their pulse is a few beats in the minute faster.

As the boy grows, he develops unlike his sister. His muscular force becomes one-third greater than hers; his flesh is firmer and his bones larger; his collar-bone becomes more curved so that he can hurl a stone or swing a club better than she can; his hips are narrow; while hers are broad, and thus he can run faster and more gracefully; he grows more rapidly, and he seeks the rude exercises which she shuns. All these traits presage his destiny to wage the rougher battles of life, and fit him to meet the buffets of untoward fortune with courage and endurance.

Some figures may here be found of interest. The French statistician Quetelet, who has devoted more attention to this subject than any other writer, gives the average weight of an adult male at one hundred and thirty-seven pounds, and the average height at five feet four inches. In England, the gentleman who has charge of the University Gymnasium at Oxford reports, that of the first one hundred young men whose names were on his book, the average height was a trifle over five feet nine inches, and the average weight one hundred and thirty-three pounds.

With these foreign measurements we can compare those of the students of Harvard University and Amherst College, New England. Dr. Gould, who examined a large number of the former, reports their average height at five feet eight inches, and their weight at one hundred and thirty-nine pounds. From the statistics of all the members of Amherst College, from 1861 to 1869, Dr. Allen found the average weight to be one hundred and thirty-nine pounds, and the average height about five feet eight inches. So that Americans appear to be between the English and French in height, but heavier than either in proportion to their stature.

The average height of American women is but five feet four inches, and their weight about ten pounds less in proportion.

A strange contradiction meets us here—a problem which science has not yet solved. It would naturally be supposed that with this more vigorous frame, and sturdier form, the vitality of the male would be greater than the female, his average life longer, his greatest age greater. It is not so. This law of population holds good in every country of which we have any statistics : About five per cent. more male than female children are born, but at five years of age more girls are alive than boys. Again, at every period of life, the "expectation of life," as insurance agents call it, that is, the average term yet to live, is greater in women than men. And, finally, of very old persons, the large majority are women. So true is this that the last census of France shows that at the age of ninety years there were three women to two men, and at the age of one hundred the number of women was more than *sixteen* times the number of men!

The characteristics of infancy, such as the delicate skin, the fragile bones, the rounded outline, the abundance of fatty tissue, are preserved in the female more generally than the male sex. It is far more accurate to say the child is mother to the woman than father to the man.

Man's Specific Function.

All these deep-seated differences, the whole great fact of sexuality with its infinite bearings on the social, the physical, and the moral life of man, look to the accomplishment of one purpose, to the performance of one function. That purpose, that function, is the *reproduction of the species*, the TRANS-MISSION OF LIFE. Around this central, mysterious power are grouped all other faculties and aspirations. It is the strongest of all instincts, the most uncontrollable of all passions, the most imperious of all demands. Nature everywhere points to it as the most sacred object of the individual's physical existence. The botanist can tell of plants rooted in such exposed and barren soils that no nourishment is afforded for leaves or fronds; but the flower and the seeds mature; the zoologist has strange stories to relate of the males of lower forms of animal life, who, when they have once completed the act of reproduction, straightway wither and die, as if this alone was the purpose of their creation.

The instinct of self-preservation itself in unnumbered instances has disappeared before the tyrannical demands of sexual love. There is an impulse in organic beings which they feel to be of greater moment than all else, weighed against which life itself is a feather in the balance, the scope of which is not bounded by the confines of the individual, but stretches into eternity and to the limits of all things. This impulse is the perpetuation of their kind—once more THE TRANSMISSION OF LIFE. It is something apart from all else in nature. Contemplating it with the inspired eye of genius, Bichat, the profoundest of modern physiologists, speaks of it as a phenomenon which science must study by itself, unconnected with the other functions of the individual. Regarding it with the practical observation of a man of the world, an eminent New York surgeon writes : "The strongest motive of human action, the most powerful mainspring within us all, is the sexual desire, with the domestic relations which rest upon it. It is stronger in its influence, controls more men, causes the commission of more crimes and more good deeds, than any other impulse." How vitally important is it, therefore, how intimately does it concern the weal of our nation, to understand its nature and its laws, its government, its dangers, its regulation! In what direction can we with greater propriety extend the domain of hygiene?

PUBERTY.

What it is.

At a certain period in the life of the youth he undergoes a change by which he acquires powers, which qualify him to take part in the perpetuation of his kind. This change is the period of PUBERTY. It is distinguished by a number of physical alterations, the most significant of which is the secretion of a fecundating fluid.

Yet we must not be understood to say that this is a prompt or sudden change. On the contrary, it is slow, extending over many years, attended by a completion of growth and a ripening of all the physical powers. Only when all these various processes are matured does the male reach the period of *virility*, that period which is the proper time for him to fulfil the duties which nature has imposed on those features peculiar to his sex. We cannot too earnestly impress on all the truth of this fact. Through ignorance of it, or neglect of it, untold misery is constantly brought upon the young, and the race itself shows the sad results of an infraction of this rule. Let us therefore define more minutely these two phases of life.

When the boy passes to the condition of youth he leaves behind him the characteristics of childhood. The skin becomes coarser and less delicate, the muscles firmer and more distinctly marked, the voice loses its childish treble, the vocal apparatus enlarges and emits a harsher sound, the bones

(19)

harden, the "wisdom teeth" appear, various parts of the body become covered with a soft down which gradually becomes rougher and thicker, and those organs peculiar to his sex enlarge.

Not less remarkable are the mental changes. Unwonted desires and sensations, half understood and confusing, awake in the mind impulses to which he has been a stranger, vague longings after he knows not what, sudden accesses of shamefacedness in circumstances where he had ever been at ease, a restlessness, and a wilfulness, indicate to the observing eye the revolution which is going on within. Perilous moment for the boy! Dangers of which he has no knowledge, which he could not understand were they explained to him, yet which will imperil all his future life and all his other faculties, are around him.

The proper age at which puberty should come varies from twelve to eighteen years, as it is influenced by many surrounding conditions. One of the most important of these is *climate.* Travelers have frequently observed that in tropical countries both the sexes arrive at maturity earlier in life than in temperate or cold countries. This explains the early marriages which are customary in those localities, and which do not appear to exert the injurious influence on the offspring which is almost constantly observed in temperate climates from premature unions. In Abyssinia and the shores of the Red Sea, which are the hottest parts of the globe, it is no unusual sight to see boys of fifteen and sixteen who are already fathers. And what is even more singular, this precocity does not appear to react on the constitution, but according to the observations of an English surgeon during the Abyssinian campaign, the masculine functions are retained with exceptional vigor to very advanced years.

In Lapland, Northern Russia, and Siberia the young men

reach the age of eighteen and nineteen years, before their sluggish constitutions undergo the changes incident to puberty, and even then it is rare that their passions are violent or long retained.

In our own country, the usual and healthy age of puberty is from fourteen to fifteen years, varying a year or two more or less as influenced by circumstances which we shall proceed to mention. One of these is *hereditary tendency.* This is constantly observed as hastening or retarding by a year or two the development of both sexes. It is to some extent connected with race, as it is found that negroes are more precocious than whites, and boys of southern parentage than those of northern. This is readily seen to be traceable to the influence of climate just referred to.

The *temperament* is also a controlling influence. Light-haired, stout, phlegmatic boys are longer in attaining the age of puberty, than those of nervous and nervo-bilious temperaments.

Occupation and *habits* have also much to do in the matter. As a general rule, the more vigorous, the more addicted to athletic exercise, the more accustomed to out-door life, and to active pursuits, the slower will be this change in approaching. This statement may be unexpected to many; they may think that vigorous health is precisely what nature would wish to assist her to complete this profound and mysterious transformation in the constitution. To all such we have to tell of a law sanctioned by the researches of all physiologists, proven by the daily experience of the physician, and which we shall have occasion hereafter to refer to frequently, for it contains the solution of many a vexed physical and social problem. This law teaches that there is a constant and a direct antagonism between the highest perfection of the individual and the exercise of the masculine function;

or, to quote the words of one of the most eminent writers on physiology, Dr. Carpenter, "The Development of the Individual and the Reproduction of the Species stand in an inverse ratio to each other."

The *constitution*, by which we mean the mass of morbid or healthy tendencies inherited from parents, consequently has very considerable weight in determining the time at which the change will take place. In accordance with the physiological law just quoted, it is very generally found that boys with weak, nervous, debilitated constitutions are apt to be precocious; and those gifted by their parents with sturdy limbs and a powerful frame remain boys much longer.

The Hygiene of Puberty.

Let it be distinctly understood, therefore, that it is altogether advisable, and the only consistent hygienic course, to defer as long as possible the development of the sexual instinct. It will surely come soon enough, and the danger only is that it will come too soon.

There are, indeed, instances of precocity, apparently without entailing debility or disease, which are not readily explained. Several cases are on record in medical works, where children at the age of three and four years manifested a complete development of sexual power. But apart from the liability to error which rests over these observations, such exceptional instances must be classed with what medical writers term idiosyncrasies, and no inferences for general guidance can be drawn from them.

Apart from moral reasons which urge the retardation of the sexual change, there are sanitary arguments of the weightiest character which tend in the same direction. Foremost of these is the danger of solitary vice, and of illicit pleasures, with their so frequent and terrible penalties. Tho less, indeed, that the boy and the youth think about, or in any way have their attention directed to the sexual distinctions, the better. Does it follow from this that it is the duty of parents and teachers sedulously and wholly to refrain from warning them, or giving instructions of a private nature? This important question has been frequently discussed, and there are now, as there always have been, men of influence who answer it in the affirmative. But it is also worth remarking that without an exception those medical authors who have given most constant and earnest attention to the diseases and disorders which arise from the prevailing ignorance in such matters, are earnest and emphatic in their recommendations to educators and to parents to give sound advice to boys, and to urge upon them the observance of certain precautions, which tend to remove premature excitements.

It is one of the most important duties of those who have charge of youths to see that neither by ignorance nor urged by opportunity or intellectual stimulants, they forestall nature's own good time. Most inexcusable is the false modesty which, on the ground of fear lest indecorous thoughts should be awakened, serves as the plea for wholly neglecting this vital department of sanitary supervision. Not unfrequently some physical ailment, some local irritation leads to an afflux of blood to the parts, which prompts the boy to thoughts and deeds far more blameworthy than any to which he could be led by grave and serious admonition.

We will briefly rehearse what sanitary regulations should be instituted in schools and in private families to prevent unnatural precocity, and to avoid the necessity of repetition hereafter, we add that these same regulations, altered more or less to suit circumstances, are of the utmost value after puberty is established, to escape unnecessary sexual excitement, and to aid in the treatment of diseases which arise, or are associated with irritability of this function. We shall on a later page refer to them in these connections.

The most potent of all means to this end is *muscular development*. Systematic, daily, regulated exercise, pushed to the verge of fatigue, and varied so as to keep up the interest of the pupil, cannot be too much insisted upon. This alone is worth all other precautions, and is almost indispensable. Now that most large schools have gymnasiums attached, and especially as light gymnastics have been so widely introduced, and can be put in practice at such small expense, there is no excuse for neglecting this precept. Parents will do well to decline sending their boys to any institution which has no provisions for physical culture.

Cleanliness is next to be mentioned. It were an excellent arrangement for every boy to be induced to take a sponge-bath, or, what is better, a shower-bath, every morning, in cool or cold water. They should be told that a sense of heat or irritation about their parts may arise from a want of thorough cleansing. One of the most distinguished authorities on these subjects, Mr. William Acton, of London, says: "My own opinion is that a long prepuce in children is a much more frequent cause of evil habits than parents or medical men have any idea of. But I have never heard of any steps ever having been taken by those having the care of youth to induce boys to adopt proper habits of cleanliness in this respect. Probably no nurse, parent, or schoolmaster, would at first relish the proposal that a boy of twelve should be told to draw back his foreskin and cleanse the part thoroughly. In my own experience of children I have found this practice so beneficial that I never hesitate to recommend it in any cases where there is the least sign of irritation from this cause."

"One of the common causes of premature excitement, even as early as infancy," says Mr. W. F. Teevan, a writer in a recent number of the *British Medical Journal* (May, 1870), "is a tight foreskin. It is a cause of much evil, and it ought always to be remedied." This can generally be accomplished by giving a boy proper directions, but, if not, there should be no hesitation in recommending a surgical operation. The rite of circumcision is in this respect extremely salutary, and some physicians have recommended its general adoption, no longer on religious but on hygienic grounds. At any rate the above advice from so eminent a quarter is deserving the highest respect, and may, with proper caution, be carried out where the observant guardian considers it applicable.

Avoidance of *irritation* from any cause is always essential. It may arise from ill-fitting drawers or pants, or from an uncomfortable seat, or from constipation of the bowels, or from an unhealthy condition of the urine or bladder, from piles, and much more frequently from worms, especially those familiarly known as seat-worms. Soft cushions should be dispensed with; cane-bottomed chairs and benches are for many reasons preferable. Certain varieties of skin diseases of a chronic character are attended by such a degree of heat and itching that the child is led involuntarily to scratch and rub the affected part. Whenever they attack the inside of the thighs or lower part of the abdomen, they should receive prompt and efficient treatment.

The *dormitory* regulations should invariably be of a character to promote modesty. Never should two or three boys be allowed to sleep in the same bed, and it were more prudent to assign each a separate chamber. They should be encouraged by precept and example to avoid needless exposure of the person and indecorous gestures. The beds should be tolerably hard, mattresses of hair or with springs

3

being greatly preferable to those of feathers, cotton, or sponge. These latter are heating, and, therefore, objectionable. The bed clothing should be light, thick comfortables being avoided, and the chambers should be cool and well ventilated. Every boy should be required before retiring to empty the bladder, as the presence of much fluid in that organ acts as a source of irritation on the surrounding parts. When a boy wets his bed during sleep, it may be taken as evidence that he either neglects this duty, or else that there is some local irritation present which requires medical attention. Sleeping on the back should be warned against, as this is one of the known causes of nocturnal excitement and emissions.

Fortunately, the prevalence of *flogging* as a punishment is by no means what it once was. We say fortunately, for through ignorance of physiological laws this method of discipline was calculated to stimulate precisely what it was intended to check. It is well known that switching across the seat is one of the most powerful excitants of the reflex nerves of the part, and is resorted to by depraved and worn-out debauchees for that very purpose. How unwise, how reprehensible, therefore, to employ it on the persons of boys, in whom such a stimulant is most dangerous. Readers of French literature may remember an instructive example in the *Confessions* of Jean Jacques Rousseau, where that depraved and eccentric, though gifted man, acknowledges to have rather enjoyed than otherwise the floggings he received when at school.

Equally important as these physical regulations is it that the boy should be assiduously trained to look with disgust and abhorrence on whatever is indecent in word or action. Let him be taught a sense of shame, that modesty is manly and honorable, and that immodesty is base and dishonorable. Establish in a school a high and pure tone of feeling in re-

gard to such matters. It can be accomplished by a skilful
master more easily than one might suppose. Let some of
the older and abler pupils have explained to them its necessity, and the risks and evils of an opposite course, and they
can readily be enlisted on the side of purity and health.

Nor should it be overlooked that the mental food presented
to the boy may serve to evoke dangerous meditations. Many
passages in the classics, many of the fables of mythology,
much of the poetry, and the prose of modern and especially
French writers, contain insinuations and erotic pictures, seductive and hazardous to the eager and impressible mind of boyhood. We have little respect for the man or woman who
"sees obscenity in pure white marble," or who can discern
only vulgarity in the myths of antiquity, or the warm deli-
neations of the poets; but what is meat for the strong man
may be poison to the child.

What is Passion?

All these precautions are to what end? To avoid exciting
the *passion of sex*. It is well to hold this clearly in view;
and it is also well to understand distinctly what this passion
is. Through a want of this understanding, the most extravagant vagaries, the most dreadful asceticism, and the wildest
debauchery, have alike claimed sanction from the holiest of
religions.

Is this passion a fire from heaven, or a subtle flame from
hell? Is this "furious task-master," as Cicero calls it, to
be regarded as an ever-present witness to our fallen nature,
as one of the imperfections inevitably rooted in our bodies by
the disobedience of our first parents? We cannot to such a
degree accuse the benevolence of the Creator; we cannot so

violate the analogy of organic life; we cannot so do in.
justice to our own consciousness.

The noblest and the most unselfish emotions take their rise
in this passion of sex; the most perfect natures are moulded
by its sweet influence; the most elevating ties which bind
humanity to holy effort are formed by it. True, it is like
the genii which obeyed the magic ring in oriental tale; so
long as the owner of the jewel did not violate its law, that
long the genii were his willing slaves, and brought him
wealth and glory; but when he became untrue to himself,
then they rose upon him, and hurried him away defenceless
to the gloomy cavern, and the unquenchable flames. The
wise man, therefore, will recognize in the emotions of youth
a power of good, and a divinely implanted instinct, which
will, if properly trained, form a more symmetrical and perfected being than could possibly be in its absence; and he
will have impressed upon him the responsibility which devolves on those who have to control and guide this instinct.

It is not at the period of puberty that passion commences.
In fact, it is hard to say, how early it may not be present;
and this point we wish to impress the more emphatically,
because parents and teachers, in spite of their own boyish
experiences, if they would but recall them, are too liable to
persuade themselves that at the age of five or ten years no
particular precautions are necessary. But the physician
knows that even in infants it is not very rare to witness excitement of the organs, which must depend on the action of
those nerves which control passion. Self-abuse not uncom-
monly prevails at the ages we have mentioned, and proves
the early development of the instinct. In such cases it is a
purely nervous phenomenon, not associated with the discharge of the secretion, which does not yet exist, nor necessarily with libidinous thoughts. But these, too, come very

soon, as any once must confess who is a close observer of boys; and at whatever age the habit exists, it is equally reprehensible.

The danger that threatens is not to be obviated by a complete repression or an annihilation of this part of our nature as something evil in itself, but by recognizing it as a natural, prominent, and even noble faculty, which does but need intelligent education and direction to become a source of elevated enjoyment and moral improvement.

Should the false modesty, the ignorance, or the neglect of those who have charge of youth at the critical period when the instinct first makes itself felt, leave it to wander astray, it is with the certainty of ensuing mental anguish, physical injury, and moral debasement. To what a hideous depth these aberrations of passion may descend we dare not disclose; for, as the apostle says, "it is a shame even to speak of such things."

Sufficient to say, that every unnatural lust recorded in the mordant satires of Juvenal, the cynical epigrams of Martial, or the licentious stories of Petronius, is practised, not in rare or exceptional cases, but deliberately and habitually in the great cities of our country. Did we choose to draw the veil from those abominable scenes with which our professional life has brought us into contact, we could tell of the vice which called vengeance from heaven on Sodom practised notoriously; we could speak of restaurants frequented by men in women's attire, yielding themselves to indescribable lewdness; we could point out literature so inconceivably devilish as to advocate and extol this utter depravity. But it is enough for us to hint at these abysses of iniquity. We cannot bring ourselves to do more; and we can only hope that the fiery cautery of public denunciation will soon destroy this most malignant of ulcers.

3*

The Man Unsexed.

To illustrate what has just been said, we can draw useful lessons from the condition of those who, through a fiendish ingenuity or some surgical necessity, have been deprived of those parts which are the font of passion; we mean eunuchs. In ancient times, and to this day in Oriental nations, these unfortunates are frequently found; they are usually slaves who have suffered mutilation at a tender age, and are employed to superintend the harems of the wealthy. When they are operated upon before the age of puberty, the changes we have mentioned incident to that period do not take place. The voice retains its childish treble, the limbs their soft and rounded outlines, the neck acquires a feminine fulness, and the beard does not appear.

On account of this retention of the voice, the mutilation was not infrequent in Europe during the middle ages, and indeed in Italy quite down to the close of the last century. The so-called *castratos* were employed to sing in the concerts, and especially in the churches, in whose choirs women were not allowed. There is a bull on record of Pope Clement XIV., especially directed against the practice, and pronouncing the ban of the church on those who encouraged it. This testifies to its wide distribution.

A number of instances are reported where persons had deliberately, either out of fanaticism or laboring under some form of mental delusion, destroyed their own virility. Ecclesiastical historians assert that the distinguished father of the church, Origen, was one example of this. He was led to do so by a too literal application of those enigmatic words reported in the nineteenth chapter of Matthew: "There be eunuchs which have made themselves eunuchs for the kingdom of Heaven's sake."

In most of these instances, and probably in all where the mutilation has been suffered when young, a decided effect on the mental and moral character is observed. Eunuchs are proverbial for their cruel, crafty, unsympathizing dispositions; the mental powers are feeble; and the physical strength is inferior. They lack both courage and endurance, and supply their place with cunning and mercilessness. They prove, indeed, that in their want of that power which connects them with posterity, they have lost something necessary to the development of the best parts of their nature. This should teach us that it is a wise provision which stimulates our duty to the future by the reward of present pleasure.

By this operation the power of sexual intercourse is not altogether lost, but there is entire sterility. The body is much more inclined to become fat, and for this reason the mutilation is practised on fowls to obtain "capons," and other animals used for food.

VIRILITY.

Signs of Established Virility.

WE have intimated that puberty and virility are by no means synonymous terms. The former is a season of change and preparation. The constitution is summoning all its powers to prepare the individual properly to protect and provide for his own wants, and to transmit life to future generations. When the growth is completed, when the beard is grown, and the bones hardened, when the vague and fleeting fancies of youth have been transformed into a well-defined yearning for home and children and a help-meet, then the season of virility has commenced. Then, and not before, is it right for the male to exercise those functions peculiarly his own; and then, only when this is accomplished as a subordinate act, conformed to moral and social law, and necessary to pure mental emotions. At the outset of his career let him learn by heart and frequently repeat these words of a celebrated physician, who spoke from a wide study of man in all his relations: "In proportion as the human being makes the temporary gratification of the mere sexual appetite his chief object, and overlooks the happiness arising from spiritual communion, which is not only purer but more permanent, and of which a renewal may be anticipated in another world—does he degrade himself to a level with the brutes that perish."

(32)

But the distinctive sign of completed manhood is in the character of the secretion which now commences.

It is not our intention to write upon physiology and anatomy. This would be foreign to a work which proposes to confine itself to the realm of hygiene. And we do not look with favor on those books which by their half-disclosures and unsavory hints, awaken a useless curiosity, which they do not intend to satisfy. But it seems necessary to speak here with distinctness of one physiological point, because it is intimately connected with the health of the male, and without some clear comprehension of it, much that we shall have to speak of in the nature of warnings and cautions would be unintelligible. We trust that an honest purpose, and scientific accuracy will guide us correctly.

The secretion peculiar to the male, known as the seed or sperm, depends for its life-transmitting power on the presence of certain minute vibratory bodies, about one-fortieth of a line in length, called spermatozoa. These are exceedingly numerous and active when the secretion is healthy. A single one of them—and there are many hundreds in a drop—is sufficient to bring about conception in the female. They not only have a rapid vibratory motion, but singular vitality. The secreted fluid has been frozen and kept at a temperature of zero for four days, yet when it was thawed these animalcules, as they are supposed to be, were as active as ever. They are not, however, always present, and when present may be of variable activity. In young men, just past puberty, and in aged men, they are often scarce and languid in motion. Occasionally they are entirely absent in otherwise hale men, and this is one of the causes of sterility in the male. Their presence or absence can only be detected by the microscope.

The organs in which this secretion is elaborated from the

blood are the testicles. Previous to birth, these small, rounded, firm bodies are in the abdomen, and only descend a short time before the child is born. They are composed of a vast number of minute tubes united together by connective tissue. The total length of the tubes is estimated at forty-eight hundred feet, or nearly one mile! Nevertheless, so small are they, that their full capacity is not more than six cubic centimetres.

The left testicle, though usually suspended lower than the right, is somewhat smaller, the difference in weight being about ten grains. The secretion is most active about twenty-five years of age, and decreases after this period as age advances. It is, however, not constant, depending very much on physical and moral causes. In some men it is periodical or intermittent, and they are therefore entirely impotent at times, without at all impairing their vigor at other times.

The testicles are subject to special diseases, which may seriously impair their action. Mumps sometimes changes from the face to them, causing painful swelling, and frequently a similar attack occurs in venereal diseases. Inflammation may arise from an injury, and also from violent and ungratified sexual excitement. All these affections may lead to loss of power and sterility, and it does not answer, therefore, to neglect them. Diseases which are not connected with the genital organs do not seem to produce any after-influence on the secretion in the adult in middle life, but in aged persons, on the other hand, this is a frequent occurrence.

A secretion is formed before puberty, but it is always without these vibratory bodies. Only after that period is it formed healthily and regularly by the proper glands. This is usually to such an extent that more or less of it passes from the person once in a while during sleep. Thousands of young men ignorantly attribute this perfectly natural evacuation to some weakness of the function. They are in error. Within certain limits, as we shall fully explain hereafter, this is a natural, healthy, and necessary effort of the system, quite as much so as an evacuation from the bowels or the bladder. It is to our present purpose to say that moderate flows of this nature are a proof of virility, when the secretion thus emitted is of proper character. Observers have noted that that produced soon after puberty is feeble, and generally fruitless, or if capable of fecundating, the child thus produced is weakly, and apt to be exposed to disease.

At the period of virility the desires should not only change in purpose, but they should be less easily excited, more completely under the dominion of reason, more readily subjugated than before. It is a gross and dangerous error to suppose that ardent desires are a sign of vigorous health. This is a delusion which should be destroyed. Those men who have the finest physiques, the most athletic frames, and are in thorough "condition," experience least acutely the spur of desire. The ancients frequently refer to the continence of the athletæ, and the gymnasts of our cities are always temperate in indulgence. On the other hand, it is a nearly constant symptom of certain dangerous diseases that the passions are unusually easily excited. The first stage of pulmonary consumption is frequently thus characterized, while it is notorious that leprosy, certain obstinate skin diseases, and slow poisoning, especially that by diseased rye-flour, morbidly influence the desires to an extent most damaging to the constitution.

Hygiene of Virility.

Those who are already in the enjoyment of good health will need but few instructions to retain their strength at this period of life. They must, however, bear in mind the approach of advancing years, and the facility to disease which ever accompanies declining age. Therefore they must avoid all excesses, restrict the indulgence of desire within moderate bounds, and if unmarried, live lives not only *continent* but *chaste*, avoiding not merely vices which are condemned both by statute and religion, but also all impure thoughts and conversations. For the latter, as we shall have occasion to show more fully hereafter, are enervating to the body as well as demoralizing to the mind. The functions of sex are so intimately allied to the mental condition that the one sympathizes invariably with the other, and what degrades one, with little short of absolute certainty impairs the other.

Then the man at middle life should be aware that to ensure either a respected or a happy old age, he must at least make up his mind to renounce forever the exercise of his sexual powers, and with this in view, he should, as years progress, steadily wean himself more and more from the control of desire, and fix his thoughts on those philanthropic and unselfish projects which add beauty to age, and are the crown to gray hairs. What more nauseous and repulsive object than a libidinous and worn-out old man, heating his diseased imagination with dreams and images which his chilled and impotent body can no longer carry into effect?

But as in the interest of the general health, and also of mental vigor, it is important virile powers be retained to the latest period of which they are capable, as the whole body shares in their strength and sympathizes in their debility, it is the duty of all to observe such precepts as will defer the loss of virility to the most distant days.

In general, in this country, we may assign the period of virility to commence at twenty-five years of age and to draw to a close at forty-five, thus extending over a score of years.

During this period the physical and intellectual activity of most men is at its height. They are capable of their best, and whether in business or in scholarship, usually accomplish the most for which they are spoken of and remembered. The children born to them during this time are more vigorous, and are endowed with more active powers, than those begotten either before or after these limits. From fifteen to twenty-five the organs yield immature and imperfect secretion, later than forty-five the passions grow rarer and briefer, and the individual suffers more acutely from every attempt to increase the species.

There are, however, some striking examples on record showing how a good constitution supported by proper care, can escape the action of this law for many years.

The Latin historian Sallust, relates of Masinissa, king of Numidia, that he married at the age of fourscore and five years, and had a vigorous infant born to him after that time.

Still more remarkable is the instance of a Frenchman named De Longueville, who lived to the age of 110 years. He married his last wife when in his ninety-ninth year, and she bore him a son when he was in his hundred and first year.

The famous Thomas Parr, of Shropshire, England, who lived to the almost unexampled age of one hundred and fifty-two years, married his second wife when above one hundred and twenty years of age. She lived with him twelve years, and although she bore no children, she asserted that during that time he never betrayed any signs of infirmity or age.

But certainly the most astonishing example of prolonged virility was Baravicino de Capellis, a nobleman of Tyrol, who died, aged 104, in 1770. He married in his eighty-fourth year a young and healthy woman, by whom he had eight children! So that it is evident that mere age does not

4

destroy virility, but that it endures with the other bodily powers.

Thus it becomes a matter of no little interest, since we see such vigor is possible, to investigate the means by which it may be obtained. With this in view, we shall proceed to some inquiries concerning

The Decay of Virility.

The age of forty-five years, which we have just stated as the average term at which sexual decadence commences, is very far from a fixed rule. Perhaps in no one cyclical change in life do individuals differ more than in this. In our great cities, where inherited debility is added to a luxurious and dissipated life, it is no unusual thing to find men of forty in whom the procreative faculty is about extinct. While, on the contrary, as we have just seen, instances are not wanting where men have married and had children, undoubtedly their own, at the advanced ages of fourscore, ninety, and even one hundred years.

"It is usually at the age of fifty or sixty," says the eminent French physician, Dr. Parise, in his treatise on old age—putting the change of life in the male at a somewhat later date than seems to us to hold good in this country—"that the generative functions become weakened. It is at this period that a man begins to mark that power decrease, and is apt to do so with a feeling almost akin to indignation. The first step toward feebleness announces to him, beyond all doubt, that he is not the man he was. He may husband his strength, and retard the effect up to a certain point by judicious living, but not avoid it altogether. The law of decrepitude is hard to bear, but it is still a law. The activity of the organs diminishes, their functions abate, they languish, and at length cease entirely. The blood flows thither in smaller quantities. The sensibility becomes blunted, the·parts wrinkle and wither, the power of erection disappears, and the secretion loses its consistence and force."

Generally, and always in the healthy state, step by step with these physical changes the passions likewise lose their force, and change in nature. Love, which in early youth was impetuous and sensual, which in middle life was powerful, but controlled and centred in the family, should at the decline of life be freed from animal propensities, assume a purely moral character, and be directed toward the younger generations, the children and grandchildren, or, when these are not, should find its proper sphere of activity in philanthropic endeavor, and patriotic attachment.

Like the ancient philosopher, the old should be able to recall the memory of departed pleasure without a sigh of vain regret, and they should adapt themselves with determined mind to the altered condition of their physical life. Let them bear in mind the reply of Cicero, who, when asked in old age if he ever indulged in the pleasures of love, replied, "Heaven forbid! I have forsworn it as I would a savage and furious taskmaster." If this prospect seems a cheerless one to the fiery youth or the vigorous adult, let him remember that desire subsides with power, and that it is still within his reach by the observance of wise precautions and a proper rule of life, to extend the period of virility considerably beyond the limit we have set to it. How this is to be done we shall presently reveal.

Whenever old age is tormented by passions which either cannot be gratified, or gratified only at the expense of health, one of two causes is at work. Either there is some local irritation from a diseased condition of the bladder or

adjacent parts of the nervous system, or else it is a sting
which previous libidinous excesses either in thought or act
have left behind. For,

> "The gods are just, and of our pleasant vices,
> Make instruments to scourge us."

In the latter case the priest, rather than the physician, is .
their proper attendant. He will tell them, as Othello told
Desdemona, that they require

> "A sequester from liberty, fasting, and prayer,
> Much castigation, exercise devout.'

But if, on the other hand—and this is much more frequently the case—these passions are excited by local or
general irritation, then the physician and the surgeon must
be consulted. Some writers call the period of decadence
"the change of life in man," and aver that it is attended
with almost as many diseases and dangers as the corresponding epoch in the physical life of woman.

At this period he is most-exposed to those maladies which
have their seat in the bladder and connected portions of the
body. Gravel and stone, difficulty in relieving the organ,
affections of the kidney, and swelling of the glandular structures, make their appearance. So, too, it is about this epoch
that gout, chronic rheumatism, plethora, vertigo, and apoplexy are most frequent. It may, indeed, be doubted if
these various signs of approaching decrepitude are any more
closely connected with the change which takes place in the
sexual organs, than are the grayness and baldness, the dimness of sight, the quavering and broken voice and uncertainty
of muscular movement, which are associated with them. But
certain it is that the association is a most intimate one, and
we are perfectly justified in saying that virility is a test of
the general physical powers, and that if it is preserved in

a healthy and vigorous condition, these signs of advancing age can be long postponed.

This is the chief, and there are many other reasons why a man should so live, and so order his labors, his nourishment, and his pleasures, as to retain to the furthest natural limit the exercise of his specific powers. So intimately are these allied to the well-being of the whole economy, that unless he is guarded and wise in their management, he will undermine his general health, and render vain all other precautions he may take. Therefore it is, that we deem it eminently proper to lay down definite directions how to retain virility.

Causes that hasten the loss of Virility.

He who would secure a green old age must commence his cares when young. Not many men can fritter away a decade or two of years in dissipation and excess, and ever hope to make up their losses by rigid surveillance in later years. "The sins of youth are expiated in age," is a proverb which daily examples illustrate. In proportion as puberty is precocious, will decadence be premature; the excesses of middle life draw heavily on the fortune of later years. "The mill of the gods grinds slow, but it grinds exceedingly fine," and though nature may be a tardy creditor, she is found at last to be an inexorable one. In the strange lines of the eccentric Irish poet, Clarence Mangan, we may say to our young readers:—

> " Guard your fire in youth, O Friends,
> For manhood's is but phosphorus,
> And small luck or grace attends,
> Gay boaters down the Bosphorus."

We enjoin, therefore, strict, absolute, unswerving chastity to the young and the celibate; a judicious marriage at virility; and an avoidance of excess or immoderation after marriage. As years increase, the solicitations of love should be more and more rarely indulged in; and they should at last be wholly avoided when they leave a sensation of prostration, or mental dulness or disturbance. If at any time during middle life or later, absence, or the death of a wife, should enforce a temporary suspension of the masculine powers, the greatest caution should be exercised on resuming their use on return or a second marriage. One of the best authorities, Mr. Acton of London, says on this subject, " Experience has taught me how vastly different is the situation of the class of moderate men, who, having married early, and regularly indulged their passions at longer and longer intervals, seldom come under the medical man's notice, from that of widowers of some years' standing, or men who have, through the demand of public or other duties, been separated from their wives during prolonged periods. When the latter class, after leading lives of chastity, suddenly resume sexual intercourse, they are apt to suffer greatly from generative disorders. The sudden call on the nervous system after years of rest, gives a shock to any constitution, and especially to those who are already somewhat feeble." These ill-consequences result, not from the mere fact of the resumption of marital privileges, but because there is often too great violence done to the constitution by an unrestrained indulgence. In all such instances, the pleasures of the marriage bed should be temperate and guarded.

Diseases which shorten Virility.

Apart from those disorders, such as acute inflammations, cancer, and sloughing ulcers, which actually destroy the organs, there are a number which excite a morbid activity;

prompting to excess or repeated nocturnal flows, resulting in premature decadence. In general terms any disease which unnaturally stimulates the carnal desires has this effect. Some of them we shall mention.

One of the most frequent is piles. These often produce a burning and itching in the vicinity, the blood accumulates in the veins of that region of the body, and acts as a mechanical irritant. For the same reason, any skin disease in that locality leads to friction and heat, which are very apt to evoke lustful thoughts and acts. So familiar even to the more ignorant classes is this, that Goethe makes use of it in the first part of Faust in a conversation between two apprentices: One says :—

> "Nach Burgdorf kommt herauf. Gewiss dort findet ihr
> Die schönsten Mädchen und das beste Bier."

To which his friend replies :—

> "Du überlustiger Gesell,
> Juckt dich zum dritten Mal das Fell?"

Undoubtedly one reason of the proverbial sensuality of the lower classes in warm climates is their want of cleanliness, which leads to various cutaneous diseases, and also to the presence of vermin.

Acidity of the urine, causing a burning sensation as it passes, gravel or stone in the bladder, and organic changes in structure are all likewise liable to impel to dangerous excess.

Diseases of portions of the system quite remote may have similar effects. Several instances are on record where violent debauches ending in debility and death have been discovered to have been prompted by a change in the structure of the brain. Physiologists are well acquainted with the curious fact that if the posterior portion of the brain be in-

jured or diseased, a distressing excitement of the venereal
passions is sometimes brought about, entirely beyond the
control of the patient, and leading him to acts quite contrary
to the habits and the principles of his previous life. This
strange sympathy should lead us to be cautious in pronouncing judgment on those who after a long course of virtue
suddenly give way to temptation. For the secret of their
action may be, and undoubtedly often is, some unrecognized
affection of the brain. Occasionally our daily papers seize
upon some scandalous story in which a minister of the gospel
is represented to have forfeited a character maintained in
purity for many years. Uncharitable comments, not unfrequently aimed at Christianity itself, are often appended to
the narrative. Yet who can tell in how many instances such
falls are owing to an overworked brain finally giving way,
and leading to actions for which the man cannot be held
responsible? Physicians to the insane well know that precisely those who in their sane moments are most pure in life
and thought, are, in accesses of frenzy, liable to break out in
obscene language. Thus Shakspeare, that great master of
the human heart, whose portraitures of insanity are mar-
vellously correct, makes the chaste Ophelia, when her reason
is dethroned, sing libidinous songs, and repeat indecent al-
lusions.

Consumption in its first stage when it is hardly suspected,
and leprosy, as well as scrofulous affections of several kinds,
and disease of the spinal cord, we have already mentioned
as provoking an unnatural, and, under the circumstances,
peculiarly injurious inclination to indulgence.

In all instances of this nature, the patient—for such he
really should consider himself—should have no hesitation in
making his case known to an intelligent medical friend. He
may perhaps, by a few simple and timely remedies, relieve

himself of inopportune emotions, and insure for himself years of strength, where a contrary course will hasten him to his grave.

Effects of Occupations and Exercises.

Very little attention has been paid by previous writers to the effects which the various occupations exert on the maintenance of virility. The importance of this consideration we have just instanced in reference to brain diseases. When mental exertion is so arduous or so long-continued as to lead to some variety of insanity, it is not unfrequently the case that an unnatural sexual excitement accompanies it. Many instances which are supposed to have been induced by solitary vice, in fact have led to and not been caused by this degrading habit.

Many years since, Professor Lallemand, a distinguished physician of Montpelier, remarked that persons accustomed to long-continued exercise on horseback, forfeit their powers early, and are apt to be afflicted with a weakness of the organs, passing sometimes into actual spermatorrhœa.

Those avocations which produce a flow of blood to the lower regions of the body, as by continued walking, or by sitting in cushioned chairs, are also weakening.

So also are those which expose a person for many hours daily to an air impregnated with the odor of tobacco, or the evaporation of spirituous liquors.

Confining occupations are inimical to prolonged virility. A change of climate once every eight or ten years by passing a winter in a southern latitude, is of great benefit to the general health as well as the specific powers. It should be taken whenever possible.

How to retain Virility in Age.

From what has been said, the reader will now be prepared to understand the essential difference which exists between a nervous function, like that concerned in the reproduction of life, and muscular power. This antagonism in their nature exists : by frequent exercise the muscular system *increases* in strength, and *decreases* in irritability; but the nerve force, by repeated calls upon it, *increases* in irritability, but *decreases* in strength. The more frequently sensation is evoked in a nerve, the greater is its sensitiveness and its *debility*. This physiological law, first distinctly enunciated by a celebrated French anatomist, is constantly overlooked. From it we learn that in order to preserve in the greatest vigor and most perfect health any nervous function, our aim should be to excite and stimulate it *as little as possible*. Nowhere does this law find a more striking illustration than in those functions which pertain to sex. And the secret, therefore, of preserving their activity to advanced years, resolves itself into *avoiding all stimulants and excitants*. By this we do not mean either to recommend asceticism, or uniform continence, but to observe temperance and discretion, to limit one's self in the use of those articles of food or drink which by stimulation ultimately debilitate, and to govern one's life by sound laws of health and morals. It is in this sense we shall proceed to speak of a sedative yet fortifying nourishment, as

The Food and Drinks which strengthen Virility.

The influence of animal as opposed to vegetable food upon life and health has often been discussed. All readers are aware that certain theorists maintain that man as a species is a herbivorous or a frugivorous animal, and that he will never attain his natural term of life and exemption from disease until he renounces all flesh-pots whatsoever. With this extreme idea we have nothing in common. But we are nevertheless of opinion that altogether too much meat is consumed by the inhabitants of the United States. In no other country are three meals of meat a day served up, as is frequently the case with us. We believe that except under circumstances where there is arduous muscular exertion, once a day is often enough to consume much animal food.

From ancient times it has been well known that a wholly or chiefly vegetable diet favors the subjugation of the passions, and hence it was recommended to persons of violent desires, and enjoined on celibate orders of priesthood. Particularly those vegetables which contain a large percentage of vegetable fibre and of water, as the cabbage, turnips, beets, melons, and carrots, and those which contain acids and some soporific principle, as sorrel, sour fruits, lettuce, chiccory, endive, and other salads, are reported to have especial virtues in this direction.

A too exclusive use of any such diet would, however, be apt to bring about physical debility, and for that reason it should not be recommended. A moderate quantity of fresh meat should be used daily, and when a choice is given, it should be taken broiled or roasted, as thus prepared it is more readily digested, and preserves the whole system in better health.

Fresh fish, shell-fish, such as oysters, and eggs, have a popular reputation in this respect, which they have obtained simply because they are highly nutritive and readily digestible. It is indeed possible, that the first-mentioned has some peculiar tonic influence, owing to a small portion of phosphorus which it usually contains, that chemical element having a powerful effect in maintaining nervous force. Islanders and sea-coast tribes, subsisting principally on fish, much of it eaten raw, are often reported in books of travel to be unusually salacious.

Those who oppose an animal diet, for a similar reason object to the use of condiments to any great extent. Here they are right. We eat altogether too much highly seasoned food. Our peppers and curries are too stimulating for our good, and we would be in the enjoyment of better health if we were exceedingly sparing in their employment. Like other excitants, taken in quantity, they confer an ephemeral and deceitful energy, certain to be followed sooner or later by a reaction and a corresponding deficiency of power. In Spanish America, where the use of red pepper is carried to an astonishing extent, its injurious effects are often witnessed by the physician. In moderate quantities, however, it cannot be objected to, but rather approved.

In the matter of beverages, the one most to be recommended is chocolate. This is, or should be made from the fruit of the cacao tree, and is closely similar to cacao and broma. A most excellent and nourishing preparation is that known as racahout, a mixture of cacao and starch, flavored with vanilla. Both the cacao and vanilla have long enjoyed a reputation as fortifying the sexual system.. Tea in limited quantities is not to be condemned, but coffee, except in great moderation, should not be indulged in, for reasons we shall presently state.

Passing now to

The Food and Drinks which Weaken Virility,

We sum up in one sentence all the highly-seasoned articles, and too exclusively animal diet, which we spoke of in the last section. The system should neither be enfeebled by insufficient or innutritious food, nor should it be stimulated by artificial means. No other excitants than the natural impulses must be summoned, under penalty of a premature decadence of force. It is obvious, therefore, that any kind of aliment which causes dyspeptic troubles, or brings on constipation or diarrhœa, or irritates the stomach or bowels should be avoided.

In this category we distinctly include most alcoholic beverages. Even the ancients recognized the debilitating effects of intoxicating compounds on the reproductive functions. "Venus drowned in Bacchus" was one of their proverbial expressions; and who is not familiar with the philosophical disquisition on drinking and lechery, which the porter in Macbeth reads to Macduff:—

"Lechery, sir, drinking provokes and unprovokes: it provokes the desire but it takes away the performance; it makes him and it mars him; it sets him on, and it takes him off; it persuades him, and it dishearteus him;" etc. (*Macbeth*, Act. II. Scene III.)

When in Rabelais' romance, Panurge applies to the learned doctor Rondibilis for some means to conquer his passions, the first resource which the erudite counsellor suggests is wine, *Par le vin.* "Because," he goes on to explain, "through intemperance in wine the constitution is chilled, the nervous force is weakened, the male secretion is dissipated, the senses are dulled, the movements are irregular, all of which interfere with the powers of reproduction." Though these are perhaps not authorities acknowledged by the faculty, they are the reports of shrewd observers, and are borne out by daily experience. Drunkards and tipplers suffer early loss of virility, and this is another argument—if any other is needed—in favor of the temperance movement.

5

To the arguments of Rondibilis—which are just as sound now as when Rabelais, himself a famous physician, wrote them three hundred years ago—we may add that modern experiments have proven that distilled spirits very frequently cause a slight inflammation of the stomach and that malt liquors, being prepared in part from an infusion of hops, contain a certain proportion of the principle "lupulin" contained in that plant, which has a specific enervating effect on the masculine functions.

Coffee *in moderation* has rather a tonic than an enervating effect; but *in excess*, it is distinctly proven by repeated instances that it quite prostrates the sexual faculties. Professor Lallemand relates an instance of a young man of thirty, who was appointed professor in a college. In order to qualify himself for his post he studied with great diligence, supporting his powers on eight or ten cups of coffee daily. After a few weeks he was seized with an irritable condition of the bladder, and not long afterwards with entire impotence. Lallemand, to whom he applied, at once stopped the coffee, to which he attributed the whole trouble, and under appropriate treatment the patient recovered. Dr. Albert Müller in a recently published work mentions that in his own experience he has witnessed several most striking instances of a similar character, and lays down the following rule as the result of his studies on this point : " Through a moderate use of coffee, virility can be strengthened ; but through a long and excessive use of it, virility may become diminished, and indeed wholly destroyed." This we can accept as a correct statement of the most recent views of physiologists. Dr. McDougall, of London, says that several of his patients afflicted with spermatorrhœa and generative debility, discovered that tea and coffee always proved hurtful to them.

It may surprise some to have us class *tobacco* among the .

foods ; but we do it in accordance with the prevailing opinions
of scientific men that it acts as a supplemental or accessory
food, hindering destruction though not assisting in repara-
tion.

Its effects on the system have been much mooted ever since
it came into general use in civilized countries, and they are
not yet very clearly made out.   But we do know that on the
whole and in most cases they are injurious, leading surely
sooner or later to chronic nervous and digestive disorders.
Physicians who have had the opportunity of watching opera-
tives in tobacco-factories, have reported that the males frequently suffer from sexual debility, and Lallemand, whom we
have already quoted, relates examples where serious disorders
and loss of functional vigor were consequent on its too free use.
We might naturally expect this to be the case, for the herb
is a powerful narcotic, and no narcotic can be indulged for a
length of time without depressing the system.   The medical
attendants of public schools have observed that in youth the
use of tobacco predisposes to frequent nocturnal emissions,
produced doubtless rather by relaxation than excitement,
and there is no question but that the same effect is apparent
though in a less degree in the adult.   Sound hygiene, therefore, banishes tobacco from the pleasures permitted those
who would retain their virility, or confines them to an indulgence in it even short of moderation.

Drugs which Stimulate Desire.

There are certain substances which act locally on the
membranes and organs associated in the performance of
the masculine function, leading to irritation of the nerves of
the part, to an unnatural excitement, and consequently to
premature exhaustion.   Sometimes these are employed for

some disorder through ignorance, and sometimes they are sought by those who would give a fictitious appearance of strength. to their animal powers, and seek by artificial irritants to restore to the nerves a sensitiveness which they no longer possess. This is a most dangerous and reprehensible habit, and one which from ancient times has been condemned by physicians and lawgivers. Yet it is astonishing that even at this day we see love-powders and philters advertised in the newspapers. In nine out of ten cases these are wholly inert, and in the tenth case they are dangerous, certain to lead to some painful, and perchance fatal malady. Instances of rapid death from their poisonous action are abundant. Phosphorus and cantharides, of which they usually consist, are both perilous drugs to tamper with, and dispensed by ignorant hands are certain to result disastrously. The death of the Latin poet Lucretius, which has been made the subject of a masterly poem by Tennyson, of Lucullus, the famous Roman epicure, and of many others, are currently attributed to this cause. By the Roman laws the manufacture and sale of these dangerous medicaments were prohibited under pain of death, but in spite of stringent enactments, their use was uninterrupted. In this country, the majority of dealers, aware of the serious results which may follow the administration of any active drug, content themselves with dispensing perfectly innocuous powders. One of these informed us that he sold two barrels of pulverized caraway seed under the name of love-powders. This fact illustrates the incredible demand for such philters even in an enlightened, and, on the whole, moral nation.

The *pastilles de serail* and other preparations brought to us from Paris, that "lupanar of Europe," as it has been severely and truly called, under whatever high-sounding and attractive names they may be sold, are equally objectionable.

We have before us the trade-receipts for a number of these preparations, and in every instance where they are anything more than mere highly spiced confectionery, they contain ingredients which cannot be used without incurring liability to serious and perhaps mental diseases. We emphatically warn against their use, as we do against every unnatural excitant of the genital functions.

The prolonged use of *astringents* and *purgatives*, to which many persons accustom themselves on account of some disorder of the stomach, or to remedy some skin affections, is quite apt to incite local irritation, and induce weakness of the sexual life. These agents, indeed, are placed by Dr. Albert Müller in the first rank of those capable of producing debilitating nocturnal losses. Their employment, therefore, especially in schools, and in nervous temperaments, which quickly respond to impressions, should be very limited, or left altogether to the medical attendant.

In some portions of Europe where rye bread is the staple food of the lower classes, no care is taken to sort out the grains of "spurred rye," or ergot, a substance which has a specific effect on the reproductive organs of both sexes. The consequence of this is seen very plainly in the population. Dr. Deslandes, in speaking of the natives of the valley of the Gironde, says : "They present a striking example how violent passions can be associated with weakened frames. Their food is scanty and lacking in nourishing properties, largely composed of rye meal from which the diseased grains have not been separated ; their faces are disfigured, pinched, and pale, and their leanness almost shocking. They present an appearance of complete physical degradation, and yet their passions are precocious, and they yield to them with a real frenzy." These wretched people are also cursed with frequent abortions, the women with womb disease, and both

5*

sexes with a variety of mortification of the extremities, which is known from its cause "ergotic gangrene." Their example proves how essential it is to health and even to morals to have what in many districts is a common article of diet prepared with care, and with a knowledge of sanitary laws.

The freedom with which in some families fly blisters and spirits of turpentine are used in domestic medicine is one of the objections to the habit of attempting to doctor one's self and others without a sufficient acquaintance with drugs. Both these substances have a specific action on the organs of sex and the bladder and kidneys. The first mentioned, cantharides, has a popular reputation as an excitant of the passions, a so-called aphrodisiac. It is not- so in any true sense, as the excitement it causes is not associated with feelings of pleasure, and moreover, its use is certain to be followed by pain and inflammation, and there are not a few examples where speedy death in great agony has supervened.

Drugs which Moderate Desire.

Rabelais' hero, Panurge, in the passage from the celebrated romance, insists on Rondibilis suggesting some other means of controlling his carnal desires than the use of wine. This the obliging doctor willingly does, rehearsing a long list of specifics, such as the *agnus castus*, the "cold seeds," and "hippopotamus skin," as of sovereign virtue in subduing passion. Unfortunately an experience of a few generations has not supported in this instance the erudite doctor's words. There are, indeed, many cases where it is highly desirable to have at our command some such medicaments, which in a sense are aids and allies to the moral nature, if not strengthening good resolutions at any rate weakening evil impulses, which is next best.

We are glad, therefore, that when the articles recommended by the older physicians fell into disfavor, modern observation discovered others with unquestionable powers in this direction. One or two of the ancient remedies have also stood their ground. Among them, the most prominent is *camphor*. This was familiar to the practitioners of the middle ages, and in a famous work on hygiene written about the time of the first crusade by the professors of the school of Salernum, in Italy, and known as the *Regimen Sanitatis*, The Laws of Health, there occurs the following line :—

" Camphora per nares, castrat odore mares ;"

" The smell of camphor makes eunuchs of men."

The most recent authority on this use of camphor is Dr. Albert Müller, whose work was published in 1869. He sums up the evidence by concluding that very small doses, half a grain to a grain, in most instances diminishes the sensibility of the organs of sex, but only for a short time, and not invariably. In some cases, which cannot be distinguished beforehand, even such small amounts produce irritability of the bladder, and therefore should not be used. On the whole, it is not a safe drug for any but a physician to administer.

The active principle of hops, called lupulin, and the pollen of that plant, have a more decided effect than camphor, and are far safer. Beer drinkers—that is, if they drink beer made by the addition of a strong infusion of hops to the malt, as is the case with good English bitter beer—soon experience a sluggishness of feeling, which often passes into indifference.

Saltpetre, or nitrate of potash, enjoys a similar reputation, but acts injuriously on the general health when taken in quantities, and for this reason should be employed with hesitation, if at all, and under advice.

There are several other drugs with the same properties, but

as they can only be used with discretion by those who have made a study of their effects upon the economy, it would neither be advantageous nor prudent to extend the list much further. We shall moreover recur to the topic when we come to treat the means for controlling certain diseased conditions of the function, and shall leave this subject by stating that in our own practice we have witnessed decided and satisfactory results from the administration of bromide of potassium. The peculiar and sometimes alarming effects of this drug on the mental powers, although they are only temporary, yet act as a drawback to its popularization. It is still a question whether permanent weakening of the memory may not be a sequel of its excessive or too long continued use. Like all substances purely medicinal in nature, we advise none to experiment with it, but to take it under the advice of a physician.

Our National Tendency to Premature Loss of Virility.

We quoted, a few pages back, the words of a French writer on old age, who placed the commencement of the period of decadence in man "between fifty and sixty." The gifted Flourens, in his work on human longevity. considers that this is far too early, did man only husband the resources of a naturally good constitution. English writers also do not speak of virile weakness in healthy men under fifty.

If it is true, and it would seem from a number of opinions expressed by medical authors whom we have consulted, that the age of commencing decay in Europe is from "fifty to sixty," then in this country we must, as a nation, be suffering some degeneration in this respect. For it is certain that of a number of elderly men whom we have consulted on this point, the majority confessed to having felt a decided decrease both in desire and sexual vigor as early as forty-five. . We venture the prediction that three out of four of our elderly readers will agree that this coincides with their own experience.

Now it is a serious question in national hygiene why this is so? The statistics of all our oldest settled states show that fewer children are born in marriages between native Americans, than in foreign-born or mixed couples. It looks as if one solution of this startling fact is to be found in the diminished activity of the male. We ourselves have no doubt of it.

The naturalist Buffon, in the last century, maintained that a careful comparison of the animals of the Old and New Worlds had convinced him that those in the latter are, on the whole, smaller, feebler, and shorter lived than those in the former. President Jefferson took some pains, and we believe successfully, in refuting this opinion; but there is really little doubt but that American born males are, as a class, liable to premature decay of the generative functions.

Nor are the causes of this early decrepitude hard to find. They are, as it were, at the ends of our fingers. And we feel in duty bound to speak of them boldly.

One of the most obvious and most undeniable is. the *excessive use of tobacco*. This acts not only on the individual, but on his sons. "In no instance," says Dr. Pidduck, a London surgeon of extensive observation, "is the sin of the father more distinctly visited on the children than in tobacco-using. It produces in the offspring an enervated and unsound constitution, deformities, and often early death." Dr. H. J. McDougall says: "Many inveterate smokers among my professional friends have mentioned to me the diminution of their venereal desires, as one of the effects of tobacco."

Another is, the *abuse of alcoholic beverages.* Not only do these, as we have shown, shorten virility, but they transmit this same tendency to the male descendants. Even when no intemperance can be charged, yet the peculiarly American habit of taking strong liquors on an empty stomach is most destructive to nervous force, and most certain to prevent healthy children.

The hurried meals and consequent dyspepsia, the use of coffee several times a day, the excessive mental strain in American business life, the increased pressure and redoubled anxieties which the desperate competition of our great marts invariably brings with it, and imposes especially on those who have families to provide for, all bring about premature old age, and create a tendency to early debility of all the nervous functions, and with them that of reproduction, which is infallibly handed down to the sons along with the money, houses, and land which a life of labor may have accumulated.

With these facts staring them in the face, it is for our native population to decide whether they will forego somewhat this desperate struggle for wealth and this self-indulgence, and thereby have to bequeath their children that which no money can purchase, and than which no costlier legacy can be left a young man—a sound constitution.

Relations of the Sexual to the other Functions.

In all that we have said before, we aimed to keep constantly in view and to impress upon the reader the intimate association which exists between the specific functions of sex, and the rest of the economy.

How close this is in the female sex is now generally acknowledged, at least by physicians. But even they are apt to overlook the nearness of the genetic power in man to all his other faculties. There is no one function which, if disturbed, leads so rapidly and certainly to general ill-feeling. The mind is sure to brood over it, and depressing melancholy, unfitness for action, and hypochondria will result.

Dyspeptic and nervous diseases without number, general debility, and many forms of insanity are more or less directly developed from some disorder of the reproductive power. Many an obscure complaint, which has led the sufferer from doctor to doctor, and cost him quantities of time, trouble, and money, without any benefit, takes its origin in some mismanagement here, of which, perhaps, in his ignorance or thoughtlessness, he is quite unconcerned.

Among many physicians, an unnecessary fear prevails lest they should offend by suggesting such a cause of disease, or a dread lest they should be thought unduly inquisitive, or a doubt fostered by some few prominent and prejudiced writers, as to whether bad effects really do come from an abuse of the sexual powers.

We can but repeat that every medical man who has given close study to the subject is perfectly convinced that there is a vast body of anguish, mental and bodily, from this source.

[AUTHORS AND WORKS REFERRED TO.—To avoid the nuisance of constant references, we append here a list of the principal authorities quoted: On the distinctions of sex, Waldeyer, *Eierstock und Ei*, p. 152; Fonssagrives, *L'Education Physique des Jeunes Filles*, Chap. I. (Quetelet's statistics); Van Buren, *New York Medical Gazette*, 1869; Bichat, *La Vie et la Mort*, p. 3. On puberty: *British Medical Journal*, Aug. 1868; William Acton, *Functions and Disorders of the Reproductive Organs*, passim; *Journal of Psychological Medicine*, Nos. I. and VI. (aberrations of sexual passion); *Wiener Medicinische Wochenschrift*, Jan. 1869 (review of *Der Urning*). On Virility: *Journal d'Anatomie et*

Physiologie, No. VI. (Prof. Mantegazza's experiments on sperm);
Hufeland, *Art of Prolonging Life*, pp. 94, 104; Flourens, *La
Longevité Humaine;* Reveillé-Parise, *De la Vieillesse;* Debay,
Hygiène et Physiologie de la Mariage, pp. 98, 445, 345 (formu-
laire aphrodisiaque); Becquerel, *Traité d'Hygiène privée et pub-
lique*, pp. 34, 54, 576; Albert Müller, *Ueber Unwillkürliche
Samenverluste*, passim ; Rabelais, *La Vie de Gargantua*, Liv. III.
Cap. XXX.; Dr. Pidduck, *On the Use of Tobacco;* Dr. McDougall,
Notes to Lallemand; the physiological text-books of Carpenter,
Dalton, Marshall, Flint, etc.]

PART II.

THE CELIBATE LIFE.

With the male rests the choice whether or not he shall seek to contract a union with the other sex for the purpose of perpetuating the species. This is a wise, and, indeed, a necessary provision of nature; for man not only is more rapidly exhausted by the exercise of his peculiar functions, but on him rests the responsibility of providing for the family he engenders. He should form no such union lightly, or before he has maturely weighed the arguments for and against it. It is our purpose to assist him here by informing him of the advantages and the disadvantages of both conditions. And first, of—

The Advantages of Celibacy.

Were this world all, and life limited by the existence of the body, the physiologist could recognize no duty more imperative than that to the species, and no demand more important than that to perpetuate its existence. But beyond this frail house of flesh is a life everlasting, and the preparations to fit ourselves worthily to enjoy it rank beyond any others. Therefore it is that the Master whose example is

6 (61)

set before us for constant imitation, while ever referring to marriage as a holy and an honorable rite, himself remained unmarried. And the most gifted of the apostles, when questioned closely on this point by the Corinthian converts, wrote to them this advice:—

"As to the question which you have asked me in your letter, this is my answer: It is good for a man to remain unmarried. * * * In speaking thus, I do not mean to command marriage, but only to permit it. For I would that all men were as 1 am. * * * To the unmarried I say that it would be good for them to remain in the state in which I also am." (1 Corinthians, Conybeare and Howson's translation.)

It is undeniable from this passage that St. Paul believed that a more devoted life—though not necessarily a purer one—could be led by a celibate. There is no doubt of it. The calls of family affairs, the necessity of providing for wife and children, the time expended in the family circle, are all so many distractions which the celibate escapes. Not a few of the men who have distinguished themselves in science and art preferred for this reason to renounce marriage. Sir Isaac Newton, Kant the metaphysician, Alexander von Humboldt the greatest of modern physicists, the statesman Pitt, the sculptor Gibson, the philologist Jacob Grimm, and many others whose names are as familiar as these, owe their celebrity in a measure to the devotion a single life allowed them to apply to their favorite pursuits.

Hence it is that the Roman Catholic Church exacts celibacy of her priests, holding that thereby not only do they learn self-control, but that they can be more free to give themselves exclusively to the welfare of those under their spiritual charge. Lord Bacon urges the same view, saying:

"Certainly the best works and of the greatest merit for the public have proceeded from unmarried or childless men."

Such lofty motives as these, however, have little weight with most men, so we hasten to proceed to one that has, that is—*economy.* It is *cheaper* to live unmarried. The spiritual Michelet in his work on woman queries, or rather flatly denies this. But let him pass for an eccentric Frenchman. An American figures too closely to be persuaded that it costs less to keep two than one. Whether the economy is not misplaced is an inquiry about which we shall have something to say hereafter.

Certain it is that this motive of economy is the chief one for most men deferring or renouncing marriage. It is particularly observable in large cities, where competition in business and expensive establishments go hand in hand. As celibacy for this cause is rarely continence, history shows it associated with a low grade of morals. Marriage had almost disappeared from ancient Rome before its fall, and to this fact a modern historical writer attributes its overthrow, so few native citizens being left to fight its battles. Paris and New York city both exhibit in their population a larger proportion of unmarried men than other cities in their respective countries, and also a more depraved state of society.

In ancient Sparta, and in some other states, laws have been enacted prohibiting celibacy, and several of the United States increase the taxes on single men after a certain age. It is presumed that if they escape so many burdens to which their married associates are condemned, they should at least pay more to support the institutions which protect all.

Love of liberty is often urged as a large item in the credit account of the celibate condition. A man can travel; he can stay at home or go out; he can smoke when he.

pleases an live where he pleases; he asks no one's permission, and is obliged to consult no one's convenience but his own. If not monarch of all he surveys, he is at least autocrat, in his own house, and lord of his own chamber. The yoke of matrimony, *vinculum matrimonii*, as the Roman law aptly called it, does not gall his neck.

All this is true, but is he any the better, even any the happier for it? Does liberty in this plea not mean license? But these are queries he must settle for himself. We cheerfully grant that his points are well taken as questions of fact. It is an old saying that he who takes a wife makes a sacrifice, and he who begets children gives hostages to Fortune. For all this, however, nature provides recompenses.

Proper Reasons for Celibacy.

We believe no modern civilized state has revived the ancient law prohibiting bachelorhood. It has been left, and wisely, to the discretion of the individual himself. For there are very good reasons why some men should avoid the nuptial tie. As a law, both moral and physical, the first indeed which man ever received, and which his inner promptings still enforce with singular vehemence, *crescite et multiplicamini*, "increase and multiply," is universally binding. But exceptional cases arise in which it may well be relaxed. We have referred to some such on the highest of all authorities, the words of Scripture.

Then, too, there is sometimes a duty to support parents, and younger brothers and sisters, which justly excuses a man from contracting any new responsibilities. Some few men are so constituted that they never experience any real deep affection for the other sex. Such do wisely to refrain altogether. An instance was the philosopher Emanuel

Kant; he even went so far as to dislike female society, and avoided it altogether. The essayist Montaigne, though married, avers that he never felt any wish to assume those bonds.

A far more serious question is that which arises in connection with hereditary diseases, or those constitutional complaints contracted during life, which taint the blood, and are transmissible to offspring. These inquiries we shall defer to a later page, premising that under some circumstances, not only do they permit, but most forcibly enjoin at least temporary celibacy.

Physical incapacity has always been allowed to be a just cause for abstaining, and, indeed, in all the States of our Union we believe the divorce laws sanction an immediate divorce when such incapacity is established, and is proven to have been in existence at the time of marriage.

Disappointed affection, whether in consequence of the proverbial inconstancy of woman, or by some casualty of nature, has ever been extolled by persons of sentiment and poetical minds as a praiseworthy argument for renouncing all future alliances. Thus the modern poet of the passions sings in Lockley Hall:—

"Am I mad that I should cherish that which bears but bitter fruit?
I will pluck it from my bosom though my heart be at its root.
Never, though my mortal summers to such length of years shall come,
As tho many wintered crow that leads the clanging rookery home."

And, from a different motive, in the sweet ballad of Edward Gray:—

"Love may come and love may go,
   And fly like a bird from tree to tree ;
But I will love no more, no more,
   Till Ellen Adair come back to me.
Bitterly wept I over the stone :
   Bitterly weeping I turned away :
There lies the body of Ellen Adair !
   And there the heart of Edward Gray !"

It is a touching constancy which thus cherishes the reminiscence of departed attachment, and maintains the image of one love inviolate in the heart. The history of many men of deep sentiment who have never married is probably this. Washington Irving is said to have ever been faithful to the memory of a lady to whom he was engaged when young, and who was suddenly snatched from his side by death.

The devotion to some high purpose, whether it be connected with the love of neighbor, the love of God, or the pursuit of science, is the highest reason for renouncing the pleasures and escaping the annoyances of family life. Examples of this kind compel our admiration, and usually the self-inflicted deprivation ennobles the character, as cheerful renunciation is ever sure to do. A devoted and eminent clergyman, remarkable for the geniality of his disposition, once replied to a friend of ours, who bantered him on his celibacy, that he was already married, that his bride was the church. He who can thus feel all his yearnings satisfied by the duties of his calling does well to abide content therewith. But let no one entertain for a moment the inexcusable doctrine that there is any other code of morals for genius, or for unusual ability, than that laid down in the Bible. There have not been wanting specious writers, who, on this plea, justify, or at least palliate, the immoralities of such men as Goethe, Byron, and Rousseau. When celibacy means anything but chastity, no matter in whom, or what the reason it is assumed, then it is a violation of physical and moral law, than which not one is more blameworthy or fraught with heavier penalties.

Disadvantages of Celibacy.

Let us at this point draw a distinction, and a wide one. Under the term celibates we include all males past the age of puberty who are not married; but it by no means follows that this celibacy means ,continence, and still less chastity. The man is continent who commits neither fornication, nor adultery, nor secret vice; but for all that, his mind may be "foul as hell within," and he may nourish his fancy on vile imaginings. Such a one is not chaste. Only he, pure in thought and in life, who withstands and overcomes the promptings of his carnal nature, deserves this noble epithet; he it is who dwells in the condition of chaste celibacy; and we say it at once, physically speaking, he alone escapes the disadvantages of celibacy, and he escapes them completely. We emphatically condemn, as a most pernicious doctrine, one calculated to work untold evil, and to foster the worst forms of vice, the theory that any injury whatever rises from a chaste celibacy. The organs are not weakened, nor their power lost, nor is there a tendency to spermatorrhœa, nor to congestions, nor to any one of those ills which certain vicious writers, and certain superficial and careless physicians have attributed to this state. No condition of life is more thoroughly consistent with perfect mental and physical vigor than absolute chastity. Those only suffer any ill results from celibacy who are impure in thought or act, and for

them, it is true, nature has devised bitter tortures, and in-
flicts them with pitiless severity.

Looking first at general results, we put the question:
Who live longer, the married or the celibate? The answer
is the same, seek it in the statistics of what country you will.
In France, in England, in Scotland, in the United States,
there are, in proportion to their respective number, more
than *twice* as many married men still living at the age of
seventy, as single (more exactly 26.9 married to 11.7 unmarried, Becquerel). This is alarming odds against the bachelors. Well might the registrar of Scotland say that it
almost means, "Marry or die."

To what are we to attribute this difference?

The causes are not hard to assign. The married man
leads a more regular life, his indulgences are more temperate, rarely excessive, his meals are better served, his wife
nurses him when he is ill, and surrounds him with a thousand tender solicitudes and precautions when he is well.
His mind is employed on his avocation, or on pleasant
thoughts and cares for his home circle. He has no unsatisfied yearnings, and he is not allowed vacant hours to sit in
moody brooding over his future or his present ills. The
sight and conversation of his children renew his own youth,
and the relaxation he finds in joining their joyous sports in-
stils into his frame something of the spirit and vigor of the
boy.

How different the life of the celibate! Engrossed in elaborate and selfish cares for his health, he destroys the precautions of months by the excess of a night. Given to secret
sins, he is exposed to destructive diseases; or else, not
satisfying his propensities legitimately, nor yet controlling
them, he plunges into reckless dissipation and license.
Which class furnishes the most insane? The celibates. In

which is death from delirium tremens more frequent? In the celibates. Who more frequently are suicides? Again the celibates. These are all statistical truths, and they tell their own story.

Looking at these parallel streams in which flow the lives of men, we may apply to them the words of Alfred de Musset's pretty poem:—

> "Il est deux routes dans la vie :
> L'une paisible et fleurie,
> Qui descend sa pente chérie
> Sans se plaindre et sans soupirer.
> L'autre, comme un torrent sans digue,
> Dans une éternelle fatigue,
> Sous les pieds de l'enfant prodigue,
> Roule la pierre d'Ixion."

Whenever through an excitable temperament, a lack of self-government, or long habit, a man feels it impossible for him to live a virtuous life, he exposes himself, if he still shuns marriage, to serious mental and physical disease. Worse than this, he doubly condemns himself in the eyes of the moralist, for he drags others from the path of virtue to share and to minister to his own debasement. "The annals of eternity alone," forcibly remarks the Rev. John Todd, in his *Hints Addressed to the Young Men of the United States*, "can tell the amount of the guilt of the sin of impurity." And, as a physician, we may add those annals alone can reveal the destruction of health and life, the misuse of talents, and the wide-spread physical evils which follow in the same train. We shall proceed to show in detail what these are; but we cannot too often repeat that they are not the consequences of celibacy in itself, but of *unchaste* celibacy. The pure in heart, like Bunyan's pilgrim, passes

these roaring lions and these ravenous fires unscathed, and
the voluptuary alone falls their victim.

It will be seen that these disadvantages attend chiefly
upon those bachelors who lead immoral lives. We need not
conceal from ourselves that the vast majority of them do so.
We are perfectly cognizant of the fact that the vices of
single men support the most flagrant evils of modern society.
Hence the sociologist finds very strong reasons to urge the
policy of all men marrying, and also of marrying as soon as
they attain the age of virility. Regarding the question as a
national one, it were to be hoped that such a regulation could
be put in practice.

[AUTHORS AND WORKS REFERRED TO ON CELIBACY.—Ed. Reich,
Geschichte des ehelichen Lebens, pp. 509, 510 ; Casper, *Med. Sta-
tistik,* Bd. II.; Becquerel, *Traité d'Hygiène privée,* p. 572; W.
Acton, *On the Reproductive Organs,* p. 73, et al. ; *Reports of the
Registrar-General ;* Rev. John Todd, *Hints to the Young Men of
the United States.*]

THE SOLITARY VICE.

WE have just spoken of the peculiar dangers to which the unmarried condition is exposed. Our purpose now is to take these up in detail, and suggest what we can toward their prevention and cure.

The first we shall speak of is one which is much more frequent before the age of virility, and even before puberty than later in life; we mean self-abuse. It is the danger to which, of the various abuses of the masculine function, boys are peculiarly liable. But it is not confined to them. We had a patient at one time under our charge in a public institution, who, although sixty years of age, was a slave to this detestable practice; and instances of men over thirty who carry it on in spite of warning, are not very rare.

There is hardly any part of our subject which is more difficult to treat than this, and yet there is none which demands more urgently plain speaking, and emphatic language. There have been, unfortunately, many wretched books put forth upon this topic filled with overdrawn pictures of its result, and written merely for the purpose of drawing the unwary into the nets of unscrupulous charlatans. There is also a wide diversity of opinion among skilful physicians themselves as to its consequences. Some treat the whole matter lightly, saying, that a large proportion of boys and young men abuse themselves thus without serious or lasting

(71)

injury, and hold, therefore, that any special warning is un-
called for. On the other hand, the large majority of practitioners are convinced that not only occasionally, but frequently, the results are disastrous in the extreme. "I could
speak," says that excellent authority, Mr. Acton, " of the
many wrecks of high intellectual attainments, and the foul
blot which has been made on the virgin page of youth, of
shocks from which the youth's system will never, in my
opinion, be able to rally, of maladies engendered which no
after course of treatment can altogether cure, as the consequences of this habit."

"I would not exaggerate this matter," says Dr. Horatio
R. Storer, of Boston, " or imply that those who have occasionally gone astray are necessarily incurably diseased, or
their souls irretrievably lost. But I do consider that the
effect upon the constitution is detrimental in the extreme."
Elsewhere he says : "Enfeebling to the body, enfeebling to
the mind, the incarnation of selfishness, hardly the person
exists who does not know from experience or from observation, its blighting effects."

In like manner the late Professor John Ware, of Massachusetts, says in a little work intended for popular instruction: " The deleterious, the sometimes appalling consequences
of this vice upon the health, the constitution, the mind itself,
are some of the common matters of medical observation.
The victims of it should know what these consequences are ;
for to be acquainted with the tremendous evils it entails may
assist them in the work of resistance." " Nothing is more
certain," writes Dr. Maudsley, " than that continued self-
abuse will produce an enervation of nervous element, which,
if the exhausting vice be continued, passes into degeneration
and actual destruction thereof."

" I myself," says the Rev. John Todd in his *Student's*

Manual, " have seen many young men drop into premature graves from this cause alone." The venerable Dr. Hufeland, in his *Art of Prolonging Life,* says : " I consider this one of the most certain means which shorten and derange life," and his words are quoted with approval by Professor Lallemand, of France, and Erasmus Wilson, of England. And we might continue the list of our quotations almost indefinitely, and all of them would be found to speak in the same train.

These are the recent and well-considered views of the ablest men in the profession of medicine. They are borne out by a number of facts in our personal knowledge. And sanctioned and fortified in this manner, we believe it a duty to speak with no uncertain sound, and we believe that our intentions cannot be misconstrued in so doing.

That there are physicians who treat lightly this censurable indulgence is nothing surprising. We could readily quote equally high authority who see no great dangers in the use of alcohol, of opium, and of illicit amours. There are many, say they, who yield to all these temptations, and yet do not obviously suffer, and ultimately reform. Is the counsellor wise who therefore pooh-poohs their perils ? Certainly not ; and for our part, we shall not, cannot, follow their example.

Its Consequences.

And yet it is no part of our purpose to give in this place the long list of symptoms, nor to describe the changes in face, expression, and form which such self-excitation brings about. We have observed that studying and gloating over the appalling catalogue has led in many instances to profound melancholy, and very rarely to reform ; and it has also led to suspicion of innocent persons. The special symptoms

7

are for the medical man to understand, and would only mis-
lead the unprofessional reader. Sufficient to say that the
earliest consequences are a languor, a disinclination to phy,
sical and mental exertion, which are soon followed by an
actual incapacity for such exertion—physical debility united
with mental weakness. Epileptic and apoplectic attacks may
also occur.

An offensive and characteristic selfishness develops in
the character; the thoughts and aspirations seem incapable
of noble flights and philanthropic instincts. The imagination
runs riot in images of debauchery, and the conversation and
reading choose by preference ignoble and vulgar channels.
The whole moral nature is debased to a more than brutal
degradation. Woman has no real charms for the miserable
being who no longer controls his passions. In the stern
words of the Rev. John Todd: "In this life a heavier curse
can hardly hang upon a young man than that of possessing
a polluted imagination. The leprosy fills the whole soul.
Time only increases it, and even the power of the gospel can
seldom do more than restrain without subduing it."

But the most fearful effects are not upon the body but the
mind. We are no alarmists. We do not wish to conjure
up unfounded terrors. But our duty would not be done,
and we would violate our conscience and our professional
knowledge, did we attempt to veil or to palliate the hideous
features of this vice. We distinctly warn that it leads to
insanity, not rarely, but *frequently*.

There is no higher authority on mental disease than Dr.
Henry Maudsley of England; and these are his words : " The
habit of self-abuse notably gives rise to a particular and
disagreeable form of insanity, characterized by intense self-
feeling and conceit, extreme perversion of feeling, and corresponding derangement of thought in the earlier stages; and

later by failure of intelligence, nocturnal hallucinations, and suicidal and homicidal propensities." So prominent and important does this learned alienist esteem this variety of insanity that he has devoted a long article to its description in the *Journal of Mental Science* (July, 1868). Not only is it insidious and frequent; it is incurable, or nearly so. "Once the habit is formed," he says, "and the mind has positively suffered from it, there would be almost as much hope of the Ethiopian changing his skin or the leopard his spots, as of the victim abandoning the vice. The sooner he sinks to his degraded rest the better for himself and the better for the world, which is well rid of him."

We have taken the pains to examine with care the latest reports of a large number of insane asylums in the United States, to ascertain precisely how many of their inmates have been driven there by this vice. The average we have found to be nearly *nine per cent.* of all the males in whom the causes were assigned; and in one prominent institution in Ohio, *fourteen per cent.*

With these fearful figures before us, with these ominous words of distinguished physicians, with the full knowledge that it is *through ignorance* that this vice is commenced and spread, who dares to say that teachers and parents should hold their peace, and suffer the youth of this land to rush unwarned into the jaws of death?

We may be met by the objection that it is quite uncommon. Fathers love to lay the flattering unction to their souls that *their* boy is above such a mean habit; principals express their pride that *their* pupils at least are free from this contamination.

Is it common in the public and private schools of the United States? This inquiry has occupied our serious attention, and as the surest plan of obtaining a correct reply, we have asked the opinion of various physicians who have had the professional care of schools. Their general sentiment is that while there are very few institutions for boys in which the vice is flagrant, or at all universal, there are fewer in which it is unknown. Generally a considerable per cent., perhaps one-fifth or one-sixth of the whole number, are given to it to an extent which is injuring their bodies or minds. The medical attendants say that in most cases they have reason to believe that judiciously and early informing the boys of the dangers of the habit succeeds in either checking it altogether, or so curbing it that the bad results are not directly obvious.

In estimating its frequency we must remember that some boys and young men resist their feelings during their waking hours, but unconsciously violate themselves *during their sleep*. Such cases are peculiarly difficult to treat, as the sufferer may be ignorant of his habit, and often some obscure general prostration is explicable in this way.

Its Prevention.

What we have to say on this subject we address to parents and educators. For on them devolves the serious responsibility of *preventing the formation* of this habit, which, when once firmly fastened on its victims, is as difficult to break as confirmed intemperance or opium eating. It is in childhood, and in early boyhood, that in ninety-nine cases in a hundred it is commenced.

We say in *childhood*, for, as we have said, the sexual passion is not absent even from the immature child. It commences almost with life itself, and so early must also the watchfulness of the parent begin. "There are," says Dr. Maudsley, "frequent manifestations of the instinct of propagation in early life, both in animals and children, without there being any consciousness of the aim or design of the blind impulse. Whoever avers otherwise must have paid very little attention to the gambols of young animals, and must be strangely or hypocritically oblivious to the events of his own early life." It is not at all unfrequent to find patients who date the commencement of their vicious indulgence from five, six, and seven years of age. Dr. Albert Müller gives the history of one who abused himself from his third year to the age of puberty, when he was destroyed by the fatal consequences of his action.

But it is more frequent about the age of puberty, when the passions become stronger, and local irritations of various kinds lead the thoughts and suggest the act. In childhood, degraded companions and vicious domestics instruct in bad practices; at puberty the natural passions often prompt, without the need of bad examples. In both cases an utter *ignorance of danger* is present, and this is the first point that the parent and teacher must make up their minds to face.

They must determine, as they expect to answer for the responsibilities they have assumed, not to blind themselves with the idea that their young charges are too innocent and too pure for such thoughts; they must not deceive themselves in the belief that sound advice here is either dangerous or needless; they must give such advice earnestly, solemnly, clearly. "I have noticed," says Mr. Acton, "that *all* patients who have confessed to me that they have practised this vice, lamented that they were not, when children, made aware of its consequences, and I have been pressed over and over again to urge on parents, guardians, schoolmasters, and others interested in the education of youth, the necessity of giving their charge some warning, some intimation of their danger.

7*

To parents and guardians I offer my earnest advice that
they should by hearty sympathy and frank explanation, aid
their charge in maintaining a pure life."

Dr. H. R. Storer remarks to the same effect : " Children
must be *taught* purity. There is no doubt that in many
of them an improper tone of thought is established even
before the period of puberty. For a boy to reach his teens
without learning from his associates something of these matters is simply impossible."

We urge, therefore, parents and teachers not to permit a
natural, and under other cricumstances very proper delicacy,
to restrain them from their bounden duty to warn their
charges of these dangers. If wisely done, there is no risk
whatever of exciting impure thoughts ; and if there *is* any
risk, it is infinitely less than that of leaving children in
ignorance.

In the first part of this work we have given at length the
hygienic precautions necessary to avoid and diminish sexual
precocity. These should scrupulously be enforced, and will
be found of great value. To none of them do we attribute
greater importance than continued, systematic, gymnastic
exercises. Use of the muscles to the point of fatigue every
day should be an unalterable regulation in schools. Not
only is the general health promoted, and the form perfected,
but the nervous forces are thus centred on providing increased nutrition for the muscular structure, and withdrawn
from the parts essential to propagation. Next to this is the
study of mathematics. This requires such mental application
and fixity of thought, that the passions remain almost wholly
at rest.

The regimen should be plain, and the imagination allowed
to remain in abeyance. Sensational love stories, and even

such warmly colored pictures as are presented in the Arabian nights, and the amorous poets had better be tabooed.

The growing custom of allowing very young people of both sexes to associate at parties, balls, dances, and similar amusements cannot be approved on the score of health. It is nearly certain to favor precocity.

Whether the education of the two sexes in the same institution would have the same effect we do not know. Those who advocate this system assert that it is extremely favorable to the maintenance of a simple and natural relation between the sexes, and consequently to the repression of the vice we are discussing. The experiment is being tried on a large scale in our country, so we may expect definite knowledge ere long. Certain it is that one of the peculiarities of the young man who addicts himself to secret vice is a desire to avoid persons of his own age of the opposite sex. His self-respect is impaired, and though others do not know it, he feels conscious of it himself, and shows it in mixed society. It might, therefore, act as a restraint on his self-degradation to have him frequently in the company of female scholars, just as association with pure and refined women is one of the best safeguards which can be thrown around the adult young man.

Its Cure.

Many a victim with flagging body and enfeebled will is ready to cry out: Who shall deliver me from the body of this death? Let them know for their consolation that very many men, now hale and happy, have met and conquered the tempter; that so long as the mind itself is not actually weakened, there is good hope for them; that the habit once stopped short of this point, the system recovers from its prostration with surprising rapidity; and that we come provided with many aids to strengthen their wavering purpose.

First, and most essential, is the advice that they must resolutely strive for *purity of mind.* All exciting literature, all indecent conversations, all lascivious exhibitions must be totally renounced. Next, all stimulating food and drink, and especially coffee and alcoholic beverages, must be dropped. The mind and body must both be constantly and arduously employed, the diet plain and limited, the sleep never prolonged, the bed hard, the room well ventilated, the covering light, and the habits as much broken into as practicable. Generally the temptation comes at some particular hour, or under some especial and well-known circumstances. At such times extra precautions must be taken to occupy the thoughts with serious subjects, and to destroy the old associations and opportunities. The instructions we have given on the earlier pages of this book for subduing the passions should be read and followed scrupulously.

There are also medical means which can be employed in some cases with good success, such as the administration of substances which destroy desire, and local applications, and even surgical operations which render the action physically impossible, but these means we do not propose to enter into, as they can only be properly applied by the educated physician, and do not form part of a work on hygiene.

As there may be some individuals, however, who cannot overcome the shame they have to reveal their weakness, and others who have no one within reach whom they can consult, we shall insert a few formulas which have the advantage of efficacy, and are not dangerous.

When it is believed that the habit is carried on during sleep, a tablespoonful of the following potion should be taken on retiring :—

Bromide of potash,	one drachm ;
Simple syrup,	one ounce ;
Water,	one ounce.

This is intended to produce sounder sleep, and also to diminish desire. The same effects are produced by the extractive principle of hops, which may be taken in the following form :—

| Elixir of lupulin, | half an ounce ; |
| Camphor water, | one ounce and a half. |

One tablespoonful may be taken at bedtime.

In most cases considerable debility is present, and they will be benefited by taking after each meal a teaspoonful of the following simple tonic :—

Tincture of chloride of iron,	two drachms ;
Sulphate of quinine,	one scruple ;
Syrup of ginger,	a half ounce ;
Water,	two ounces.

The question whether marriage should be advised as a cure for masturbation is one which we are often asked. We are in most cases inclined to reply, no. In the first place, the condition of matrimony is too noble, too holy, to be debased by recommending it for any such purpose. Can the wife wooed and won with any such ignoble object in view ever hope to be loved as a woman and a wife should be loved? It is a base and flagrant outrage on society for the physician to give such recommendation. Would he yield his own daughter to any man who sought her for such a purpose? How then dare he counsel it?

Again, we believe that when the habit is not deeply rooted, an earnest endeavor, backed by rigid observance of the rules we have laid down, will enable a youth to conquer himself and his unnatural desires. But if it *is* deeply rooted?

We quote for our reply the words of Dr. Henry Maudsley, who gives no uncertain counsel : " Certainly marriage need not be recommended to the confirmed masturbator in the hope or expectation of curing him of his vice. He will most likely continue it afterwards, and the circumstances in which he is placed will aggravate the misery and the mischief of it. For natural intercourse he has little power or no desire, and finds no pleasure in it; the indulgence of a depraved appetite has destroyed the natural appetite. Besides, if he be not entirely impotent, what an outlook for any child begotten of such a degenerate stock ! Has a being so degraded any right to curse a child with the inheritance of such a wretched descent ? Far better that the vice and its consequences should die with him."

These are hard words, and we are glad to believe that they are harder than need be. We have certainly known some few instances where after abuse for many years and to an excessive degree, men have married, had healthy children, and been weaned from their unnatural appetite.

We wish most clearly to be understood that even after great excesses of this nature, a young man *may* recover perfect health, and that where the habit has been but moderately fostered, in nearly every case, by simply ceasing from it, and ceasing thinking about it, he *will* do so. Therefore there is no cause for despair or melancholy.

It is hardly credible, and yet it is true, that there are medical men of respectability who do not hesitate to advise illicit intercourse as a remedy for masturbation. In other words, they destroy two souls and bodies, under pretence of saving one ! No man with Christian principle, or even with a due respect for the statutes of the commonwealth, can approve for a moment such a course as this.

Careful regulation of life according to sound hygienic

rules, aided perhaps with appropriate medication which the physician can suggest, will generally effect good results.

When everything else fails we have no hesitation in recommending surgical treatment. This is of various kinds, from repeated blistering to that ancient operation which Latin writers tell us was practised upon the singers of the Roman stage, called infibulation. This is of such a character as to render the act impossible or nearly so. Castration, which some have suggested, need never be resorted to. By one means or another we can say that there are exceedingly few cases, except the actually insane, who cannot be broken of their habit, and considerably or wholly relieved of its after effects.

A serious obstacle in the way of such reform is the unwillingness of sufferers to ask advice for fear of disclosing their weakness. They are ashamed to tell the truth about themselves, and, when they do apply to a physician, conceal the real cause of their debility, and deny it when it is asked. To such we may say that if they cannot have implicit faith in the honor as well as the skill of a medical adviser, they had better not consult him, for on their frankness his success will often depend.

[AUTHORS AND WORKS REFERRED TO ON THIS SUBJECT: Acton, *On the Reproductive Organs*, p. 62; Dr. Horatio R. Storer, *Is it I?* Dr. John Ware, *Hints to Young Men on the Relations of the Sexes;* Tissot, *Sur l'Onanisme;* Rev. John Todd, *The Student's Manual;* Henry Maudsley, *Physiology and Pathology of the Mind,* and *Journal of Mental Science,* July, 1868; Müller, *Ueber Unwillkürliche Samensverluste,* pp. 23–34; Esquirol, *Les Maladies Mentales;* Reports of the Insane Asylum of the U. S. for 1868, 1869, etc.]

SPERMATORRHŒA.

If the functions which connect us with our species are a source of pleasure when properly governed, so they are also the causes of acutest agony when disordered, or even when we only imagine they are so. "It is a weakness of our sex," justly remarks a well-known American surgeon, "to be over-sensitive upon everything which pertains to the generative function. A man will be more alarmed by a trifling ailment there, than if told that he has tubercles in his lungs."

Fully aware of this, and relying on the general ignorance on this subject, the most unblushing misrepresentations have been published by unscrupulous men for the sake of extorting money from terrified dupes. Nowhere do we see the lamentable effects of popular ignorance more sadly displayed than in the groundless alarms which so many young men suffer lest they are afflicted with the disease now very widely known even among unprofessional readers as *spermator-rhœa.* It is our object to do away with these fancied terrors, while at the same time we shall not hesitate to point out where real danger may be.

The long word itself means an involuntary loss of the secretion peculiar to the male. It may occur only in sleep, or else at stool, or when the passions are much excited, or when the parts are accidentally irritated. And at the outset we must correct an extremely prevalent error. We

(84)

have often been consulted by young men who were badly frightened because they had once, or twice, or three times a week, or more rarely, involuntary losses during their sleep, usually associated with vivid, passionate dreams. They feared they were the subject of some terrible disorder; they believed they were losing their virility, and were fast becoming melancholy and debilitated. Their appetites were poor, their rest disturbed, their minds wandering.

Now all these symptoms were purely the results of a distempered fancy. There is *no danger* in such discharges when moderate. They are not a sign of weakness, but of strength. They are natural to every healthy young man, and rarely lead to any bad results. They do not constitute the disease spermatorrhœa, and there is no necessity for a moment's anxiety about them.

Spermatorrhœa itself is a *very rare* disease, although it is undoubtedly a very serious one when it does occur. The patient cannot recognize it for himself, and it is therefore useless and foolish for him to worry his mind about it. If he feels his health running down, and fears this may be the cause, let him frankly state his case to some physician in whom he has confidence, and not worry his own mind about it. It is no disgrace, and nothing to be ashamed of, as it arises nearly as often in perfectly continent as in unchaste men.

The loss of the secretion then takes place more frequently than we have mentioned, without dreams, and on very slight provocation. It is associated with all the symptoms of an enervated nervous system, extending to a loss of memory, of mental power, and even of epilepsy and insanity. The countenance is pale or sallow; the features drawn; the eyes dull; the spirits depressed. Exercise of the functions is impracticable, or nearly so. Profound melancholy, altered

8

sexual feeling—often an aversion to society of either sex—
and impotence, may also present themselves. But here, as
before, we shall avoid any long and terrifying catalogue of
symptoms. When a man feels one-half of the disturbances
of system that spermatorrhœa brings, he should, as we have
said, have medical advice, and the physician already is acquainted with the characters of the disease.

We said a patient cannot decide whether he has this complaint. Every one of its symptoms may be produced by
other affections, and that physical sign which is so particularly terrifying to patients, and which when they see, they
conclude at once that all is over with them, the discharge
of a white glairy fluid, is most deceptive and uncertain.
Many comparatively innocent causes may give rise to just
such discharges. Altered conditions of the kidneys and
bladder, local inflammations, and specific diseases may do so.
Nothing but a careful examination under the microscope
can decide whether or not such a discharge is the seminal
secretion. And if it does exhibit those peculiar appear-
ances—the spermatozoids—which distinguish this fluid, they
may arise from accidental and innocent causes. Finally, if
it is shown beyond a doubt that it is a clear case of spermatorrhœa, unless there are severe general symptoms of depression, there is still nothing at which to be frightened. Men
have lived on for years in perfect health with daily losses of
the kind. Professor Niemeyer, relates that he knew personally a conductor on a railroad, who, for at least ten years, lost
a considerable quantity with every stool, without any observable bad effect on his general health. He was married, and
his wife had several healthy children. The British surgeon,
Mr. W.F. Teevan, expresses his opinion that a habitual escape
of semen when straining at stool "occurs to most men during
some period of their lives without producing bad results."

This illustrates how grossly those swindlers impose upon the public, who would make the ignorant believe that any loss of the kind is attended with disastrous effects. Our advice is, Do not fret about yourself, and keep your thoughts and actions pure, and you will not suffer.

But while we say all this, and say it most emphatically, our duty would be but half done did we not warn in equally clear language against the evils which lead to the real disease. Though it is rare, it is, when present, most destructive to happiness and to health, and, what is more to our purpose, it is *always preventable*. We shall speak, therefore, of

What brings it about?

Undoubtedly in most instances this is self-abuse. It is another of the bitter penalties which nature has attached to this unnatural crime. What is more, these cases are the most hopeless, simply because the victims cannot break the fatal chains which bind them. The tongues of men or angels, the solemn warning of the gospel itself, are unavailing. The only choice that is left is death not very remote, or a surgical operation which absolutely prevents them handling the parts. This last resort has succeeded when everything else has failed. But such is the state of mind of most victims that they cannot nerve themselves to submitting to it.

A second cause is excess in indulgence. This may be in the marital relation, but far more frequently it occurs in the unmarried who are more apt to indemnify themselves for long self-government by renouncing all restraint when opportunity offers. Not a few wretched old bachelors wreck themselves in this manner. This class, too, are particularly exposed to another cause which leads to the same result—secret diseases. The after-consequences of these when neglected or ill-treated, often enough produce a weakening of the part, and a loss of power to retain the secretion. So, too, the indulgence in impure imaginings, and allowing the passions to become frequently excited, surely bring about a similar debility with a like tendency.

All these are causes which imply a degraded mind and disgraceful habits. But it must be understood that this disorder may arise where no blame whatever attaches to the individual. The change in the urine which takes place when the substance termed oxalic acid is secreted in large quantities renders the fluid irritating, and may lead to spermatorrhœa. So unquestionably may stone in the bladder, ulcers and worms in the lower bowel, and some local inflammations arising from colds. Prolonged diarrhœa, neglect of cleanliness, certain skin diseases, the inordinate use of coffee, alcohol, or tobacco, excessive mental application to the neglect of exercise, and a hereditary predisposition, may all or any of them lead to the same result, without the individual being the least in fault. The judicious physician always bears this in mind, and we mention it, so that no unfounded fear lest he should be suspected or convicted of debasing practices may restrain the young man who fears he is suffering from this much-dreaded complaint from candidly laying bare his anxieties to his medical counsellor.

And if it be these habits which are the source of his suffering, he should have no hesitation in making a frank statement, for the physician's office is as inviolable as the confessional, and he knows too well that ignorance is at the source of this habit, to condemn or despise one who is or has been under its fell sway.

How to prevent it.

The suggestions we have to offer here are rendered almost unnecessary by what we have said of its causes. Many of them—all of them, indeed, except the hereditary predisposition—are within the power of the individual to avoid, if he only knows enough to begin in time. The instructions we have previously given in detail about the general hygiene of the passions will apply to those who are threatened by weakness in consequence of excesses, either social or solitary. When the water or adjacent irritations are to blame, these can promptly be remedied by any intelligent physician ; and when the habits of food or drink are injurious they must be amended.

Even when there is a natural weakness which leads to over frequent losses, very much can be accomplished by cold bathing, regular exercise, an unstimulating diet, and rigid purity. It is safe to say that this is one of those diseases which never occurs in a person who submits his life to thorough hygienic regulations ; and it is, therefore, a disease which we hope soon to see almost unknown to the young men of our day.

How to cure it.

Although this is the physician's business and not the patient's, and although it is no part of our plan to instruct or to advise the sick to heal themselves, there are some remarks we have to make under this head, which if borne in mind and observed, will very materially assist the doctor, and aid those who cannot obtain the services of one. There is hardly any complaint in which treatment will be less satisfactory, unless the patient co-operates with his adviser. He *must*

8*

renounce injurious and irregular habits, shun evil companions, keep watch and ward over his emotions, avoid as he would the pest all prurient literature, and live a chaste life. If ho will not or cannot do this, he is lost.

Hardly less important is it that he should strive by occupation, innocent recreations, study, and refined society to divert his thoughts from his symptoms. Nine-tenths of the misery which spermatorrhœa brings arises directly or indirectly from mental sources. If it cannot be thrown off it can be dodged, and no effort or expense should be spared to seek genial and proper diversions. Nearly all such patients have a *penchant* for reading semi-medical books, and take a gloomy satisfaction in perusing over and over again the long trains of appalling symptoms which some writers have gathered together as indicative of seminal losses. If such reading strengthened the will to resist temptation, or acted as a salutary warning, we should not say a word against it. But this is conspicuously not the case. It only serves to make them still more hypochondriacal and unnerved. Let it be altogether eschewed.

Of the methods of cure, one has acquired an unfortunate publicity through its ignorant and often injurious employment—this is by cauterization. Many sufferers have had their pains greatly and uselessly increased by its injudicious application, many more have submitted to it when they had no disease at all, and were only hypochondriacal, and tormented by imaginary evils. It is rarely that it need be employed, and should never be thought of for a moment when in the hands of an advertising or itinerant charlatan.

Our most emphatic warning—and we cannot lay too much stress upon it—is to shun irregular empirics and those who advertise themselves as "specialists" in this department. Most scandalous cases of extortion, mal-practice, and black-mail come up before the police courts of our city nearly every year, and show most plainly how these insatiable leeches cajole and frighten their victims to the last degree, and for all their money furnish no sort of relief. Let the sufferer appeal to some regular physician of good repute, and preferably, one whom he personally knows, rather than run any such risks.

When the seminal losses occur during sleep, they can generally be checked by taking the following prescription after each meal, care being had not to allow it to touch the teeth, which it is apt to injure :—

| Muriated tincture of iron, | twenty drops ; |
| Water, | one tablespoonful. |

A cold bath should be taken just before retiring, the water being poured along the spine from a height, for three to ten minutes. The bladder should be thoroughly emptied, and a position on the back avoided, as this posture allows the urine to accumulate and press upon that portion of the bladder which is most sensitive. It is sometimes necessary when one cannot break himself from assuming such a position during sleep, to wear a plate with a projecting piece, fastened on the back with a strap or belt, or what is equally good, to tie a towel around the body with a hard knot in it just over the spine.

Several means have been devised to prevent erections during sleep, and instrument makers vend for this purpose "spermatorrhœal rings," which have on their inner surface sharp points. These are worn at night, and the pain caused by the points wakes the person as soon as the erection commences.

Such contrivances rarely answer the purpose on account of their inconvenience, and the difficulty of procuring them when wanted. A better and cheaper plan has lately been suggested by Dr. Wood, in the *Canada Medical Journal.* He reports having used successfully in two cases of this kind, one a very desperate and intractable one, in which all other measures had failed, the following simple method: "I took a strip of isinglass adhesive plaster, two inches long by half an inch wide, moistened it, and applied it along the back of the member. It worked like a charm, and the young man has not been troubled since, when the plaster is on. He is now entirely recovered and at work at his trade."

This method will also prove of service in those obstinate cases where self-pollution is carried on during sleep, and at no other time. Mr. Acton relates the case of a young man who could break himself of this only by tying his hands to a cord passed around his neck; and Prof. S. M. Bemiss, of the University of Louisiana, mentions in the *New Orleans Journal of Medicine,* one of his patients, a boy of eighteen, who had brought on epilepsy by nocturnal masturbation, to prevent which they tied his hands and feet nightly to the bed posts.

The French surgeon, M. Doisneau, has recently published a description of an instrument he uses for this purpose, which interrupts the circulation to the genital organs, and thus renders erection impossible. He has used it with signal success in several cases. It consists of a strap passing between the thighs, to which are fastened two tightly-stuffed balls, which compress the arteries leading to the member, and cut off the supply of blood.

This bandage is applied over the shirt upon retiring for the night, and by means of straps we can obtain a compression sufficient to render an erection very rare, if indeed it ever takes place, the circulation being so interrupted that the parts remain benumbed, and as though paralyzed by sleep.

[AUTHORS AND WORKS REFERRED TO IN THIS SECTION: Dr. Van Buren, *Lecture on Spermatorrhœa*, *N. Y. Med. Gazette; Correspondence on Spermatorrhœa, Med. and Surg. Reporter*, May and June, 1870; Prof. Niemeyer, *Text Book of Practical Medicine*. vol. ii. ; Lallemand, *Practical Treatise on Spermatorrhœa ;* Dr. Marris Wilson, *Diseases of the Vesiculæ Seminales*, chap. iii. v. vi. ; Dr. Albert Müller, *Ueber Unwillkürliche Samenverluste;* Bemiss, in *New Orleans Journal of Medicine*, Oct. 1869; *Half Yearly Compendium of the Medical Science*, Jan. 1867; Erichsen, *System of Surgery; St. Louis Medical Archives;* Dr. Wood, *Canada Medical Journal;* Mr. Teevan, *British Medical Journal*, May, 1870. Doisneau's apparatus is described in *Le Courier Médicale*, 1869; and the *St. Louis Medical Archives*, same year.]

SECRET DISEASES.

Their Effects and Frequency.

A MASKED pestilence, a subtle infection is stealing upon the health of the nation, poisoning its blood and shortening its life, spreading from husband to wife, from parent to offspring, from nurse to infant, working slowly but with a fatal and an inexorable certainty. This pestilence is the specific contagion of diseases which arise from impure intercourse.

Were this its only source, and did it stay its ravages with the guilty parties, we might say, it is a just penalty, and calls for little sympathy. But this is not so. By the inscrutable law of God, which decrees that the sins of the father shall be visited on the children, even unto the third and fourth generation, these diseases work attainder of blood, become hereditary, and blight the offspring. They pass from the guilty to the innocent by lawful intercourse, by vaccination, by circumcision, by nursing, by utensils, even by a kiss. Hundreds of examples are recorded in medical literature, where the infection has spread by just such means. Not a single physician of experience who has not witnessed wife and children poisoned by the husband's infidelity.

Here again we fear that we shall be called alarmists, and severely criticized for exciting unnecessary apprehension. We care not. This is no imaginary evil we combat, nor is it any paltry or insignificant one. We do but repeat, and with

(94)

moderated emphasis, what others have already said. We
have before us a work which is anything but sensational,
and which was written by men who stand second to none in
our land for professional and personal character. It is the
Fifth Annual Report of the Board of State Charities of Massachusetts (1868). The Board are speaking (p. lvi.) of "that
hideous disease which must have come from the most veno-
mous fang of the serpent which bit the heel of mankind,"
and they go on to say :—

"Woe to the bodily tabernacle in which it once enters ;
for it is one of those evil spirits which not even prayer and
fasting can cast out. With slow, painless, insidious, resist-
less march, it penetrates into the very marrow of the bones,
and poisons the fountain of life beyond purification. All
may look fair without and feel fair within, but the taint is
there, and it affects the offspring. The effects of this disorder in corrupting the human stock, and predisposing offspring to disease, are more deadly than is usually believed.
They are hardly exceeded by the effects of alcohol. Nature
readily 'forgives unto the sons of men other sins and blas-
phemies wherewith soever they may blaspheme,' but this
one, like 'him that blasphemeth against the Holy Spirit,
hath never forgiveness, but is in danger of eternal damna-
tion, for he hath an unclean spirit.' "

And this is said, be it remembered, in a public document,
for general distribution. Can we then be blamed if we remove without compunction the veil which hides the hideous
features of this malady ? Would we not deserve extremest
censure in a work of this nature if we hesitated so to do ?

We would gladly add, to counterbalance what we have to
say on this point, that such maladies are rare. But who
would believe it ? Is it not notorious that there is no hamlet
so remote, no frontier settlement so isolated, that it is free of

this scourge ? In the great cities it is fearfully prevalent. Including both sexes and all grades of society we do not doubt that more than *twenty-five per cent.* of their whole population is more or less tainted with it, and the greater number *innocently.* Nor is it at all confined to the indigent and the degraded. Its hold is just as firm, though concealed and held in check, in the fashionable clubs and stately mansions of the opulent, as in the alleys and back slums of the dregs of our population. No man, no woman, we care not what his position or his life may be, is secure from its loathsome touch.

How great, therefore, is the error of those who speak of it as a penalty which is confined to low vice only ? And how short-sighted the policy which bids us to

> " Skin and film the ulcerous place,
> Whiles rank corruption, mining all within,
> Infects unseen."

This social problem interests the *public.* *They* must appreciate the danger, *they* must unite and act, *they* must take up arms in solemn earnest, and determine to curb and limit, and if any way possible utterly stamp out, this spreading evil. What information seems to us of use for this purpose we shall proceed to give.

Their Nature and History.

The contagious diseases which are propagated by the sexual relations are two in number, and are technically known as gonorrhœa and syphilis. They both commence by some local manifestation, and may not proceed further; but about as often they rapidly extend to the whole system, and produce effects upon it which are as permanent in character as those by vaccination or other specific virus.

By far the most insidious and destructive is syphilis. This is supposed by some writers to have been unknown in Europe until about the period of the discovery of America. And not a few historians maintain that it was conveyed from the natives of the West Indies to the inhabitants of the Old World by the sailors of Columbus. Certainly about that time it broke out with unparalleled virulence in the camps, courts, and brothels of Spain, Italy, France, and England. No country was willing to father it, so the English called it the " French disease ;" the French, "le mal de Naples ;" the Italians, "la mallattia della Spagna."

There is good reason, however, to believe that neither Columbus, the Indians, nor any one of these nations was solely to blame in the matter. Probably it had lurked unrecognized and under comparatively innocent forms through all races and ages. At the epoch referred to, the massing of great armies by Francis I. and Charles V., and the increased commerce, acting together with some change in the human constitution itself, led to a violent outbreak in its most virulent form. Some have imagined that the ancient leprosy, so often referred to in the Old Testament, was one of its forms; and others, that it was derived from the glanders in the horse, transplanted into the human economy. But these theoretical views are of little public interest, and it is enough to remember that, about the year 1500, a very malignant type of the disease arose and spread with fearful rapidity, and that since that time it has been rightly deemed one of the scourges of the human race.

The other form of secret disease, gonorrhœa, was well known to the ancient Romans, and to the lawgivers of the middle ages, and old English statutes of the fourteenth century concerning brothels distinctly refer to it as "the perilous infirmitie of burnynge." It, too, appears to have increased in frequency and severity about the same time as syphilis, and is to-day certainly much more severe than it was even in the dissolute commonwealth of imperial Rome. So far have a riper civilization, a more advanced medical science, and a purer morality failed to curb these insidious complaints, that they are now probably more widely distributed than ever before, and little, if at all, abated in violence. The only point which we have actually gained—and this certainly is much—is to treat them with greater success than hitherto.

The Course and the Consequences of Secret Diseases.

We believe that if the public generally, and especially young men, were better aware of the dangers they incur from illicit indulgence, there would be a determined effort at reform both in municipal and personal life. We cannot think that sane, intelligent men, to say nothing of morality, would, for the gratification of an ephemeral desire, risk the well-being of their whole lives and the health of their offspring. It must be ignorance of danger which blinds them. The fools rush in where the wise men fear to tread.

Our intention, therefore, is not to rehearse a harassing and disgusting train of symptoms of no value except to the medical man, but to state in plain terms the general course and the frequent consequences of these diseases.

We have already said both commence by local manifestations of some kind, which, after a time, are followed by a general contamination of the system. This is the case with both, but in different degrees. The after-effects of gonorrhœa are much the less severe, and are confined wholly to the individual. It does not leave any hereditary taint. But it may bring about life-long suffering. The passage from the bladder becomes inflamed and contracted; that organ itself is very apt to partake of the inflammation, and become irritable and sensitive; spermatorrhœa and impotence with all their miseries may follow, and the whole economy may partake of the infection.   An eruption on the skin and an obstinate form of rheumatism, both wholly intractable to ordinary remedies, are more common than even many physicians imagine. Not unfrequently those troublesome chronic rheumatic complaints which annoy men in middle and advanced life are the late castigations which Nature is inflicting for early transgressions.

These results, though serious enough, are too personal to demand public action.   But not so with those which flow from syphilis.   They are so wide reaching that every philanthropist must feel it his duty, when once made aware of them, to urgently insist on some general measures—if such can be devised—which will abate them, and protect the innocent thousands on whom they are visited.

We shall first speak of the effects of syphilis on the individual.   They are divided into three classes ; first, the local attack, which commences as a small ulcer on the part touched by the virus. Next in order of time are the secondary symptoms ; · they may show themselves in three or four weeks, and may lurk unnoticed for that many months; the poison attacks the skin and soft parts of the body, producing rashes, ulcerations, swelling of the glands, sore throat, disorders of the stomach, liver, and other internal organs; the hair loosens and falls out, the spirits are depressed, and the brain may be attacked, leading to imbecility, epilepsy, or insanity.   At this stage, shallow ulcers are apt to form on the tongue and just inside the lips. The discharge from them is a poison and can convey the disease; and so can a drop of blood from the infected person.   Let one in this condition kiss another, or drink from a cup, or use a pipe or a spoon, and pass it to another, the danger is great that the disease will thus be transmitted. An instance is recently reported in a French medical journal of a glassblower who was suffering from such ulcerations. As is usual, in all respects he appeared in good health, and was received into a manufactory. In these establishments the workmen are accustomed to pass the tube through which the glass is blown rapidly from mouth to mouth. He had been there only a few weeks when the physician to the factory was applied to for "sore mouths," and found to his horror that this single diseased man had infected in the process of blowing bottles, *nine* others. Let such an example be a salutary warning to neatness and caution, as well as an illustration how often innocent persons can become the victims of this loathsome complaint. Let it also be an admonition to charity, and against hasty condemnation of the sufferers.

The third step in the progress of the disease is when the bones are attacked. They often enlarge, become painful, and may ultimately ulcerate. Especially between the knee and the ankle, and on the head is this the case. By this time the whole body is poisoned, and an ineradicable taint is infused in the system. The constitution, though still apparently strong, is liable to give way at any moment. There is no longer the same power to repair injuries which there once was. The bones are brittle, and slow to heal. We knew of a young man of promise who was in this condition. One day, in merely attempting to pull off his boot, he snapped his thigh-bone, weakened as it was by the disease. For nearly two years he lay on his bed, and was only released by death. Let any one who wishes to see a picture of what a human being is who is brought to this wretched condition by his vices or his misfortune, peruse the sketch entitled " A

Man about Town" in Mr. Warren's remarkable book, "The
Diary of a London Physician." If after reading that masterly
delineation he still feels willing to incur the risk of such a
loathsome fate, then to him other words of warning are vain
and needless.

"Syphilophobia."

While we do not wish to mitigate by one line the dark
colors of this picture, we still have a word of consolation
which we shall interpolate here. By no means every case
of disease runs on to this dire form; constitutions differ exceedingly, and on some the effects of the poison are brief
and passing. A hideous phantom haunts some men lest
they should have this disease lurking in their system. They
watch with terror every swelling and eruption on themselves
and their children. None but the observant physician can
appreciate what horrors prey upon them. We know the
son of a distinguished professor, a young man who lapsed
from virtue but once and contracted a mild form of the disease, who became a hopeless lunatic from this constant
dread. This is what is called "syphilophobia," and is a by
no means infrequent cause of insanity, suicide, and reckless
living. The charlatan finds in such a man a ready victim
for his extortionate demands. As a rule, these sufferers
avoid telling their family physician, and prefer to consult
some distant and unknown adviser. Hence they often fall
into the hands of bad men, who play upon their fears, swin-
dle them out of their money, do them no good whatever, and
when all else fails to satisfy rapacious demands, levy black-
mail, under threat of disclosing their condition. This
course of rascality is so common that we warn all our
readers against trusting their health, fortune, and reputa-

tions with any man, no matter what his claims, of whom
they have no better guarantee of his honor and skill than
his own word therefor, and some dozens of fraudulent certifi-
cates from unknown parties. In nine cases out of ten all
such fears are groundless and unfounded.

The Sin of the Father Visited on the Children.

If there is any field where the philanthropist and reformer
is most urgently demanded, it is to limit the infant mortality
which prevails to such an alarming extent in our great
cities. In New York, Boston, and Philadelphia over one-
fourth, in Cincinnati nearly one-third (30 per cent.) of all
the children born alive perish within the first year of life!
What a portentous fact is this? What are the causes of
this frightful mortality?

We will mention one. A physician of wide experience
has calculated, after careful inquiry, that fourth on the list
of causes is *hereditary syphilis.* But even this statement
does not at all convey an adequate idea of the effect of this
disease on limiting and corrupting population. Of the infants which are stillborn, the number is very great, and of
these, the *most frequent* cause of death, according to that
cautious writer, Dr. Berkeley Hill, is syphilis.

But even if the child survives its first year, the danger is
not past. It may be the picture of health till five or six
years of age, or to the period of puberty, or even to adult
age, and then first reveal the long-concealed poison which
has lurked in the system ever since its being began. That
poison shows itself under a hundred protean forms. It may
be in eruptions on the skin and foul ulcerations, or in obstinate "colds in the head," in swelling of the bones, in a peculiar affection of the eyes leading to blindness, in brittle and

loose teeth, in the protean symptoms of scrofula, in idiocy, stunted growth, and in insanity.

Such are the legacies which parents who through vice or misfortune have been cursed with this disease have to hand down to their offspring. "The fathers have eaten sour grapes, and the children's teeth are set on edge."

Face to face with these facts, it becomes of the highest general interest to learn what the laws of such transmission are, so far as they have been discovered by careful observation.

They are curious. It is possible for a man in whose constitution the taint of disease exists, but is latent, to have perfectly sound offspring. But if he has any symptoms of the disease in any stage, it is probable, nay, almost certain, that his children will show the effects of it, although their mother remains healthy.

Much more generally the mother takes the disease either from the father, or from the unborn child in whose body lurks the paternal taint. But unless she does so before the seventh month of her pregnancy, she will escape.

When both mother and father display unequivocal signs of the disease, the case of the child is desperate. There is hardly any hope of its being born sound.

When such a child is born, it is a dangerous source of infection for all around it. The nurse who applies it to her breast, the friend who kisses it, the attendants who handle it, are in imminent danger of becoming in turn victims of the loathsome disease.

The only person who can nurse or even touch it without danger is the mother who bore it. It is in this form of infantile syphilis that the disease is most easily communicated. In the strong, and yet not too strong language of Dr. Colles, a well-known English surgeon : " The readiness with which syphilis in infants can be communicated by contact cannot be exceeded by any other disease with which I am acquainted. I look upon it as *equally infectious with the itch itself*." And Dr. Barton adds: "A common mode by which the syphilitic infant spreads the disease is by being *kissed* by the girl that carries it, or by others."

If this is so—and there is no doubt of it—is it not time that the public received some warning about it? Are we to shut our mouths and see these perils to public health hourly increasing, and say nothing, do nothing?

Let such a child by careful attention and sound hygiene survive to adult life, and become in turn the father or mother of a family, even then unrelenting nature may not be satisfied. There are undoubted cases on record where the disease was handed down, in spite of every care and strict virtue, to the *third* generation, and perhaps to the *fourth*.

It appears in multiplied forms of disease. "We are compelled to conclude," says Dr. Barton, summing up in his recent work the many observations on the transmission of syphilis, "that *a very considerable proportion* of those chronic diseases of the eyes, skin, glands, and bones, to which the epithet *scrofulous* has been applied, are really the results of inherited syphilis."

And all this misery, all these curses long drawn out, these consequences so dire to innocent generations, the penalty of one moment of illicit pleasure, the vengeance of a violated law which knows justice but no mercy!

With these deplorable possibilities in view, it becomes a serious question

How soon can a Man, once Diseased, Marry?

A French specialist of eminence does not hesitate to reply: Never. We cannot agree with him. In a large number of persons the disease is transient, mild, curable. In others it may be severe and obstinate, but finally yields entirely to judicious treatment. Only in a small minority is it utterly ineradicable. That it is so, however, in this minority, and that it is extremely difficult to say positively, who does not belong to it, is unquestionable. We doubt if any man having once had decided infection can positively say that he has entirely recovered from it. .

We know a respectable physician who, when commencing practice, contracted syphilis on the finger in attending the confinement of a diseased woman. It became constitutional, but by active treatment he apparently completely cured it. He married, and has four to all appearance healthy children. Fourteen years after all symptoms had disappeared, on an occasion when his general health was lowered by loss of rest and anxiety, the disease broke out anew. There is not a doubt but that during the whole of that period it had been lurking in his blood.

English writers who have given the question we are considering a great deal of attention on account of its vast social importance, and the frequency with which it is asked, have settled on the following rule, which we believe may be accepted as of general validity, and may be acted on with very little hesitation : The shortest period between the latest epoch of the contraction of disease and marriage must be three years ; and at least one full year must elapse between the disappearance of the last symptom of the complaint and the marriage.

We recommend also to all who apply to us for advice on this difficult subject, to test their constitutions thoroughly, and see if they have any seeds of the malady in their systems. This can be done by bathing daily for a month in warm natural sulphur waters ; for example, the hot springs of Arkansas, those on the St. John River in Florida, or those so well known to the fashionable public in Virginia. These have the property of producing a peculiar eruption on the skin, if syphilis is present; and if this does not appear, we may be very certain that there is no virus in the system.

How to Prevent these Diseases.

What we have said of the extent, the virulence, and the calamitous results on the individual, his offspring, and the nation, of these diseases, must evoke in every mind the earnest desire to see some regulations devised and carried out which will limit, and, if possible, annihilate this destructive scourge. The nature of syphilis leads us to hope for this consummation. It is strictly *contagious* in nature, transmitted, that is, by contact only. The problem, therefore, resolves itself simply how to avoid contact.

Unquestionably the chief though by no means the only source of contagion is in prostitution, a subject therefore which we shall shortly proceed to consider at length.

It is important, however, for all men to be aware of the fact, that gonorrhœa not at all unfrequently arises from other cause beside contagion. Ignorance of this has within our knowledge led to cruel accusations, utter disruption of families, and untold misery. Dr. Ricord mentions the case of a young man who even committed suicide, because he was seized with this disease on his wedding trip, and ignorantly concluded that his bride was unchaste. When relations are had with a woman who suffers from an acrid discharge, or at the time of her monthly illness, or when the indulgence is excessive, or the excitement over-intense, it is by no means unusual for the male to have as the result an inflammation and discharge, which are quite the same as this disease, even being communicable.

A very recent writer, Prof. A. W. Stein, of New York, says in an address read February, 1870, before the New York Medical Journal Association : " It cannot be too often mentioned that gonorrhœa is not always the result of illicit or impure intercourse. It is of the greatest importance that we should fully appreciate this fact, for the most disastrous consequences have resulted from ignorance of it." All writers are agreed that the conditions we have mentioned in the female may give rise to it.

Such causes, therefore, should be scrupulously avoided; and also we should be not over-apt to condemn the person, male or female, who thus must bear the suspicion of unchastity.

Personal Means of Prevention.

Foreign writers have spoken much of the means for the personal prevention of diseases of this character. Very minute directions are given, and certain chemical preservatives recommended, by the application of which immediately after exposure, the virus which conveys the disease is neutralized, and deprived of its poisonous properties. Certain mechanical appliances have been brought before the professional public by American surgeons for the same purpose, and their use has been defended by the well-known surgeon. Dr. Bumstead, of New York, on the ground that " the passions always will control, as they always have controlled, the moral sense of the greater part of man and womankind, and as the effects of vice are by no means confined to the guilty, their prevention is no unworthy subject of consideration." While conceding the force of this expression of so eminent a teacher, we still fear that such information, if given publicly and promiscuously, might tend to remove one of the barriers which now keep men in the path of rectitude. We therefore believe such instructions should be kept for individual instances, and reserved for those cases; in married life, where, on the one hand, an abstinence on the part of the husband might lead to bitter feeling, or destruction of domestic ties from suspicion and jealousy; and on the other, should he not abstain, he might involve her in his own misfortune.

They are also justifiable when a wife has a discharge of the character we have mentioned, which is liable to produce a disease apparently specific in character, in her husband. Some men are extremely sensitive to any exposure of this kind, while others suffer it with impunity.

Instances may also occur, and, to our knowledge, do occur, where men engaged to be married, and the day fixed, contract shortly before their wedding one of these diseases. A thousand social reasons combine to prevent them obtaining a delay; they are often not aware of the full extent of the danger to which they will expose their bride and their *children;* they are not very conscientious; such marriages are often for policy or *convenience,* and they marry. If they could save their wives' health, they would. They generally can, and it is the least that can be asked of them to do so.

Yet as we have said, with these contingencies in our mind, we have not felt it would be right to detail the means recommended, lest we should in some degree shear of its proper terrors *illicit* intercourse.

[Authors and Works referred to on these topics.—Dr. Wm. A. Hammond, *On Venereal Diseases;* Wm. Acton, *On Prostitution;* Durkee, *On Gonorrhœa and Syphilis;* Dr. Berkeley Hill, *On Venereal Diseases;* Barton, *Nature and Treatment of Syphilis;* Colles, *On Syphilis;* Cullerier, *Atlas of Venereal Diseases;* Dr. J. F. Bumstead, *On Venereal Diseases;* Lancereaux, *Traité de la*

Syphilis ; Dr. P. Diday, *Nouvelles Doctrines sur la Syphilis,* and *Infantile Syphilis ;* Ricord, *Lettres sur la Syphilis ; The Westminster Review* for July, 1869, January and April, 1870; Stein, in *New York Medical Journal;* and numerous monographs, reports, discussions, and articles in the recent medical periodicals.]

THE SOCIAL EVIL.

WE have now pointed out with dispassionate yet earnest words the deplorable consequences of misgoverned sexual instinct on the individual, on his family, on his children, and through these on society and the race at large. There remains for us to turn a still darker page, and to reveal an abyss of misery, iniquity, and disease, from which the philanthropist too often turns away with a shudder. This abyss is *prostitution*, the great social evil of our day, invading all grades of society, contaminating with leprous touch the fairest of our land, destroying the pure joys of the domestic hearth, the well-spring of disgusting maladies, the inexhaustible source of all manner of evil.

Too often the clergyman and the statesman prefer to shut their eyes and shun the unpleasant topic. This is not our purpose. Such a course can command no admiration and effect no good result. Rather will we risk the charge of over-plainness of speech than hesitate to exhibit the nature, the extent, and the consequences of this infecting ulcer in the body politic of our land. Our statements are based on careful studies of original documents, and the opinions of those physicians and philanthropists who have devoted most time to combating this pest. We shall aim to exhibit it as it actually exists in our midst, choosing the most trustworthy and the most recent sources of information, and premising that all our statements are taken directly from original authorities.

(110)

Prostitution in the United States.

There is no branch of social science that offers greater difficulties to the investigator than that which concerns itself with the number, the life, the fate, and the condition of fallen women. It has ever been so. Thousands of years ago King Solomon the wise said—

"Lest thou shouldst ponder the path of her life, her ways are movable, that thou canst not know them." (Proverbs v. 6.)

The great majority of them entirely elude the searches of the police, and conceal their calling under some outward garb of honest occupation. Before we proceed, therefore, to estimate the numbers in our large cities, we must explain the different classes in which they are divided.

The police reports of our great cities divide them into "public prostitutes," "waiter-girls," and "kept women," or "private mistresses." The first mentioned alone can, for obvious reasons, be known as such to the police. They are those who ply their avocation with such publicity as to become familiar to the agents of the law. Many of the mistresses dress as well, drive as elegant equipages, and behave in public as decorously as any ladies. The "waiter-girls" can only be classed as to character according to the good or bad reputation of the refreshment houses where they are employed. There are certain saloons—Captain Kennedy, Superintendent of the New York Metropolitan Police, says thirty-three in that city and Brooklyn—in which the chief business is licentiousness. They were a few years ago very abundant in St. Louis, and the wretched women in them were known locally as "beer jerkers;" but the excessively injurious effects of such establishments became so notorious that they were all shut up. Only the lowest class of depraved women are found in such dens.

The haunts of those one degree above these girls are known to the police as "houses of prostitution;" and ranking above these again in the observance of decorum are the "houses of assignation." In the former, the inmates either go forth at night to seek their victims, and are known merely as "boarders;" or they remain within, and await chance comers, and are then called "parlor boarders." The mistress of the house furnishes room and board to her inmates, and sometimes clothing, for which articles she takes care to keep them in debt to her. Liquor of the vilest manufacture is always kept on hand at extravagant prices, and the girls are forced by threats and promises to urge its sale. Gambling is not uncommon, and "panel thieving" is carried on with great adroitness in very many of them.

All the inmates of these infamous houses bear assumed names, and it is a matter of constant observation how "movable" they are, as our translation of the Proverbs has it. They go from house to house, and from city to city, driven by an aimless restlessness. They are of all nationalities, Americans and Germans predominating, the Celtic race, that is, the Scotch, Welsh, and Irish, being in the minority, in proportion to the general population.

What is surprising, in Philadelphia, New York, and probably other northern cities, there are houses fitted up with considerable expense in which all the inmates are mixed, negro and white blood, quadroons and octoroons. They are patronized exclusively by white men.

The houses of assignation, according to the police reports of New York, are yearly on the increase, while the houses of prostitution are decreasing. In the former, the proprietors pretend to keep no boarders, but to have a number of female acquaintances, who, to eke out a scanty income or for motives of pleasure merely, sell their bodies. This story in ninety-nine cases in a hundred is notoriously false, and the women in such houses are as often common street-walkers as anything else.

With these explanations in mind, we shall proceed to estimate the magnitude of this great evil in some of our cities, and thus show the imperative importance, in a hygienic as well as a purely moral view, of taking some measures to curb it. According to the police reports of 1869 there are in New York and Brooklyn 496 houses of prostitution and 107 houses of assignation. The whole number of women certainly known to the police as public prostitutes is 2107; but various competent authorities estimate the actual number of those who subsist in great part or entirely on the wages of sin, at the enormous number of *thirty thousand*.

This calculation, allowing for difference in extent and character of population, agrees closely with that made by the Midnight Mission of Philadelphia in the same year. The officers of this charity are of opinion that there are not less than *twelve thousand* in that city.

In Cincinnati a municipal law orders a register to be kept at police headquarters, on which the name and address of every well-ascertained public prostitute are inscribed. In 1869 the number so registered was 485; which, if the same proportion of public to private prostitution prevails as in New York, gives for the total number of fallen women seven thousand.

But Chicago has the unenviable notoriety of being the city in the United States where this degraded class is most numerous. Prof. Edmond Andrews, M. D., of that city, estimated that in 1867 there was one public prostitute to 230 inhabitants, or more than twice as many in proportion to

the population as in New York city or Philadelphia, and
more than in any of the corrupt capitals of the Old World,
Paris not excepted!

It is unnecessary to carry this dreadful enumeration any
further. We have said enough to display beyond question
the appalling extent of this sin, and an elaborate discussion
were out of place here.

We shall next proceed to describe

Its Effects on the Woman.

Dr. Sanger, a physician of New York, who has had favorable opportunities for investigation in that city, asserts that
the whole population of public women changes once in four
years; in other-words, that every year one-fourth of them
disappears, and are replaced by fresh accessions to the fated
crowd. What becomes of this fourth which in some way
vanishes from the knowledge of the police? Dr. Sanger does
not hesitate to say that most of them *die*. Our study of
the subject leads us to doubt this. The majority either
move to other cities, are imprisoned, become private mistresses or wives, or escape to a life of honest labor.

It may astonish some to hear us say that they become
wives. But this is not very unusual. Sometimes they marry
much above their original station in life. We positively
know that out of one class which graduated at a leading
Eastern college not many years since with less than a hundred members, *three* have married women whom they knew
to be prostitutes. Scions of some of the most respected
families in New York, Philadelphia, and Boston have committed the same.folly. The results of such alliances are of
course disastrous without exception.

Though this disposition of the majority we believe to be

true, yet a large minority do die. If one considers for a moment the irregularities, excesses, and exposures to which they are subjected, he cannot doubt this. Many of them are constantly diseased with venereal maladies; they often drink to intoxication; they are exposed to inclement weather with insufficient clothing; they are frequently injured in brutal brothel fights; they are neglected when sick. Their chance of life must necessarily be greatly lessened.

But this, though serious enough, is by no means the worst effect. It is the almost hopeless *moral* death of the prostitute which is the darkest result of her mode of life. The woman who once loses her virtue can never recover her self-respect; but she, who for money has prostituted her body as a trade, seems to lose hold of all moral principle, and even natural affection. She consorts by necessity and preference with thieves, gamblers, and the vilest classes of men. She rarely makes the effort to rid herself from the jaws of death, even when assistance is offered. The ancient heathen wrote over the doors of brothels: *Hic habitat voluptas,* Here pleasure dwelleth; but the Christian knows that a far truer inscription were that which Dante says is written over the gates of hell :—

" Leave every hope, ye who enter here."

It is this utter demoralization which invests with such difficulty every attempt to redeem these creatures. And we must look it squarely in the face in all our schemes for reform.

The most striking exhibition of their unnatural debasement is the almost entire lack of maternal feeling in these women. Their avocation by its constant excitement prevents conception as a rule, and this is a beneficent law of nature. For the wretched offspring of such mothers could hope for nothing but misery. When born, the infants are usually sent to a foundling hospital, or to a "baby farming" establishment, or killed outright. The latter does but anticipate a fate almost certain at the hospital. The infant mortality on Ward's Island, New York, is over 90 per cent. Very nearly *all* die. And the result is the same in Boston, Philadelphia, London, and Paris. The causes, in most instances, are hereditary syphilis and neglect.

Its Consequences to the Man.

In speaking of the effects of the social evil on women, we have been repeating common-places which every reader knew or suspected. But there remains. an exhibit of its consequences to be made, which is often lost sight of, or imperfectly apprehended; we mean its effect on the men who support it.

This is, if anything, even more deplorable than on the woman. The words of the wise king are every whit as true now as they ever were, and we would that ministers of the gospel had the nerve to choose them oftener as a text :—

"The lips of a strange woman drop as a honey-comb, and her mouth is smoother than oil;

"But her end is bitter as wormwood, sharp as a two-edged sword;

"Her feet go down to death, her steps take hold on hell;

"Remove thy way far from her, and come not nigh the door of her house;

"Lest thou give thine honor unto others, and thy years unto the cruel;

"Lest strangers be filled with thy wealth, and thy labors be in the house of a stranger;

"And thou mourn at the last when thy flesh and thy body are consumed." (Proverbs v.)

" Whoso is simple, let him turn in hither: and as for him that wanteth understanding, she saith to him :

" Stolen waters are sweet, and bread eaten in secret is pleasant ;

" But he knoweth not that the dead are there ; and that her guests are in the depths of hell." (Proverbs, ix.)

And who are the guests ? The gambler, the thief, the policy dealer, the ruffian; and with these, the college student, the bank clerk, the member of the fashionable club ; aye, and also the father of the family, the husband of a pure wife, the head of the firm, the member of church ; all these, every night, in all our great cities. Can any of these think to escape the contamination ? Vain chimera. It is as certain as death. If nothing else remains, the moral stain is indelible. As the poet Burns most truly says :—

> " It hardens a' within,
> And petrifies the feelings."

But often there are physical consequences more immediately troublesome than this. The prevalence of contagious disease among these women is shocking. It is safe to say that one in three or four is suffering under some communicable form of them. " And how fearfully," exclaims the Rev. Dr. Muhlenburg in his sermon on the Midnight Mission, " is the wrath of God seen in these physical consequences ! The most loathsome sight which the diseased human body, in man or woman exhibits, the most horridly disgusting, are the living corpses in which victims of lust are putrefying to their graves." We have already said enough on this point, and we pass to another.

Besides being morally degrading, and physically dangerous, illicit indulgence is pecuniarily ruinous. These women accustom themselves and their dupes to reckless expenditure, and of course they sink together into poverty. Nor let the shrewd and cautious business man think himself safe. It is notorious that a large class of these women are kept by their paramours exclusively for the purpose of *levying black mail.* The middle aged, respectable married man is allured by some decoy, his name is learned from his clothing or by the panel thief from his pocket book, he is tracked to his home or place of business, his history and family connections are hunted up, and with these facts at his command the unscrupulous pair have their victim in a net which he dares not break, and they bleed him to their heart's content. No one not intimately acquainted with the vices of our great cities can have any idea of how many men of the "highest respectability" are daily suffering the torments of the damned from the threats and extortions of such villains.

Let this public exposition be a warning to those who are tempted by the woman in the attire of a harlot and subtle of heart who says :—

"Come, let us take our fill of love until the morning; let us solace ourselves with loves.

"For the good man is not at home, he is gone a long journey.

"He hath taken a bag of money with him and will come home at the day appointed."

If he yields, he will soon discover that the snares are spread as they ever were for those void of understanding.

The Causes that Maintain It.

The social problem we are considering must be studied in its origin in order to prepare any method for its solution. We ask, therefore, what is it leads so many women, usually, almost necessarily, young, healthy, and handsome—for they

mnst be all these to ply that trade—to open or secret sin?
Rev. Dr. Muhlenberg, in his sermon already quoted, answers
thus: "Some with no excuse, others, if not with excuse, yet
with palliations either in their bringing up apart from Christian influences, and amid constant exposure to temptation;
or, from their having been the victims of seduction; or from
the extremities of destitution; or, allow me to add, in a fond-
ness for finery, copying their sisters in higher life, who, by
their example of vain show in dress, have more to answer for
in this matter than they suspect."

It is popularly supposed among men that in the greater
number of cases it is the strong passions, the insatiable lusts
of these women, which lead them to take up this mode of
life. Such an opinion displays entire ignorance of woman's
nature and facts. It is, probably, the rarest of all the causes
which lead to public immoral life. It is true that many of
these women claim and pretend to exhibit great erotic passion, but this is nearly always fictitious, adopted as an attraction, merely a "trick of the trade." The excessive frequency
with which they indulge blunts their sensibility and pre-
cludes the possibility of much real feeling.

Probably the most common and fatal temptation to young
women is simply *money.* They can gain more, and can, consequently, dress finer, live more idly, and fare better for a
while by this than by any other means at their command.

Then there are a very great number who are brought up
to the business. The Board of Health of the Citizens' Association of New York estimate there are at least thirty thousand children between the ages of five and twelve in that
city who are subject to no parental control, receive no instruction either religious or secular, and are constantly exposed to the corrupting influences of a hotbed of vice. Ten
years later they become a vast army of prostitutes and thieves.

So long as this is the case, it were indeed vain to expect the cessation of the evil.

Seduction and violence are constant, but not the most important, sources of supply. Country girls and female immigrants are not unfrequently "allured to boarding-houses where scoundrels, with lying promises, or with lures of money, with the baits of vanity, with the stupefying cup, or with violence, rifle them of their all, and leave them, lost strangers in a strange land, for other harpies to devour" (Rev. Dr. Muhlenberg.) It is notorious to those familiar with the vices of our cities that there are so-called "employment offices," or "intelligence offices," which are in reality snares for the unwary, and that the proprietor (male or female) is in connection with a house of ill-fame, and sends to such places those whom he thinks will be entrapped.

Opulent satyrs, cloyed with ordinary means of vice, and bent on provoking exhausted senses with novelty, offer large bids for youth and virtue; stimulated by them, a class of evil old women make it their business to be on the watch for giddy and vain girls, and set before them every temptation to forsake the path of chastity.

From these various sources the numbers of the lost are constantly maintained in our great cities, and constantly increased.

Is it a Necessary Evil?

Divines, philosophers, and physicians have united in the expression of the opinion that prostitution is a necessary evil, not only in the sense that it is unavoidable by any known regulation, but that it is necessary to the interest, even to the morality, of society at large. St. Augustine, the eminent father of the Latin church, in his book *De Ordine*, says: " Suppress prostitution, and you will plunge society into libertinage" (*aufer meretrices, turbaveris omnia libidinibus*). The severe Cato recommended that young men should visit the brothels when their passions were ardent, so that they might not be tempted to invade the sanctity of marriage.

"I regard prostitution," says Mr. Acton, "as an inevitable attendant upon civilized, and especially closely packed population. When all is said and done, it is, and I believe ever will be, ineradicable." And to like effect the Rev. Dr. Muhlenberg, of New York: "The 'social evil' is ever in proportion to the wealth and luxury of a community."

Such opinions are discouraging, and are not to be accepted as the solution of the problem. There is absolutely no moral evil which is *inseparably* connected with human society. Herbert Spencer, in his "Social Statics," points out with lucid and logical language the *perfectibility* of the human species. And it is a libel on man, "made in the image of God," to say that there is any crime, especially so flagitious and enormous a crime as this, from which it is impossible for him to refrain. Granted that our efforts to escape it have hitherto been abortive; yet there is no cause for despair; we simply have not set about it right.

The doctrine of St. Augustine above quoted seems to us monstrous, and contrary to known facts. In what countries are the obligations of marriage most sacredly respected? Is it in those where brothels are most abundant? We trow not. Are the large cities, where such dens are located, more conspicuous for marital chastity, than the rural districts where none exist? The proposition is an absurdity.

In examining this whole subject with an impartial desire to ascertain the exact truth, we have failed to find a single redeeming feature in the vice of prostitution, without it be that there are women wretched enough, friendless enough, desperate enough, to be forced to this mode of life to escape

11

starvation. And this is indeed sorry praise to give it. It only gives them a chance to sell their birthright to heaven for a mess of the devil's pottage.

The opportunity of illicit intercourse never protects marriage. Chastity, not allowed sensuality, is the safeguard of the household. The more a young man sees of abandoned women, the less is his faith in woman in general, and the more reckless becomes his libertinism.

How can it be Stopped?

The theories which have been propounded for the abating of this formidable and hydra-headed evil have been numerous and diverse. We shall confine ourselves to the examination of a few which have been brought forward within the past few years.

The boldest is that advocated by a "Christian Philosopher" in a work published in 1869, called "Monogamy and Polygamy Compared." This anonymous writer maintains that Christian precept and example both advocate a plurality of wives, that such a system has really no seriously objectionable features, and that by absorbing all the female population into the married state it effectually kills prostitution by depriving it of any material. This theory we do not deem worthy of sober attack.

Valuable for its practicality is the plan of repression suggested by Dr. George J. Ziegler, of Philadelphia, in several medical periodicals in 1867. He urges that the act of sexual connection be, *ipso facto*, the solemnization of marriage, and that when any such single act can be proven against an unmarried man by an unmarried woman, the latter be at once invested with all the legal privileges of a wife. By vesting this power in the woman, no man would risk himself in the company of a dissolute, scheming girl, who might force him to a marriage, and ruin him for life. There are many strong points in Dr. Ziegler's article, to which we refer our readers for full particulars (see list of authors at the close of this section). The strongest objection to it would be that it would considerably increase the temptations to destroy family purity, married women being the only ones who could be approached without danger of being forced into a misalliance.

Last year (1869) Dr. Charles Drysdale, of London, a sociologist of eminence, brought forward a proposition intended to inflict the death-blow on prostitution ; it consists, to give his own words, in a general determination to have "early marriages, and very few children (indeed, none at all, perhaps, as in France, for some years), and greater facility for divorce, as obtains at present in Indiana, and some other States of the United States."

We question very much whether these three recommendations would not have the very contrary effect from that desired. We have made considerable inquiry of private individuals from the States of our Union to which Dr. Drysdale refers, and all our informants seem convinced that the facile divorces have in nowise helped the morals of the community. We have already shown that precisely in Chicago, where divorces are notoriously easy to procure, the number of prostitutes in proportion to the population is greater than in Paris itself. How premature marriages, and the absence of the endearing ties which children knit between father and mother could increase purity of thought and chastity of life, we confess ourselves quite unable to perceive.

The fourth method suggested is based upon the undoubted fact that it is *money*—which may stand for bread and butter, or for fine clothes, or for intellectual gratification, or for any of the numberless pleasant things it can furnish (among which a quiet conscience and a sound body are not included)— *money*, that in the majority of cases is the real tempter. Give women, say the reformers of this school, the same opportunities to earn their living, to satisfy their tastes, to *make money*, as men have, and the number will be few, who will be obliged, or who will care, to make it by destroying their reputations, their peace of mind, and their bodily health.

Finally, there are those who believe in throwing all theories aside, and going to work at once in collecting these lost sheep of the Master into mission houses and halls, in setting forth to them the temporal and eternal dangers of their lawless life, in providing those who will accept with remunerative labor, and situations adequate to their capacities, and in trying upon them the effects of sound religious instruction. Such are the Midnight Missions which have been established by zealous and pious Christians in most of our cities; such the Magdalen asylums supported by the Protestant denominations; and such the "Houses of the Good Shepherd," organized for the same purpose by practical Catholics.

These admirable institutions all accomplish a good work, although in comparison with the magnitude of the harvest, the laborers are indeed few. We have attempted to form some idea of their actual efficacy by examining such reports as we have been able to obtain. From these it appears that the Midnight Missions rescue from a life of sin nearly three-fourths of those who enter the Homes; and we are informed by a responsible Catholic authority that the proportion of the saved in the Houses of the Good Shepherd are between two-thirds and three-fourths. But satisfactory as this is, it is discouraging to see how few can be induced to enter these doors of escape when they are opened. The Midnight Mission Home in Amity Street, New York, in its report for the year 1868, shows only one hundred and twenty-two receptions; though it is true that these excellent charities, like so many others, are sadly cramped for want of means.

Shall it be Regulated by Law?

In mere despair at discovering any means of entire repression, and very properly unwilling to shut the eyes and refuse to see this hideous and advancing tide of immorality and disease, many governments have chosen the policy of recognizing its existence, and subjecting it to such regulations as have been thought best devised to limit its growth, and diminish its destructive consequences.

There have been recently published several very elaborate discussions concerning the success of these plans of legislation as they are carried out in Europe. In general terms, they aim to have the name and residence of each prostitute registered, to have the houses licensed, and their inmates subjected at certain intervals to medical examination. Those found diseased are at once sent to a venereal hospital, where they are detained until cured. In Paris, the registered prostitutes are furnished with a ticket, giving name and residence, and this they are obliged to carry always with them, and show when called upon. They are not allowed to accost men on the streets, nor to employ in public places any of the wiles of harlotry. The houses (*maisons de tolerance*) are strictly watched by the police, and the charges are fixed, and posted up in a conspicuous place. These onerous enactments have failed on account of their stringency. The girls are subjected to so much surveillance that they seek in every way to escape from public into pri-

11*

vate walks of crime. Consequently, while in the last ten
years, the number of registered women in Paris has been
steadily decreasing, the number of private prostitutes, called
grisettes, lorettes, femmes entretenues, etc., have vastly and
alarmingly increased.

The contagious diseases act, which against violent opposi-
tion has been introduced into England during the last few
years, and which has been highly praised by some, and as
severely condemned by others, is still under probation.   It
provides that any woman, against whom an informant has
deposed that he has reason to believe her a public prostitute,
may be summoned by the superintendent of police, and be
forced to submit to medical inspection, and to be placed
under surveillance. If found ·diseased, she is ordered to a
hospital, where she is obliged to remain until the medical
officer pronounces her well.   It has been justly urged against
this act and the other acts associated with it, that they en-
croach too much on the freedom of the individual.

In the United States we have been very shy of approaching this delicate and difficult topic.   Our legislators imitate
the ostrich, which, when it wishes to escape its enemies, is
currently reported to hide its head in the sand, thinking that
if it cannot see them they cannot see it.   The results of
this policy are that in Chicago, New York, Philadelphia,
and all our largest cities, gross vice stalks our streets with
unblushing tread, the strange woman lays her snare for
innocence and youth at every street corner, disease is more
common and more deadly than in any regulated European
state, and the proportion of prostitutes rivals that of any
other civilized nation in the world.

It is quite time, therefore, that we lay aside this most
mischievous and dangerous modesty, or pretended blindness,
and set about some decisive measures if not to purge away,

at least to limit, control, and render as powerless as possible this infecting ulcer. Two things we can do : we can prevent the open tempting in our public streets, the fearful facility of vice which now prevails; and we can limit the spread of contagious disease. For the former, we require police regulations, firmly carried out, forbidding the accosting of men on the streets, indecent behavior in public, and immodest dress. For the latter we must have periodical medical inspection of prostitutes, and wards or hospitals to which those found diseased can be sent until they are recovered.

Here are two distinct, practical, thoroughly practicable aims for legislation, and every one who has the good of his species at heart, and is not utterly cankered by obsolete prejudice, cannot but grant their urgent importance and great value.

It has been supposed by the French surgeon, Auzias-Tu-renne and his disciples, that, so far as syphilis is concerned, this could be successfully checked by the process known as "syphilization."

This method is based on the theory that after the syphilitic poison has been artificially introduced into the system by repeated puncturing, the individual will thereafter be protected against it, just as he is protected against smallpox by the practice of vaccination.

A number of experiments have been carried out in France, Italy, and Sweden, with this view. Necessarily it is chiefly limited to public prostitutes, as no other class of the commu-nity would submit to such an ordeal. It was hoped that by its universal adoption public women would be made incapable of contracting, and hence incapable of transmitting this variety of venereal poison.

The results, though still somewhat uncertain, have not equalled these anticipations. While unquestionably the process does, to some extent, and for some time, materially lessen the liability to contract the disease, it does so unequally in different individuals, and the protective influence dies out after, at most, a few years.

Even if successful it would be difficult of application, and its effects on public morals are open to question. Therefore, we may dismiss it as a means of repression too visionary to merit serious consideration.

But, after all, it is not by police regulations, nor sanitary rules, nor legislative enactments, nor even, we fear, by gathering the fallen from the highways and byways of our crowded cities to hear the gospel, that we shall ever put an end to the social evil. We have been casting about for a thousand devices by which we could thrust virtue down the throats of others, while ourselves continue our cakes and ale in peace. We have ever been ready to point the finger of shame at the erring sister, we have ever been eager to rush forward and cast the first stone, but have we ever pondered for a moment on the words: "He that is *without sin* among you?"

Ah! here we touch the heart of the matter. Would you learn the only possible method of reforming sinful women? Three words contain the secret: *Reform the men.* In them, in their illicit lusts, in their misgoverned passions, in their selfish desires, in their godless disregard of duty, in their ignorance of the wages of sin, in their want of nobleness to resist temptation, in their false notions of health, is the source of all this sin. Teach them the physiological truth that chaste continence is man's best state, morally, physically, mentally; correct the seductive error which talks of indulgence as "natural," venial, excusable; show them that man is only manful when he sees the right and does it; train them to regard *self-government* as the noblest achievement of all; educate them fearlessly in the nature and regulation of those functions which pertain to the relations of the sexes; do this, and we shall soon see that we have gained a vantage ground over against which the powers of evil cannot stand.

Every great social reform must begin with the male sex; theirs it is to take the step in advance, and they must do it with self-knowledge, with intelligence, and with no false sentiment. Here, especially, they must act. The sin is wholly of their own making. All the misery, all the lost souls, all the blighting consequences present and to come, of prostitution, are chargeable solely and wholly to the uncontrolled sexual instinct of the male. What duty, then, is more imperative to the clergyman, the educator, the statesman, the enlightened philanthropist anywhere, than to study this instinct, to learn how to guide it in youth and age, and how to direct it in its natural and healthy channels?

[AUTHORS AND WORKS ON PROSTITUTION REFERRED TO.—Dr. Sanger, *History of Prostitution;* Dr. J. Jeannel, *De la Prostitution au dix-neuvième siècle ;* Acton, *Prostitution in its Moral, Social, and Sanitary Aspects;* Parent-Duchatelet, *De la Prostitution en Paris;* Dr. Ed. Andrews, *Letter on Prostitution*, Chicago Medical Examiner, Oct. 1867; Rev. Dr. W. A. Muhlenberg, *Woman and Her Accusers*, a Sermon for the Midnight Mission, 1869; Dr. Ziegler, *Medical and Surgical Reporter*, 1867; Dr. Charles Drysdale, *Medical Press and Circular*, May, 1869; Westminster Review, *Prostitution and How to Cure It*, January and April. 1870; the Annual Reports of the Superintendent of Police. the Boards of Health, and the Midnight Missions of New York, Philadelphia, Chicago, Cincinnati, etc., for 1867-69.]

PART III.

THE MARRIED LIFE.

The Preliminaries of Marriage.

A MAN first becomes a man and a woman a woman in marriage. Only when united by that mysterious rite does each find nature satisfied, and all the faculties and functions meetly exercised. By such union those powers which are directed without the individual, those strong sentiments which are the reverse of the selfish and introverted portions of our constitution, are called into action. The husband and the father no longer labors for himself alone, no longer even principally for himself. There are others who, he feels, have claims upon his time, his thoughts, his possessions, more imperative even than himself. He first provides for these, and for their sakes willingly and often undergoes deprivations and self-denials. To the philosopher who occupies his mind with the study of the motives of men, their self-abnegation must appear at once one of the most singular and most beautiful traits in our nature. That we may justly appreciate the rite which we are about to describe, we shall first speak of

The Meaning of Marriage.

The composite character of the nature of our species does not allow us to answer this in one sentence. We are formed

(131)

of organic, terrestrial bodies, and of subtle spirits. To the former portion of our nature, marriage is the condition best adapted to the perpetuation of the species: it is a union of two persons of opposite sexes which calls into play the peculiar functions of each, thus furnishing the necessary factors for the production of a third individual of the same species. The physiologist sees this and nothing more. He may even dare to say that there is nothing more.

In this he egregiously errs. Were this all, it would have little booted the legislators of all time, and the divine voice itself, to have enacted stringent and numerous regulations having reference to the married state. *Such a union extends its influence throughout the whole fabric of social and political life, and strikes its roots deep into the moral nature of the race. If we are asked for a specific definition, we have found none better than that given some years since by the Count of Portalis in the French legislative body. It runs as follows : "Marriage is the union of a man with a woman, who associate themselves in order to perpetuate the species, to aid each other by mutual assistance, to support together the chances of life, and to endure the same fate." In this clear and practical statement we perceive precisely what every one who proposes to form this relation should feel himself or her self thoroughly prepared to assume.

It is only in the most abject members of the human race that we find the marriage tie almost obliterated, and in none, we believe, is it wholly null. There are, indeed, tribes in East India where the practice of polyandry, or of one woman having several husbands, is usual, but even among these, promiscuous intercourse is prohibited. The rudest savages respect and enforce fidelity, they believe that adul- . tery is a crime, and hold the family circle to be sacred.

In proportion as morality and civilization advance, so

1o the sanctity of marriage, and the appreciation of the beauty of marital chastity. The Roman Catholic and Greek churches consider the rite one of the holy sacraments of the church, and the apostles and the early fathers of the church unanimously refer to the married condition as honorable, pure, and praiseworthy; while no denunciations were too scathing for those lewd men and women who seek to degrade it by violating its ordinances. Just in proportion as such elevated sentiments as these are abroad in a community, just in proportion as love is pure, marriage honored, and the bed undefiled, will all the other Christian and patriotic virtues be admired and practised. And no more ominous sign of decay and deep corruption in a nation can be seen, than when there is a wide-spread aversion to marriage, an oft-repeated sneer at the happiness it brings, a current doubt as to the fidelity of those who are united in its bonds.

We believe and hope that perhaps excepting one or two of our largest and most profligate cities such a state of thought does not exist in our land. Most young persons of both sexes look forward to marriage as a desirable condition, and when they have entered it, they accept cheerfully its burdens, observe honorably its injunctions, and are far happier than if they had remained single. Few matters give more anxiety than the fear that for some reason this favored condition may never be reached, that some disability exists which disqualifies one from its acceptance. This is not unfrequently a fruitful source of disquietude to young men, and therefore we deem it well to discuss here the

Physical Fitness and Unfitness for Marriage.

The physiological and also the legal understanding of marriage is, that it is a union *for the purpose of offspring.*

12

Therefore both the lawyer and the physician must condemn any marriage in which this purpose is not at all, or only imperfectly carried out. In other words, *virility* is a necessary preliminary to marriage. Not merely should the age of puberty be passed, but the whole body should be so developed, and the special functions so matured, that intercourse may not prove injurious to the male, nor his unripe secretion be unequal to the formation of a healthy child.

Impotence, we shall speak of hereafter, but here we insist on *virility*. Marriage works sure and irreparable injuries on the constitution of boys or very young men. Their lives are shortened, their health enfeebled, their mental powers frequently impaired. Then their children are usually puny and sickly, apt to have hereditary weakness, and not to attain advanced years.

The most advisable *age to marry* has been much discussed by writers in all ages. We shall not repeat their conflicting opinions, many of them purely theoretical, but say at once that in this country in the majority of cases, the full stature and complete development of physical powers are not attained before the age of twenty-five years, and that from that to thirty-five is the decade in which a man may the most suitably seek a wife.

Physicians are not unfrequently appealed to on the question whether a person of feeble constitution will be benefited or injured by marriage. Many families have hereditary taints, and not a few young men through misfortune or temptation have incurred maladies which they fear may be aggravated by the novel relations under which they will be placed, or possibly transmitted in some form to their offspring.

So far as such inquiries relate to those diseases which ordinarily arise from impure intercourse we have already replied to them in the previous portion of this work. In cases of a consumptive, a scrofulous, or an insane tendency, it is probable that a predisposition to such weakness will be passed down, and quite certain that they will, should a like tendency exist in the wife. But it is not likely that any of these diseases will be aggravated or hastened by marriage ; on the contrary, very many facts could readily be adduced to show that in both sexes, providing that the other partner has not the same tendency, such constitutional disorders are decidedly mitigated and often altogether avoided by a union. The exercise of the generative functions in marriage has a powerful derivative effect, and not rarely alters for the better a feeble constitution. Epilepsy, nervous depression, and even occasional insanity have been known to be greatly relieved or removed by a judicious union.

When, however, such debility arises from a progressive and natural decay of the body—in other words, when it is the consequence of advancing age—the very worst results may be apprehended from such a step. There are matrimonial engagements occasionally contracted by elderly men which are eminently satisfactory both physically and mentally. But in such instances the man must be healthy and vigorous, or else, like King David, he must content himself with the proximity alone of her who is his partner in life, otherwise he will soon fall a victim to some serious disease. Dr. Reich, in his learned work on the Degeneration of the Human Race, finds an active cause of the increasing number of diseases and weakened muscles of our generation in the growing tendency now-a-days to postpone marriage until time and perhaps indulgence have diminished the forces, and exposed the system to succumb readily to any unusual drain upon its resources. Therefore, after the age of thirty-five, a man in poor health, or with an obvious tendency to disease, shonld be extremely cautious how he contracts a lien of this nature.

Malformations of various kinds, whether by nature or accident, not unfrequently occasion poignant distress of mind lest they constitute an insuperable barrier to matrimony. Generally, such anxiety is unfounded. A diminished or an excessive growth of the parts rarely is carried to such an extent as to constitute a barrier to intercourse. The absence of one or even both of the testicles may arise from the fact that they have never descended from the interior of the abdomen, where they are always located before birth. This retention of their original position does not necessarily interfere with their functions, however. Sometimes the prepuce is long, thick, and adherent to such a degree that it seriously interferes with the exercise of the function. In such cases it should be submitted to the examination of a surgeon, as an operation may be required. A more rare condition is when the orifice of exit is not at the extremity, but on the side or close to the body. This usually does not prevent connection, but does produce sterility. It, too, can often be removed by a skilful surgeon.

The size of the organ sometimes excites fear lest matrimony could not be completed. But there is no permanent proportion between size and vigor. Generally an unusual size is accompanied with debility, and it is not infrequently observed, indeed it may be said to be the rule, that persons of vigorous powers have small but well-shaped parts. Those who have studied the models of classical antiquity will have noticed that the most perfect representations of manly strength present these parts even unusally small. The negro race have the parts larger than the white, but they do not proportionately increase in size on erection. A small and shrivelled condition in either race is a sign of impotence.

The Choice of a Wife.

Although the boy Cupid is notoriously blind, and shoots his arrows wildly, yet it is not amiss for the prudent man to take such an important step as marriage with his eyes open. A vast amount of domestic infelicity, and a vast amount of social vice, which is the consequence of this infelicity, would be saved were people a little more discreet and sensible in their selection of those with whom they propose to join irretrievably their lives and fortunes. So far as mental and moral qualities are concerned, we shall have little to say, others, and they better qualified than ourselves, having given abundant advice on these topics, but in what relates to the physical, we have some hints to offer, which, if observed, will go far to insure a fortunate alliance.

The young man who goes forth in search of a wife should not overlook health, nor undervalue beauty in the woman he seeks. Without the former, he will lose half the pleasure which otherwise would be his lot; with the latter, the attractions which bind him true to his own hearth will be redoubled. A sickly, nervous, peevish, inefficient wife—qualities which are naturally associated—is not a help-meet, but a dead weight to a man; a homely, or even an indifferent-looking woman runs a risk of being slatternly, of disgusting her husband, and of alienating him. The powers and the charms of personal beauty deserve to be appreciated and applauded far more than is the wont, and when it is remembered that real beauty means also sound health, we cannot hesitate to answer the young man who asks us deprecatingly, "Would you have me marry for beauty?" with a round affirmation: "You probably cannot do better."

The *relative ages* of the two should be thought of. No young woman should marry before she is twenty, and it is

12*

not wise for a man to select a wife who is his elder. Such unions usually result in estrangement. A seniority of between five and ten years on the part of the husband is most highly to be recommended.

A writer whom we have already quoted, says: "I think there should always be an interval of about ten years between a man of mature age and his wife. Women age much more rapidly than men, and as the peculiar functions of matrimony should cease in both parties about the same time, such interval as this is evidently desirable." But we are of opinion that a difference of less than ten years is more suitable. As above remarked, from five to ten years may be taken as the limit.

It is also well to be aware of the fact that when the husband is the elder, the children are more likely to have a majority in the male sex. Why this is, we shall have occasion to explain subsequently. Then, too, man retains his powers and passions longer than woman, and his fidelity is more assured when she is fresh and blooming, than when she has already become old while he retains his vigor. These are low motives, it may be said, but they are such as we know influence our sex powerfully, and we must therefore enlist them on the good side.

Marrying Cousins.

The question whether *intermarriage of near relatives* can be approved is one which within the last few years has excited lively discussion among physicians. The most skilful are found on opposite sides, and the arguments adduced against it seem very strong. While granting this, we must express our own views candidly that they only *seem* strong. and that if closely scrutinized they are found to be based on erroneous statistics, and compiled by persons who are prejudiced already in favor of their own views.

In a similar work to the present, addressed, however, to the other sex, we made use of the following language, which exposed us to severe criticism from several eminent statisticians and medical writers: "The fear of marrying a cousin, even a first cousin, is entirely groundless, *provided there is no decided hereditary taint in the family.* And when such a hereditary taint does exist, the danger is not greater than in marrying into any other family where it is also found. But as few families are wholly without some lurking predisposition to disease, it is not well, as a rule, to run the risk of developing this by too repeated unions."

Decided as this language is, our further investigations since we made use of it do not lead us to weaken its force. On the contrary, we find ourselves supported in it by one of the most cautious and dependable authorities in the medical world, the *Lancet* of London. In the editorial columns of a late number of that journal the following statement is made as the result of the most recent and extended researches on that point:—

"The marriage of cousins, providing both are healthy, has no tendency to produce disease in the offspring. If, however, the cousins inherit the disease or the proclivity to it of their common ancestor, their children will have a strong tendency to that disease, which might be fostered or suppressed by circumstances. There can be no question that cousins descended from an insane or highly consumptive grand-parent should not intermarry; but we cannot see any reason for supposing that either insanity or consumption would result from the intermarriage of healthy cousins."

In conclusion, while for a man to marry a near relative when they both belong to a consumptive, a scrofulous, or a weak-minded race, is eminently reprehensible, it is not contrary to ascertained laws for him to unite himself to his cousin when the family is thoroughly healthy.

Long Engagements.

" Plighted troth" is a poetical and romantic subject, but there is such a thing as carrying a prolonged fidelity under the terms of an "engagement" to a dangerous excess. We do not now refer to the moral perils, the increased temptations which arise from the more intimate familiarity and over-confidence of lovers—though these are real and objectionable —but to the direct injury they bring on a young man. It is impossible for him to indulge in these caresses and fondlings without violently exciting his passions, and they in turn react on the secretory functions. The consequence is that not unfrequently repeated nocturnal emissions, spermatorrhœa, and loss or impairment of power result. At the very moment when he should be in full possession of his strength, he finds that hope too long deferred, balks itself. This caution is especially needed by those who at an earlier period of their life have injured themselves by solitary vice or sexual excess.

There are strong physical as well as moral reasons why we would urge the lover, however, unwelcome such advice, and however certain to be disregarded, to hold his loved one at arm's length, and to deny himself those little fondlings and toyings which he can secure. Innocent though they are, and pure as the affection is, they still cheat nature with unfulfilled promises, and bring with them retribution. The advice of that distinguished surgeon, Mr. William Acton, on this point, is forcible. He says: " All medical experience proves that for any one, especially a young man, to enter into a long engagement without any immediate hope of fulfilling it, is physically, an almost unmitigated evil. I have reason to know that this condition of constant excitement has often caused not only dangerously frequent and long-continued nocturnal emissions, but most painful affections of the testes. These results sometimes follow the progress of an ordinary two or three months' courtship to an alarming extent. The danger and distress may be much more serious when the marriage is postponed for years." Instances of the same kind have come under our own experience, and convince us that even such strong language as that we have just quoted, does not state the possible injury too decidedly.

The Male Flirt.

The evils we have just mentioned find their origin in *ungratified sexual excitement.* This is always sure to be attended, if frequently repeated and long-continued, by injurious consequences. Whether it be from an engagement, from disappointed affection, from too great familiarity with the other sex, or from entertaining lascivious thoughts, any such excitement leads to weakening of power, and sometimes to actual disease. Degeneration or chronic inflammation of the gland, spermatorrhœa, emissions, and impotence, are all possible from neglect of hygienic rules in this regard.

Here, therefore, is a reason—one of many—why we should discountenance the disposition among young men to become the heroes of half a dozen engagements and love passages. In so doing they violate social laws, trifle with the best affections of our nature, give others endless anguish, and also run the chance of hurting themselves for life.

The society of refined and pure women is one of the strongest safeguards which a young man can have, and he does well when he seeks it; but it should always be motives of simple friendship and kindly interest which impel him to cultivate it. When he considers that the time has come that his means and circumstances allow of marriage, he should then look intelligently for her with whom he would care to pass the remainder of his life in perfect loyalty. He should be impelled by no wanton impulse, nor dissipate his time in worshipping at every passing shrine, but in sincerity and singleness of heart seek an early alliance with her to whom he is ready to swear to be ever true.

For every man does well to reflect, before he assumes the vow, on

The Paramount Duty of Fidelity,

which every husband owes his wife, quite as much as every wife owes her husband. The lax morality of society excuses in the one what it unequivocally condemns in the other, but the Christian and the physiologist agree in allowing no excuse for either.

Nothing is more certain to undermine domestic felicity, and sap the foundation of marital happiness, than marital infidelity. The risks of disease which a married man runs in impure intercourse are far more serious, because they involve not only himself, but his wife and his children. He should know that there is nothing which a woman will not forgive sooner than such a breach of confidence. He is exposed to the plots, and is pretty certain sooner or later to fall into the snares, of those atrocious parties who subsist on black-mail. And should he escape these complications, he still must lose self-respect, and carry about with him the burden of a guilty conscience and a broken vow. If we have urged on the celibate the preservation of chastity, we still more emphatically call upon the married man for the observation of fidelity.

[AUTHORS REFERRED TO IN THIS SECTION.—Edward Reich, *Geschichte, Natur-, und Gesundtheitslehre des ehelichen Lebens;* Napheys, *The Physical Life of Woman;* Acton, *On the Reproductive Organs;* Reich, *Ueber die Entartung des menschlichen Geschlechts;* A. Debay, *Hygiène du Mariage.*]

THE CONSUMMATION OF MARRIAGE.

Its Signification.

In both law and medicine the prime object of marriage, regarded from a social point of view, is the continuation of the species. Hence, until the preliminary steps to this end are taken, the marriage is said not to be consummated. The precise meaning of the expression is thus laid down by Bouvier in his Law Dictionary: "The first time that the husband and wife cohabit together after the ceremony of marriage has been performed, is called the consummation of marriage." A marriage, however, is complete without this in the eye of the law, as it is a maxim taken from the Roman civil statutes that consent, not cohabitation, is the binding element in the ceremony; *consensus, non concubitus, facit nuptias.*

A sage morality throughout most civilized lands prohibits any anticipation of the act until the civil officer or the priest has performed the rite. The experience of the world proves the wisdom of this, for any relaxation of the laws of propriety in this respect are fraught, not only with injury to society, but with loss of self-respect to the individual. Those couples who under any plea whatever, be it of the nearness of the day or the imagined veniality of the liberty, allow themselves to transgress this rule, very surely lay up for themselves a want of confidence in each other, and a source of mutual recrimination in the future.

True as this is shown to be by constant experience, yet

(144)

there have been and still are communities in which the custom was current of allowing and even encouraging such improper intimacies. In the early middle ages it was common in all grades of society, and is mentioned as leading to dissolute habits and consequently condemned, in the laws of King Charlemagne, known as the Capitularies.

The Emperor, Frederick III. of Austria, after he was affianced to Leonora, Princess of Portugal by diplomatic envoys, refused to complete the marriage unless he was permitted to first ascertain whether she would prove a satisfactory wife. And that the same rights were occasionally insisted upon by the other sex is shown by the example of the Lady Herzland von Rappoltstein, who, in 1378, declined to carry out her agreement to wed Count John IV. of Habsburg, on the ground that, after opportunities given, he had proved himself to be incapable.

There are still remote districts in Germany where the peasantry retain the institution known as "trial-nights," *probenächte*, and "come-nights," *komm-nächte*, on which a girl's lover will visit her, and each may be convinced of the physical fitness of the other for marriage. A century ago a similar custom prevailed in parts of New England and in the German settlements in Pennsylvania, as has been lately shown by Dr. Henry A. Stiles, of Brooklyn, in his work on *Bundling*, by which term it was known. Washington Irving, in his *Knickerbocker History of New York*, several times refers to it also.

Now, we believe, happily no trace of the habit exists in our land. Only in a singularly simple and unsophisticated state of society could it be perpetuated without leading to flagitious immorality, and we may regard it as one of the beneficent results of the extensive diffusion of knowledge, that the merit and the advantages to both sexes of absolute

13

continence before marriage are at present universally recognized in this country.

Ignorance Concerning Marriage.

While this precocious knowledge was at one time not condemned as it deserved to be, and as it now is, proper information on the subject is still singularly lacking. As Mr. Acton correctly remarks: "It is but seldom, and then incidentally, that these matters are treated of in books. Nevertheless ignorance, or false ideas respecting them, has caused much evil, and much domestic misery. It is generally assumed that instinct teaches adults how these functions should be exercised. But from several cases that have come under my notice, I should say that many would be entirely ignorant but for previously incontinent habits, or from such notions as they pick up from watching animals." He gives as an instance one of his patients, a member of the Society of Friends, who had been married for some years, and who, out of mere ignorance, had never consummated the ceremony.

Parallel examples come to the knowledge of most physicians who have long been members of the profession. It is no very extraordinary experience to be called to a case of confinement, and to discover that the woman is, strictly speaking, still a virgin. The celebrated accoucheur, Professor Meigs, of Philadelphia, used to relate in his lectures several instances of the kind from his own practice. And so recently as last year (1869), we find a communication by Dr. H. L. Horton, of Poughkeepsie, New York, in the *Medical and Surgical Reporter*, describing a similar case in which he was attending physician. The husband, when questioned, stated that his wife had always found the act painful, and expressed his disappointment, while in fact, although she was at term and was shortly delivered of a healthy child, an examination showed she never had actually yielded.

The same Journal, in a later number, contains an article by Dr. Quimby, of Jersey City, where after several years of marriage, under like circumstances, a coldness and ultimate separation arose. Indeed, nearly always, domestic disappointment is the consequence of this ignorance.

We had one instance brought to our notice where, through ignorance and timidity, nearly a year had elapsed after the persons had married, and yet it had not been consummated. The husband knew something was wrong, and it led to a separation which came near being final.

As when nature is balked in this manner, there must be a hindrance to normal domestic relations, it is proper that parents should see that young persons of both sexes who are about to enter matrimony have a proper understanding of its duties.

The Marriage Relation.

Usually marriage in this country is consummated within a day or two of the ceremony. In Greece, the excellent rule prevails that at least three days shall be allowed to elapse between the rite and the act, and it were well if this rule were general. In most cases the bride is nervous, timid, exhausted by the labor of preparation and the excitement of the occasion, indeed, in the worst possible frame of body and mind to bear the great and violent change which the marital relation brings with it.

The consequence is that in repeated instances the thoughtlessness and precipitancy of the young husband lay the foundation for numerous diseases of the womb and nervous system, and for the gratification of a night he forfeits the

comfort of years.   Let him at the time when the slow paced
hours have at last brought to him the treasures he has so
long been coveting, administer with a frugal hand and with
a wise forethought.   Let him be considerate, temperate, and
self-controlled.   He will never regret it, if he defer for days
the exercise of those privileges which the law now gives him,
but which are more than disappointing if seized upon in an
arbitrary, coarse, or brutal manner.

There is no more infallible sign of a low and vulgar man
than to hear one boast or even to mention, the occurrences
which transpire on the nuptial eve.   Who does so, set him
down as a fellow devoid of all the finer feelings of his own
sex, and incapable of appreciating those of the other.   While
the newly married man should act so that his tender solici-
tude and kind consideration could only reflect credit on himself were they known, he should hide them all under a veil
of reticence more impenetrable than that which ancient
legend says concealed the mysterious goddess of Sais.

The husband should be aware that while as a rule the first
conjugal approaches are painful to the new wife, and therefore that she only submits and cannot enjoy them, this pain
should not be excessively severe, nor should it last for any
great length of time—not more than one or two weeks.
Should the case be otherwise, then something is wrong, and
if rest does not restore the parts, a physician should be
consulted.   It is especially necessary that great moderation
be observed at first, an admonition which we the more urgently give, because we know it is needed, because those
specialists who devote their time to diseases of women are
constantly meeting patients who date their months and
years of misery from the epoch of marriage.

The Tests of Virginity.

There is a wide-spread, an erroneous, and a most mischievous notion accepted among those not acquainted with anatomy, that unless marriage is a bloody rite, it is indicative of previous unchastity on the part of the bride. We have had instances brought to our knowledge by correspondents, where the most poignant agony, and the most cruelly unjust suspicions were the consequences of this unfounded belief. It seems to have become general from the perusal of those portions of Deuteronomy which lay down the Mosaic ritual of marriage, in which this test of virginity was considered final.

But there is every difference between the ancient Jewish maidens, brought up to an active live, married very young, and of a peculiar temperament, and our young women educated with lax muscles, and delicate frames, to habits of indolence and debility. The consummation of marriage with a virgin is by no means necessarily attended with a flow of blood; and the absence of this sign is not the slightest presumption against her former chastity. In stout blondes it is even the exception rather than the rule; and in all young women who have suffered from leucorrhœa, the parts are relaxed, and flowing does not occur.

So, too, the presence or absence of the hymen is no test. Frequently it is absent from birth, and in others it is of exceeding tenuity, or only partially represented. There is, in fact, no sign whatever which allows even an expert positively to say that a woman has or has not suffered the approaches of one of the opposite sex.

They are all quite as deceptive as that still practised in Albania, known as "the sieve test." A skin is stretched tightly across the top of a sieve, and the bride is requested to stand upon it. If the skin yields, she is a virgin. As it is very sure to do so, the Albanian bridegrooms are perfectly convinced of the chastity of their wives.

The true and only test which any man should look for is modesty in demeanor before marriage, absence both of assumed ignorance and a disagreeable familiarity, and a pure and religious frame of mind. Where these are present, he need not doubt that he has a faithful and a chaste wife.

Obstacles to the Consummation of Marriage.

We have now to consider the cases where for some incapacity on the one side or the other, it is not possible to consummate marriage. When an incapacity of this kind is absolute or incurable, says Bouvier in the Law Dictionary, and when it existed at the time of the ceremony of marriage, both the ecclesiastical law and the special statutes of several of the American States, declare the marriage void and of no effect, *ab initio*. But the suit must be brought by the injured party, and he or she naturally incapable cannot allege that fact in order to obtain a divorce.

An incapacity for marriage may exist in either sex, and it may be in either, temporary or permanent. We shall first examine it

On the part of the Female.

The most common cause of a temporary character is an excessive sensitiveness of the part. This may be so great that the severest pain is caused by the introduction of a narrow sound, and the conjugal approaches are wholly unbearable. Inflammation of the passage to the bladder, of some of the glands, and various local injuries, are also absolute but temporary barriers. Any of these are possible, and no man with a spark of feeling in his composition will urge his young wife to gratify his desires at the expense of actual agony to herself.

Conditions of this kind require long and careful medical treatment, and though it is disagreeable to have recourse to this, the sooner it is done, the better for both parties.

A permanent obstacle is occasionally interposed by a hymen of unusual rigidity. It is rare, indeed, that this membrane resists, but occasionally it foils the efforts of the husband, and leads to a belief on his part that his wife is incapable of matrimony. A suit for divorce was brought in a Pennsylvania court some years since on this alleged ground. An examination by experts, however, revealed the fact that no actual incapacity existed, but merely a removable one, from this cause.

A complete or partial absence of the vagina forms an absolute and generally incurable obstacle to conjugal duty on the part of the woman. Such a condition may arise from an injury received earlier in life, and which has allowed the sides to contract and grow together; or she may have been so from birth. Surgeons have devised various operations for the relief of this malformation, but they are usually dangerous and of uncertain results. No woman should seek a matrimonial connection when thus afflicted, and when it is not discovered until after marriage, the proper course is either a separation or a voluntary renunciation of marital privileges.

On the Part of the Male.

These are far more numerous than in the female, and form an important branch of our subject. Probably no one topic in sanitary and physiological science gives rise to more distressing and generally more causeless fears than the anxiety lest one may not be able to fulfil the duties of married life. A philosophical medical writer says : " In losing the command of this function at an age when it should be vigorous, man loses his self-respect, because he feels himself fallen in importance in relation to his species. Therefore the loss of virile power, real or supposed, produces an effect more overpowering than that of honors, fortune, friends, or relatives ; even the loss of liberty is as nothing compared to this internal and continual torture. Those who suffer from injustice or misfortune can accuse their enemies, society, chance, etc., and invent or retain the consciousness of not having deserved their lot; they have, moreover, the consolation of being able to complain, and the certainty of sympathy. But the impotent man can make a confident of no one. His misery is of a sort which cannot even inspire pity, and his greatest anxiety is to allow no one to penetrate his dismal secret."

We are well convinced that there are many to whom these words apply, and also that there are many who suffer these pangs needlessly, or who at least are anxious without cause. We shall therefore proceed to speak in detail of the conditions of the male which render him averse to the procreative act, incapable of completing it, unable to attempt it, or barren in its results, under the headings, lethargy, debility, impotence, and sterility. And

1. Lethargy.

There are some individuals who are rarely or never troubled by the promptings of nature to perpetuate life, and yet are by no means incapable of doing so. They are indeed few in number, and are usually slow in mind and of an extremely lymphatic and lethargic temperament. They experience very little desire and no aversion toward the opposite sex. In a less degree, this trait is a national one. The poorly fed peasants of the north of Europe are remarkable for the little store they set by the indulgence of passion. Such a condition need cause no anxiety, and calls for no treatment.

A want of desire does, however, often occur under circumstances which give rise to great mental trouble, lest it be permanent. It may have many causes, some mental, others physical. Prolonged and rigid continence, excesses either with the other sex or in solitary vice, a poor and insufficient diet or the abuse of liquors and the pleasures of the table, loss of sleep, severe study, constant thought, mental disturbances, as sorrow, anxiety or fear, the abuse of tobacco, drugs, etc., all may lead to the extinction of the sexual feelings. So, too, may certain diseases of the organs, especially those brought about by impure intercourse, and by organic changes, the results of age, and also, in some persons, a natural intermission in the secretion of the procreative fluid, and occasionally, a dislike of the person to whom one is united. Athletic exercises, severe and long-continued, have always been known to bring about a temporary lethargy of the reproductive system, and persons who grow obese nearly invariably find their passions diminish until they almost wholly disappear.

Of these various causes, lethargy arising from muscular or mental exertion, from continence, from emotion, and from high living, need give no anxiety, as when the causes are removed, the natural instincts will quite surely re-assert themselves. "Men who gain their bread by the sweat of their brow," says a medical writer, "or by the exhausting labor of their brains, should know full well that they cannot hope to be always in a fit state to perform the sexual act.

During certain periods when occupied with other matters
the thoughts can dwell but little on such subjects, and no
disposition exists to indulge anything but the favorite or
absorbing pursuit, mental or physical, as the case may be.
After a lapse of time different in various individuals, such
thoughts arise again, and the man who yesterday was so indifferent to sexual feelings, as practically to be temporarily
impotent, now becomes ardent."

When such absence of feeling springs from self-abuse, from
excessive alcoholic drinks, sexual indulgence, the employment of drugs, or the use of tobacco, it is more serious and
more lasting. Then there is not only a temporary cessation
in the secretion, but the action of the internal organs has
been altered to a degree which may prove permanent.
Some may think in classing tobacco under this head, we are
going beyond what facts warrant. But our own observation,
as stated on a previous page, leads us to indorse the views
of Mr. William Acton, who uses the following language :
" I am quite certain that excessive smokers, if very young,
never acquire, and if older, rapidly lose any keen desire."
The treatment in all such cases can only be successful when
the sufferer is willing, *and able* to renounce definitely and
completely, the habits which have brought about his condition. Of course, the hygienic advice we have to offer to all
our readers is, never to allow themselves to be led into excess, and if they have already been guilty of such folly, the
sooner they renounce it the happier and healthier they
will be.

When lethargy arises from age or local disease it must be
met by a judiciously regulated medical treatment, which we
cannot detail here.

2. Debility.

It is not uncommon to find desire present, and yet the consummation of marriage to be impossible from a want of power, although the individual is by no means impotent. This condition is called "false impotence," and often causes great alarm, though generally unnecessarily. In persons of nervous temperaments, though otherwise perfectly healthy, the force of imagination, the novelty, the excitement, and the trepidation attendant upon the ceremony of marriage completely overpower them, and they are terrified to find it impossible to perform the duties of their new relation. Sometimes this state of the system lasts for days, weeks, and months. Recollecting perhaps some early sins, the young husband believes himself hopelessly impotent, and may in despair commit some violent act forever to be regretted.

In the superstitions of the middle ages this temporary incapacity was deemed to be the work of some sorcerer or witch. In France the spell was known under the name of *nouement d'aiguillette*, and many a poor wretch has expiated this imaginary and impossible crime with severe tortures and life itself. The French perhaps, as a nation with a prevailing nervous temperament, may have been subject to such an affection more than others. Montaigne in one of his essays speaks of it as something very common, and with the enlightened spirit which characterized him, derided the superstitions with which it was associated by the vulgar. He says in his essay on the force of imagination: "I am not satisfied, and make a very great question whether those marriage locks and impediments, with which this age of ours is so fettered that there is hardly anything else talked of, are not merely the impressions of apprehension and fear." This rational explanation was not received generally then, because the trouble was imputed to witchcraft; nor now, because it is attributed to permanent incapacity. But in all nations and ages the nervous system is and has been liable to such sudden prostrations.

Herodotus, the Greek historian, relates that Amasis, King of Egypt, having married a Greek virgin famous for her beauty, by name Laodicea, found himself deprived of all power to complete the marriage. Under the impression that she had used some enchantment, he ordered her beheaded. But Laodicea begged time and opportunity to erect a statue to Venus, before the completion of which she assured Amasis, his faculties would be restored him. The king granted her request, and she thus saved her life.

Such instances not unfrequently come to the notice of the physician, and if he is a judicious one, he refrains from calling into requisition any of those powerful drugs which act as stimulants to the functions, but rather writes for some carminative, and assures the patient of its efficacy. His promises are rarely falsified, for the mind once convinced that the corrective has been found, the nervous debility departs.

The case is different and more serious in that form of debility attended by premature loss of the secretion, or a defective erectile power. To be sure, this too may arise from the novelty of the act, want of power of the will, undue excitement, apprehension, fear, or disgust, and in these instances, its treatment is obvious. But it is also one of the commonest consequences of excess, of venereal diseases, especially gonorrhœa, of solitary vice, and of all those causes which we have previously enumerated as exerting a debilitating influence on the masculine function. Concerning its prevention and treatment we refer to what we have already said in the second part of this work. Usually this form of debility is associated with considerable irritability, that is, persons so afflicted are on the one hand very readily excited by the presence of the other sex, or other causes, and yet are weak, and unable satisfactorily to complete the conjugal duty.

All such persons should sedulously avoid every kind of artificial excitement, make free use of cold water as douche and hip-bath, and often they require special surgical treatment, or the employment of electricity or galvanism. Sometimes this irritability arises from an accumulation of matter under the foreskin, or from the too great tightness of this part. Debility may result from wearing trusses for ruptures, as these mechanical appliances interfere with the circulation, and hence impair the secretion of the fluid. Should this impairment extend to the degree of threatening entire loss of power, the question would arise whether the hernia should not be cured by what is known in surgery as the "radical operation."

A diet exclusively or largely vegetable is supposed by many to weaken the powers, especially of such vegetables as are chiefly made up of fibre and water, as cabbage, turnips, beets, etc. So, too, any diet which is not nourishing interferes with the functional vigor. The monks of La Trappe are obliged by the rules of their order to abjure meat altogether, and to subsist upon a loaf of black bread and water each day. They are famous for the rigidity of their vows, and the success with which they maintain them.

3. Impotence.

Actual impotence during the period of manhood is a very rare complaint, and nature very unwillingly and only after the absolute neglect of sanitary laws gives up the power of reproduction. Whatever mercenary quacks may write for

14

base, interested motives, and however they may magnify the ill-results of abuse, it is very uncommon to find complete and permanent inability to consummate the marriage rite.

Professor Lallemand gives the following definition of this condition: "True impotence consists of want of power, not once, but habitually; not only with prostitutes, but with those whom we most love; not under unfavorable circumstances, but during long periods of time, say five, fifteen, or twenty years." It is well that it is rare, for as Prof. Niemeyer remarks: "Not only sensual women, but all, without exception, feel deeply hurt, and are repelled by the husband whom they may previously have loved dearly, when, after entering the married state, they find that he is impotent. The more inexperienced and innocent they were at the time of marriage, the longer it often is before they find that something is lacking in their husband; but, once knowing this, they infallibly have a feeling of contempt and aversion for him." It is the knowledge that they are becoming contemptible and disgusting to their wives, that brings so many young husbands, fearing they are impotent, to the physician. And as Professor Niemeyer goes on to say, unhappy marriages, barrenness, divorces, and perchance an occasional suicide, may be prevented by the experienced physician who can give correct information, comfort, and consolation when consulted on this subject.

Therefore we are careful to repeat that actual, permanent impotence is very rare in early and middle life, that nature is long-suffering in this respect and slow to bring in her revenges for even very gross violations of her laws. In by far the most numerous instances, supposed cases of impotence and actual cases of inability to consummate marriage depend for their cause either on lethargy or debility of the function, and are temporary, or at any rate curable.

When a single man fears that he may be unable to fulfil the duties of marriage, he should not marry until this fear is removed, as the very existence of such a suspicion will strongly tend to bring about the weakness which he is so anxious about. Rather let him state his condition fully to some intelligent physician, and always preferably to one whom he knows and in whose skill and discretion he has confidence, and *never* to the specialists whose advertisements he reads in newspapers, and whose only aim is to foster his terrors to the extent of frightening him out of large sums of money without doing him a pennyworth of good. And under no circumstances should he adopt the scandalous and disgusting advice which immoral associates may give him, to experiment with lewd women in order to test his powers. Such an action must meet with unequivocal condemnation from every point of view.

Should there be good medical reasons to believe that he is actually impotent, he must not think of marriage. Such an act would be a fraud upon nature, and the law both of church and state declares such a union null and void. Yet even 'with this imperfection, he need not give way to despair, or to drink. There is plenty to live for besides the pleasures of domestic life. Thousands of men deliberately renounce these. There are careers of usefulness and of pleasantness in abundance in which he can pass his days and hardly miss those joys which are denied him. Certainly it would be far more deplorable to lose sight or hearing than this faculty so rarely and sometimes never called into play. There is good cheer, therefore, even for such unfortunates.

That the causes of such loss may be guarded against, in so far as they are preventable, as every man is bound to do, we shall briefly recapitulate them.

First, *old age*. As we have explained in the first part of

this work, the period of virility in man, like that of child-bearing in woman, is naturally limited to but a fraction of the whole term of life. The physiological change which takes place in the secretion in advanced years deprives it of the power of transmitting life, and at last the vigor of the function is lost. The spermatozoa, which in manhood are bodies formed, as we have said, of a conical head and a long, vibrating extremity, lose the latter portion of their body, and become mere rounded cells, without the power of independent motion. With the impotence of decrepitude, however, we have little to do, and as to its prevention—cure, there is none—we refer to what we have already said in the earlier portion of this book, in regard to prolonging virility.

The second cause is *venereal diseases*. M. Liégeois, who has most closely examined the effects of these diseases on virility of any recent writer, considers that they lead, more frequently than any other class of maladies, to permanent, incurable impotence. They may do so either by an actual destruction of the part, or by exciting inflammation in the secretory apparatus, or by attacking the adjacent structures.

Malformations are another cause. These may be natural, dating from birth, or accidental, from injury, or from some necessary surgical operation, or from design, as in the case of eunuchs. They are so various that we cannot give any special directions for such cases. When the secreting glands are absent from birth, there may or may not be impotence, but generally it is present. Cases are on record, however, where men in this condition have married and had large families of children. Stock-raisers, however, look with well-grounded suspicion on the males of the lower animals which present this malformation.

The influence of *self-abuse* in producing impotence has been much overrated for selfish purposes by writers who cared nothing how much mental suffering they caused, so that they only bled their victim's purse. This habit causes perversion of feeling, and debility, but does not affect the character of the secretion, except when carried to great excess.

"The diminished power of the onanist is usually first increased to temporary impotence by reading popular medical treatises on the results of his vice," says Professor Niemeyer, and it is the manifest truth of this remark that leads us to believe that some better information than that now generally current on this topic will do good, and save many from months of needless anguish. This is true also of spermatorrhœa. It leads to debility, but exceedingly rarely to permanent incapacity.

M. Liégeois, in the paper from which we have already quoted, says this complaint, "as a general rule, does not modify the secretion." All that is required in the temporary condition of incapacity which arises from this cause is to cease from the evil, to commence a course of tonic medicines, and to place the body under the best hygienic conditions. Given these, and the most alarming symptoms will disappear, with a rapidity as gratifying to the mind as it is beneficial to the body. Of course we do not deny that in some *very few* cases the insidious corruption of the system has progressed to such an extent that recovery is hopeless; but they are so uncommon that few physicians meet with them.

Every one knows that repeated excesses in indulgence enfeeble the powers, and result at length in actually annihilating them. Dissipated single men, professional libertines, and married men who are immoderate, usually pay the penalty of oft-recurring violation of natural laws, by a complete loss of virility long before the average period. We can but admonish such, that they indulge at their own peril, and that years of ceaseless care cannot repair the damages which months of intemperance have brought about.

We have already referred to the fact that obesity diminishes the generative faculties. It may altogether extinguish them. Trainers of domestic animals are well aware that there is an antagonism between the fat producing and the reproductive powers. Capons are more readily fattened than cocks, steers than bulls. So it is in the human race. Both men and women, as a rule, commence to grow stout about the time their reproductive powers flag; and eunuchs always increase in flesh.

Dr. Dancel, in his treatise on obesity, says this condition of body may lead to impotence, either mechanically, by causing such an unwieldy growth that the conjugal relation is rendered impossible, or by diminishing desire and power.

As far back as classical antiquity, this fact was familiar to physicians. Hippocrates, the father of medicine, cites a number of instances where a too robust habit had brought about virtual or actual impotence. Fat children sometimes never manifest in after years any desire for the opposite sex, and there are examples of young men of thirty who were completely devoid of feeling from the same cause.

The remedy for such a condition is to observe a regimen which will reduce the flesh without impairing the strength. This can be accomplished with ease and certainty by a judicious application of what is now familiarly known as the "Banting system." The details of this can be readily ascertained from Mr. Banting's pamphlet, or from other sources.

"I have never failed to observe," says Dr. Dancel, in this connection, "that a man, not yet old, who is delivered by a judicious diet of even twelve or fifteen pounds weight, is astonished at the advantageous change which has taken place in his virile powers since he has commenced to grow thinner."

So that we can add a judicious regulation of the weight of the body to the precepts we gave on an earlier page, "how to prolong virility."

There are some special causes of impotency not generally known, and therefore not guarded against. The habitual use of opium or hasheesh induces a general prostration of the nervous system, and a debility of the powers of generation, which in the slaves to those pernicious habits passes into complete impotency. General mal-nutrition of the body (*sine Cerere friget Venus*, is an ancient classical expression), lead poisoning, diabetes, and some diseases of the spinal cord, also may bring about this condition.

Arsenical poisoning has the same effect, and it is worth while to remember that poisoning from both lead and arsenic are more common than people generally believe, on account of the very extensive use made of the salts of those metals in the arts. We have known and read of repeated instances of lead poisoning from drinking water brought in lead pipes, and of arsenical poisoning from the coloring matter in green wall paper, and such familiar sources. Nearly all the hair-tonics and hair-color restorers sold so extensively contain sugar of lead, and may produce the results of that poison by their outward application.

4. Sterility.

In the legal treatises we have consulted in order to ascertain the view which that profession takes of various questions concerned in virility, it appears that no distinction is made between impotence and sterility. Bouvier in his Law Dictionary expressly calls attention to this inaccuracy. The researches of physicians have recently placed it in a strong light. It is perfectly possible for a man to consummate marriage, when it is utterly impossible for him ever to have children. His power of transmitting life is gone forever.

The condition of sterility in man may arise either from a condition of the secretion which deprives it of its fecundating powers, or it may spring from a malformation which prevents it reaching the point where fecundation takes place. The former condition is most common in old age, and as a sequence of venereal disease, or from a change in the structure or functions of the glands. The latter has its origin in a stricture, or in an injury, or in that condition technically known as hypospadias, or in debility.

We wish distinctly to add that neither self-abuse nor spermatorrhœa, nor excess in natural indulgence leads to sterility. In all these conditions, the secretion is, barring exceptional cases, perfectly capable of transmitting life; though we may presume certainly not such vigorous life as in healthy and moral individuals.

Dr. Marion Sims, of Paris, has recently given much attention to sterility in man, and his researches have thrown much light on the subject. As, however, they will particularly interest the profession, we shall not spare space for them here, but proceed to the discussion of the practical question: Ought a man who believes himself sterile to marry? He is able, we will say, to consummate his union, but can have no expectation of offspring.

This inquiry is not rarely put. Old men who contemplate matrimony must take it as their own. Men with certain deformities have also to discuss it. They cannot explain their condition to the women they love; hardly can they disclose it to the most sympathizing and discreet medical friend.

Our suggestions to them may relieve them from the necessity of either. The only question really at issue is, whether they should deprive a woman of the sweet satisfaction of having little ones of her own to love and cherish. Therefore if she be of such mature years as to have passed the epoch when she can hope for such joys, certainly there is no objection to the match. But if young, with all the motherly yearnings and capacities unsatisfied, it will be a cruel and a dangerous thing to condemn her to a childless life.

It is possible, however, even where there is sterility in the male, providing the secretion is not absolutely devoid of life-producing properties, for the husband to have children. This, one of the latest and most brilliant discoveries in this branch of medical science, has been successfully carried out by Dr. Girault, of Paris, whose essay " on the artificial production of the human species" was published in 1869. It would lead us into details of altogether too technical a character to do more than mention the fact.

Those professional readers who would look into the subject further will find the references at the end of this section. Suffice it to say, that with such resources at hand, no man need hesitate about matrimony on account of sterility, unless that condition arises from a permanent and absolute degeneration of his functions.

So far as the propriety of employing such means are concerned, we cannot doubt that under many circumstances they are perfectly justifiable. They do not in any way violate nature, or go contrary to her plans, but assist her in carrying them out. Frequently it is of the utmost importance to the happiness of a married couple that they should have a child. When it is found that the sterility in either partner is owing to one of the causes which the plan of Dr. Girault can alone counteract—and it may be either the fault of wife or husband—there can be no good reason urged against carrying it out.

Where sterility depends upon a deficient secretion of the seminal fluid, the patient may have a fair chance of improvement, always provided no organic disease is present. A regulated diet, tonics, and a change of climate will do much; but it is the judicious application of electricity from which most is to be hoped.

"It appears not unreasonable to expect," says Dr. Julius Althaus in his recent work on Electro-therapeutics, "that the secretion of semen may be restored when lost, or improved when deficient, by the use of galvanism. A deficient secretion of milk in the breasts of a female, of cerumen in the ears, of nasal mucus, and of saliva, may be stimulated by the application of electricity. The same effect may naturally be looked for by acting with the continuous current upon the secretory glands of the semen."

The value of this medicinal agent in debility and failure of the generative powers has long been recognized by professional men. As long ago as the close of the last century it was even extravagantly vaunted as a restorer of virility.

It acts as a powerful stimulant, and when combined with proper general treatment holds out a promise of improvement and often of cure, in most cases where no structural change has taken place. But it is a useless and even a dangerous remedy in ignorant hands.

Excessive passion in either sex leads to sterility. Sometimes this passes to a condition of true monomania, technically known as *erotomania*. In such cases it is usually connected with some serious disease of the brain or spinal cord, and may well give grounds for uneasiness.

When in men, it is known under the names of *priapism* and *satyriasis*. The unfortunate subjects of these distressing complaints arc constantly goaded by passion; their thoughts dwell most of the time on lascivious images; sleeping or waking they are besieged by passion; and yielding to their desires so far from assuaging only incites them more, until the constitution breaks down under the unnatural strain. Male Messalinas, they are *fatigati, sed non satiati.*

The secretion under such circumstances is non-fecundating, as a rule, showing the condition to be one of disease. And further proof to the same effect is the fact that it may arise in persons who have lived continent lives.

Whenever such is the case, it is the part of prudence to abstain as far as possible from any indulgence whatever, to take a regular course of treatment, to have a thorough examination, and in all respects to regard one's self in the light of a sick man. Those who ignorantly and rashly imagine that such excessive sensations are a mark of vastly increased vigor, and felicitate themselves on the change, will have bitterly to rue their error in after years.

Special Treatment of Loss of Power.

What has been said about the causes of loss of power will to a considerable extent indicate the care necessary to prevent it, and to improve it.

But besides these there is a specific course of treatment which, if persistently and intelligently carried out, is productive of good results.

Except in those cases where there is an organic change in the parts, or where it is the result of advanced age, there is every hope that the power can be restored. The weakness is a nervous weakness; it depends upon a want of strength in the nervous system; and by having this clearly in mind we may accomplish much.

It is well known that *marriage* often has an excellent influence on the slighter affections of this nature. As Prof. Lallemand says, "the regular and legitimate employment of the functions will alone give all the energy of which they are susceptible, and to this general law the function of reproduction forms no exception."

Yet it is necessary to make the distinction here that whenever it is not nervous debility, but local irritation or inflammation which has brought on loss of power, no recommendation could be more injudicious than this of marriage. The excitement will most certainly severely aggravate the trouble.

Another consideration is, that while it is permissible to marry in most cases of debility or temporary impotence, such a course cannot be recommended out of consideration for the young wife and future offspring.

Who has a right to ask a happy and charming young girl to forsake home and friends in order to rescue a lascivious young man from the penalties of his own turpitudes? Who, being a father, would tolerate such a proposition a moment if it concerned his own daughter?

Then the act of procreation is physically the most exalted one of life. Its demands on the nervous force are greater, and it requires the expenditure of more of the vital power. When this is the evident plan of nature, what offspring can we reasonably expect from flagging and exhausted functions?

While, therefore, marriage as a hygienic measure is desirable, it should be preceded or accompanied by treatment of a more direct kind, specially directed to restore the nervous force. This can be successfully done by various agents.

One of the best is *electricity*, of which we have already spoken. It does not suit where there is irritation or inflam-

mation, but for debility, pure and simple, there is hardly any
more satisfactory therapeutic means. After the patient has
once been taught by a skilful practitioner the particular
method of application which suits his individual case, he can
apply it himself. Good batteries can now readily be obtained
at a reasonable price.

Next in value is *phosphorus.* This agent, so dangerous
if carelessly or ignorantly employed, is of the greatest service
when wisely used. It is precisely the element which the
nervous system expends, and therefore that which it requires
to invigorate it. When there is a feeling of exhaustion after
the act, or incomplete preparation for it, or when debility
unattended with inflammation is present in any of its forms,
we find it of the highest value.

It may be administered in various preparations, but there
is only one which it would be suitable or safe for the non-
medical reader to attempt. As we have remarked on a previous page, *death* has in various instances resulted from its
injudicious employment. The one we shall mention is
"phosphoric acid lemonade." The formula is

Dilute phosphoric acid,	fifteen drops ;
Syrup of ginger,	a tablespoonful ;
Water,	a tumblerful.

This makes an agreeable beverage, and may be taken
three times a day, *but not oftener;* nor should the amount
of the dilute acid be increased.

The other powerful excitants of the nervous system which
are prescribed in such cases are all so dangerous if incau-
tiously used that we shall not mention them. They form
part of the physician's reserves, and can only be taken when
the patient can be closely watched to prevent any injurious
effects.

15

[AUTHORS AND WORKS QUOTED ON THE ABOVE TOPICS.—Bouvier, *Dictionary of Legal Terms;* sub voce, Marriage and Impotence; Reich, *Naturgeschichte des Ehelichen Lebens,* pp. 92, 95,
Acton, *On the Reproductive Organs,* p. 109 ; Dr. Horton, *Medical
and Surgical Reporter,* Aug. 1869, and Feb. 1870. On Virginity,
Tardieu, *Les Attentats aux meurs ; Marriage Rites of all Nations,*
New York, 1869, chap. III.; Professor Lallemand, *On Spermator-
rhœa;* Dr. S. Durkee, *On Gonorrhœa and Syphilis;* Alfred Maury,
La Magie et l'Astrologie au Moyen Age, On the *nouements
d'aiguillettes;* Montaigne, *Essais,* Liv. I. chap. **xx.**; Herodotus,
Bk. II. ; M. Liegeois, *Half-yearly Compendium of Medical Science,*
Part IV. Sect. II. ; Dr. Dancel, *Traité de l'obesité,* chap. iv.; Dr.
Marion Sims, *On Sterility in Man,* in the N. Y. *Med. Jour.,* 1869 ;
Dr. Girault, *Etude sur la Generation artificielle dans l'espèce
humaine.* Paris, 1869, and *Medical and Surgical Reporter,* June,
1870 ; Dr. Julius Althaus, *Treatise on Medical Electricity,* pp.
620-625, second edition, 1870.]

HUSBANDS AND WIVES.

Wᴇ shall now suppose that the young couple have passed through the trials and dangers of the "honey-moon," as it is familiarly called, and have settled down to the staid conduct of life as "old married people." In this condition they will find themselves surrounded by circumstances very different from their former experiences as single persons, and it behooves them to give careful attention to the precepts of hygiene now, lest peculiar temptations and novel trials lead them to the commission of acts for which they will be bitterly but fruitlessly sorry in after years. Therefore we commence our instructions with some remarks on

The Hygiene of the Chamber.

This should be a large, well-ventilated room, with a southern or western exposure, which can receive the direct sunlight for several hours of the day. At least twelve hundred cubic feet of air ought to be allowed each occupant, so if two sleep in the room, and the ceiling be twelve feet high, about fifteen feet square is a desirable size. If one or more children sleep in the same room the dimensions should be proportionately increased, or extra pains should be taken to secure a rapid change in the air of the room. No doubt much of the mortality which characterizes the courts and alleys of our great cities is due to the narrow and crowded rooms in which the tenants sleep; and no matter how many other causes of disease are removed, so long as this remains, we cannot expect to see a proper and normal degree of health established.

In this country it is customary for married persons to sleep in the same bed. In Europe, in the higher classes, they nearly always occupy separate rooms. Louis Philippe, the "citizen king" of France, who thought it policy to assimilate himself in mode of life to the middle classes, chose to make his family an exception to this rule, and, during his reign, visitors to the Tuileries were duly pointed out the great double bed in which the king and queen slept. Probably under most circumstances it is well to adopt the American habit, as such nearness of body leads to a nearness of spirit, and mutual trust and love are fostered by the fact of contiguity.

Only when disease, or some avocation which leads to disturbed slumbers, is to be taken into account, do we recommend the opposite plan. Some physicians suppose that consumption is contagious, and of course many chronic skin diseases notoriously are so; and if present, it is too severe a demand for the sufferer to make that a healthy person should needlessly be exposed to the danger of illness.

Physicians, who are called up nearly every night, can hardly with propriety insist that their wives shall partake of this annoyance inseparable from their avocation. But we forget. We need not extend to them advice on the subject of sanitary rules, as with these they are supposed to be already familiar.

Cleanliness of person is a point about which married people of both sexes cannot be over-scrupulous. When in health, we urgently recommend them to use a bath every morning or every evening. An unpleasant odor almost always attends those who neglect this direction, and certainly few small things can sooner or more inevitably lead to aversion than a bad smell. Persons whose feet, or whose perspiration is generally foul, can obtain relief from this by seeking medical advice. When it is their own fault, as for instance from chewing tobacco, or from frequent indulgence in spirits, they will stand sadly in their own light unless they renounce these indulgences. The man who likes his quid better than his wife is not much of a man.

Frequent changes of underclothing are desirable on this account as well as for general hygienic reasons, and any pains bestowed on keeping the attire neatly arranged and well cared for will not be lost. Women have more delicate sensibilities than men, they are more readily pleased or repulsed by little things, and the husband who is anxious to maintain pleasant relations in his home circle will do well not to neglect the cares of the toilet.

We pass from these considerations of general hygiene to those which more particularly have to do with the state of marriage ; and first

Of Marital Relations.

At the outset of this important subject, we stop to correct a gross, but widely received popular error. Every woman, every physician, nearly every married man will support us in what we are going to say, and will thank us for saying it.

It is in reference to *passion in woman.* A vulgar opinion prevails that they are creatures of like passions with our-selves ; that they experience desires as ardent, and often as ungovernable. as those which lead to so much evil in our sex. Vicious writers. brutal and ignorant men, and some shame-less women combine to favor and extend this opinion.

15*

Nothing is more utterly untrue. Only in very rare instances do women experience one tithe of the sexual feeling
which is familiar to most men. Many of them are entirely
frigid, and not even in marriage do they ever perceive any
real desire. We have in numbers of instances been so informed by husbands, who regretted it, and were surprised
at it.   •

Loose women, knowing that their business is increased if
they feign the pleasure to be reciprocal, often give occasion
for the opinion we are combating, in the minds of young and
inexperienced men. As Mr. Acton well remarks : " There
are many females who never feel any sexual excitement
whatever ; others again, to a limited degree, are capable of
experiencing it. The best mothers, wives, and managers of
households know little or nothing of the sexual pleasure.
Love of home, children, and domestic duties are the only
passions they feel. As a rule, the modest woman submits to
her husband, but only to please him ; and, but for the desire
of maternity, would far rather be relieved from his atten-
tions."

This is doubly true of women during the periods when they
are with child, and when they are nursing. The whole force
of the economy at these times is taken up with providing
sustenance for the new being, and there is no nervous power
left to be wasted in barren pleasures. In those exceptionable cases where this does not hold good, every excitement
is visited upon the child, and it has to suffer in health and
growth for the unnatural appetite of the mother.

The above considerations, which all married men will do
well to ponder, should lead them to a very temperate enforce-
ment of their conjugal rights. They should be always considerate, and not so yield themselves to their passions as to
sacrifice their love to the woman they have married. Let us

here quote the words of Dr. Horatio R. Storer, of Boston, on
these rights : " Restrained within due bounds as to frequency,
they serve to give a charm to life, and to impart fresh
courage for enduring its vicissitudes ; but to gain these, one
single rule must be observed. It is this : That the husband
compel his wife to do nothing that she herself does not freely
assent to. A forced union is even worse than solitary vice.
No true conjugal enjoyment can exist unless it is mutual.
The true rule is to take only what is freely given."

In a similar strain speaks the distinguished old English
divine, Jeremy Taylor, in his excellent " Rules and Exercise
of Holy Living :" " Married people must be sure to observe
the order of nature and the ends of God. He is an ill husband that uses his wife as a man treats a harlot, having no
other end but pleasure. The pleasure should always be
joined to one or another of these ends—with a desire of children, or to avoid fornication, or to lighten and ease the cares
and sadnesses of household affairs, or to endear each other ;
but never with a purpose, either in act or desire, to separate
the sensuality from these ends which hallow it. Married
people must never force themselves into high and violent
lusts with arts and misbecoming devices, but be restrained
and temperate in the use of their lawful pleasures."

We cannot improve upon this admirable advice, so sound,
and so fitly expressed, by one of the wisest and purest of
men ; nor, though other authorities are numerous enough to
our hand, do we consider they are called for.

It is impossible, necessarily, to lay down any specific rules
for the government of others in this particular ; but we may
state generally that no husband should force his wife to submit to him against her will, nor should he even ungently
persuade her : and for himself, whenever he feels immediately
after the act, or during the next day, any depression, or de-

bility, or disturbance of the health, it is a certain sign that he is overtasking himself. Taking men on an average, we counsel them for their own sake, when in middle life and usual health, not to indulge more than once or twice a week, and in old age and feeble health (no matter if they do experience desire), by no means so often, or not at all.

There are certain periods when a complete cessation should be observed. One of these is during the monthly sickness of the woman, and for a day or two after that epoch. It is well known that among our American Indians at such times the squaws leave the lodge, and remain entirely segregated from the household ; and among the Israelites the Mosaic law pronounces a woman unclean for a number of days after her periodical illness has ceased.

The origin of these customs, no doubt, was that observation proved that intercourse at such periods leads to disease in the male ; and modern science, after having, as usual, denied for some time this ancient opinion, has at last proven its correctness. "It cannot be too often mentioned," says Dr. Alexander Stein, of New York, in a paper read before the Medical Journal Association of that city, February, 1870, "that venereal disease is not always the result of impure intercourse, but may arise from contact with a female during the existence of a discharge which is not specific, as, for instance, during menstruation." All other writers of note coincide with this view, and therefore the caution is necessary absolutely to abstain at such times.

During pregnancy and nursing, conjugal relations should be as few as possible. Some writers condemn them altogether, but this we consider an extravagance. They do no harm, providing that they neither on the one hand unduly excite the woman, nor on the other are repulsive to her.

In the former case they injure the growth of the fœtus before birth and sometimes provoke a miscarriage, and after birth are quite sure to deteriorate the quality of the milk to the serious damage, perhaps, of the infant. If repulsive, they lead to domestic unhappiness, loss of mutual respect, and sometimes to violent nervous excitement on the part of the wife.

After a natural confinement, at least two full months should be allowed to elapse before the resumption of the marital relations, and if the labor has been an unusually severe or a complicated one, it is prudent to extend this interregnum yet another month.

During and after the change of life, it is also important to observe an unwonted moderation. During that period any unaccustomed excitement of this character may be followed by flooding, and other serious symptoms, while after the crisis has been passed, the sexual appetite itself should wholly or almost wholly disappear.

In what we have said it may be complained that we harp too constantly on one string—that we are forever repeating and urging moderation, temperance, restraint, self-denial— that if marriage is going to be one constant torment of Tantalus, with the beaker of pleasure ever filled and ever presented to the thirsty lips only to be whisked away again the next moment, leaving the ardent longings cruelly deceived, then that the charm of the condition is gone, and it is better and easier to deny one's self entirely than to irritate by half-indulgence.

Or it may be thrown up to us that all this counsel is useless because men will *not* be moderate in lust, and will *not* practise self-restraint in order to spare feelings which they cannot understand, and a delicacy which they cannot appreciate, in a person over whom the law gives them, in this respect, an absolute power. Very well, we are prepared to enforce our advice with arguments drawn from another source.

We must counsel moderation not only as a moral and amiable trait, and as a bounden duty which man owes woman, but more than that, as an imperative obligation which every man owes himself. That he may know precisely what may befall him from a disregard of the precepts of temperance, we shall mention a few of

The Dangers of Excess.

The unmarried man, who purchases at a high price, and rarely, the pleasures of illicit love, is generally supposed to be the only sufferer from excess in the venereal act. Far from it. He is by no means alone. More commonly than is currently believed, the married man has to settle an account for immoderate indulgence.

To quote the words of a physician of wide experience : " Too frequent emission of the life-giving fluid, too frequent sexual excitement of the nervous system, is most destructive. Whether it occurs in married or unmarried people has little or nothing to do with the result.

"The married man who thinks that, because he is a married man, he can commit no excess, no matter how often the sexual act is repeated, will suffer as certainly and as seriously as the debauchee who acts on the same principle in his indulgences, perhaps more certainly from his very ignorance, and from his not taking those precautions and following those rules which a career of vice is apt to teach a man. Till he is told, the idea never enters his head that he has been guilty of great and almost criminal excess; nor is this to be wondered at, as such a cause of disease is seldom hinted at by the medical man he consults."

The nature of excess may be twofold; either it is a long-continued indulgence beyond the average power of the man to withstand, and which slowly but surely undermines his health, strength, and life ; or it is brief and violent.

It is too often supposed that if only for a night, or a few nights, or a week or two, a man gives the reins to his passion and overtaxes his functions, a few days' rest will restore him. It does seem to, but often only *seems*. The ultimate consequences of libidinous excess, even when that excess is of very limited duration, are becoming more and more apparent to physicians.

Dr. Thomas Laycock, Professor of the Practice of Medicine in the University of Edinburgh, in an article published quite recently on this subject, states it as the result of his clinical experience, that "a great excess for a few days only, acting like a 'shock,' may manifest its consequences in the nervous system at a long distant subsequent period. A sudden, short, yet great excess may be more dangerous than more moderate, albeit excessive indulgence, extending over a long period. In certain constitutions, although only indulged in legitimately and for a short period, as after marriage, such excess may act like a shock or concussion of the spinal cord, or like a blow on the head, and may give rise to serious chronic diseases, as epilepsy, insanity, and paralysis."

The ordinary results of an abuse of the conjugal privilege are, in the man, very much the same as those brought on by self-abuse. Locally there is over-excitation, irritability, and possibly inflammation. The digestion becomes impaired, dyspepsia sets in, the strength is diminished, the heart has spells of palpitation, the spirits are depressed, spermatorrhœa may arise, the genetic powers lose their vigor, there is unusual sensitiveness to heat and cold, sleep is not refreshing, and a jaded, languid indifference takes the place of energy and ambition.

One of the most striking and characteristic effects is indicated in the throat and by the voice. There is a very close sympathy, and one not readily explained between the voice and the procreative function.

We have already mentioned the change from tenor to bass which takes place at puberty, and never occurs in eunuchs. Excessive indulgence often first shows itself by an impairment of vocal power, and a sense of dryness and hoarseness in the throat. Self-abuse and nocturnal losses produce the same effects in men otherwise continent. Often a chronic bronchitis or a loss of volume and strength in the voice is due to some disorder or overstraining of the masculine function, and the proper remedies must be directed in accordance with this fact.

A vast amount of ill-health arises from this unsuspected cause, and it is one of the benefits which we hope will accrue from a more public discussion of this topic than has yet been attempted, that there will be a general appreciation of the truth that a man for his own sake should exert self-denial in marriage.

Still more should he do so for his wife's sake. Very many women lose their health, and some, no doubt, their life, through the constant solicitations of their husbands. One of the ablest physicians of our country who has made the diseases peculiar to women his special study, Dr. Storer, says: "Among these diseases is a very large class occasioned or aggravated by excessive sexual indulgence." Of course we do but refer to this fact here, as we have elsewhere treated of woman's peculiar functions and the disorders to which they are liable, but we wish all men to know that often they may injure their wives' health irretrievably by a self-indulgent course, and with this run the risk of ruining their own domestic happiness.

A foolish notion sometimes prevails that it is necessary to health to have frequent intercourse. We have already said that there is no condition of life more thoroughly in accordance with perfect vigor than chaste celibacy. Next to this comes moderation in married life. It is never required for sanitary reasons to abuse the privileges which law and usage grant. Any such abuse is pretty sure to bring about debility and disease.

They may be long coming, and the connection may often be obscure, but it is undeniable. The ancient Greek physicians were acquainted with the peculiar form of paralysis now technically called "locomotor ataxy," and attributed it to excess in venery. Modern observers have indorsed their opinion, and have traced beyond doubt the relation of cause and effect in a number of instances.

The question may now be put

What is Excess?

As a matter of figures it is difficult to answer, but there is no difficulty whatever in stating explicitly the laws of hygiene in the case.

The power of the masculine function in different men varies greatly. Extraordinary accounts are given by some writers, and individuals are very apt to exaggerate their capacities.

It is well known that Augustus, surnamed the Strong, last King of Poland, had three hundred and fifty-four children, on which Carlyle justly remarks, in his *History of Frederick the Great*, that Augustus certainly attained the maximum in bastardy of any mortal on authentic record.

One of the Latin historians records of the Emperor Pro-

16

clus, that in the war with the Sarmates he violated one
hundred virgins in fifteen days. Such exhibitions of brutal
lust are discreditable to the race, and nearly always disastrous to the individual.

In point of fact it is impossible for even the most vigorous
man to repeat the sexual act more than five or six times
within twelve hours. Should it be attempted more frequently
no spermatic fluid passes, but merely a glairy mucus, often
tinged with blood, or even pure blood. Pleasure there is
none, and danger there is much.

Attempts have been made by legislators and divines to
fix definitely a limit to the conjugal approaches which should
be binding on all. The physician knows the impossibility
of such a regulation. What one man can support with
impunity will ruin the health of another. Each one must
be a law to himself.

We have known men who for years hardly omitted a single night to approach their wives, and yet seemed none the
worse. These are exceptions. If we are asked to give
some general average which may serve as a guide, we should
say that for a man past the first flush of youth, whose mind
or body is engaged in regular labor as severe as that of
ordinary business, once a week is as often as he can pru-
dently expend his force in sensual pleasure; and often he
will find it of advantage even to restrict himself more than
this, as we have previously stated.

Generally speaking, the hygienic rule is, that after the act
the body should feel well and strong, the sleep should be sound,
and the mind clear. Whenever this is not the case, when
the limbs feel languid, the appetite feeble or capricious, the
intellect dull, and the faculties sluggish, then there is excess,
and the act should be indulged in more rarely.

Those who observe strictly this rule will need no other, and will incur no danger from immoderate indulgence.

[AUTHORS AND WORKS REFERRED TO.—Becquerel, *Traité d'Hygiène;* Acton, *On Prostitution;* Dr. Storer, *Is it I?* p. 117; Jeremy Taylor, *Rules of Holy Living,* p. 50; Dr. Stein, *New York Medical Journal,* June, 1870 · Dr. Napheys, *Physical Life of Woman,* p. 78: Dr. Laycock, *Dublin Quarterly Journal of Medical Science* (May, 1869), *on the Dangers of Libidinous Excess;* Acton, *On the Reproductive Organs* (p. 212), *on Clergyman's Sore Throat;* Thomas Carlyle, *History of Frederick the Great,* vol ii. p. 95: Müller, *Ueber Unwillkürliche Samensverluste* (pp. 50–62), *on Venereal Excess.*]

THE HUSBAND AS A FATHER.

THE differences of the sexes, the emotions which depend upon these differences, and the institution of marriage are primarily and directly existent for the purpose of transmitting life, or, to put it more plainly, for having children. Every married couple must distinctly and constantly impress this truth upon their minds, and be governed by it in their life. Whatever relations they bear to each other, whatever duties they may have to society and themselves, all of them are subordinate to the paramount obligation of having and raising a family. We care not what excuse may be imagined in order to escape this duty, it is inadmissible. Nothing short of positive incapacity can exculpate either party.

It is not only their duty to have, not merely a child or two, but a family of children; but also, to do all in their power that their offspring have all the natural advantages which it is possible to give them. It may not be generally known that this matter touches some of the most intimate and earliest relations of the married couple. But, now-a-days, physicians at least are fully satisfied that the season and manner of conception, the condition of father and mother at the time, and several attending circumstances, exercise a most important influence on the newly formed being. In order that this topic, which we believe to be one of the highest interest to all, may be properly understood, we are obliged to depart from the rule we have generally

(184)

laid down for ourselves—not to trespass on the domain of the physiologist—and give a brief explanation, so far as that is possible with the present possessions of science, of that most mysterious and wonderful phenomenon, conception.

The Nature of Conception.

The old writers had a proverb : " Every living being originates in an egg." Without allowing this maxim the latitude it claims, it is perfectly true so far as the human race is concerned. Every one of us commenced our existence in an egg. The human egg, however, has no shell, and is not, as with fowls and many lower animals, deposited outside the body. The female matures one or several at each of her monthly periods, and they pass from the sac which has hitherto contained them on their way to the outer world. They are so minute that they are hardly visible to the naked eye, and so delicate in structure that they readily perish. They remain a longer or a shorter time in their passage from the spot where they are formed to their destination, sometimes requiring but a day or two, at others probably a week or two.

During this passage, should they come in contact with the secretion of the male, the vibratory bodies which we have described as spermatozoa surround the egg, penetrate into it perhaps, and fecundate it. At this moment conception has taken place, and a new member of the species has commenced its individual life.

Now the interest of this process to us in the present connection rests on the indisputable fact that the qualities of the male element are very largely influenced by the condition, mental and physical, of the father at the time ; and that these qualities materially change for better or worse, as the

16*

case may be, the development of the egg, and the growth, faculties, character, and destinies of the newly-formed individual.

One of the best proven and most disastrous examples of this is seen in children who have been conceived at the time the father was partially intoxicated. There is no doubt whatever that under such circumstances the child is pretty sure either to be *idiotic*, or to have epileptic fits, or to be of a feeble mind and irritable nervous system. What a curse does the unblessed cup here entail upon the family! How horrible the reflection, in after years, that the idiot boy or the tortured girl owes its wretchedness to the intemperate indulgence of the father!

The children of men who have exhausted themselves by excesses, or solitary vice, or insufficient food, or severe bodily and mental strain, are not what they would have been if these deteriorating elements had been removed. Very intellectual men rarely have large families, and though to some extent talent is an inheritance, the children of such are apt to be either quite below or quite above mediocrity.

The offspring of men who marry late in life usually manifest some signs of the decrepitude which marked their senile father. They are not long-lived, and are rarely healthy. Their teeth and hair fall early, and they are perhaps never conspicuous for sturdy muscles and power of endurance.

Not dissimilar are those which are conceived at a time when the father is recovering from or is threatened with a severe illness. It is characteristic of the period of convalescence from some affections, that the passions are quite ardent. A sound hygiene forbids their gratification. For not only may this result in a relapse, or a lingering debility, but it may bring into the world a child condemned to an early death, or a lingering and painful life.

The seasons of the year exercise a very manifest action on the secretion of the male element. In domestic and wild animals this is familiar to every one. To a less extent it is observable in the human race. Tennyson refers to it in " Locksley Hall :"—

"In the spring a young man's fancy lightly turns to thoughts of love."

Mr. Acton, possibly acting on the hint of the poet, has taken the trouble to collect the statistics on this point as found in the registration reports of Great Britain. He reaches the curious result that there are about seven per centum more conceptions in that country during the spring months than during any other quarter of the year. And Dr. Edward Smith, of London, has pursued the subject further, and ascertained that the mortality of infants conceived in the spring time is decidedly less than that of those whose existence has commenced at any other period of the year. It would thus seem that a well-defined law indicates that the male, as a rule, is more capable of perpetuating his species when the icy winter loses his hold of the land, and the warm breath of the south wind evokes, as if by magic, sweet violets and gay daffodils from the dark and cold earth.

An even temper, peace of mind, and calm desires are usually supposed, and with every probability, to conspire favorably for the destinies of the offspring. Jeremy Taylor, in the work we recently quoted, says : "Those mixtures are most innocent which are most simple, most natural, most orderly, and most safe."

It is both disgraceful and dangerous for a man to use his wife as a libertine does a prostitute. How can he expect her to retain her respect for him, who shows none for her? How can he suppose that she will remain pure, if he practises corrupt arts, and artificial excitants?

"Husbands should know," says the Seigneur de Brantome in one of his curious books, "that when they abuse their wives by lascivious actions and discourses, they injure themselves, and violate the purpose of marriage; and if their wives fail in fidelity in consequence of such corruptions, husbands have no right to demand redress, for they have brought this punishment on themselves."

Too frequently, we fear, young men regard this sacred union as merely a safe and easy means of indulging their appetites. If they carry out such an idea, they may discover too late the magnitude of their folly.

It is a vicious and a vulgar error which pretends that the unnatural ardor, the anxiety, and the sweetness of the stolen fruit, which are associated with illicit love, tend to produce a more felicitously constituted being. Illegitimate children are notorious for their mortality. The deaths among them during the first year are far greater in proportion than among the progeny of the married, as has been demonstrated by the writers of the Report of the Board of State Charities of Massachusetts (1868). Some celebrated bastards there have been, it is true, but they are the exceptions, and generally they have a taint of viciousness or of monomania running in their blood, which spoils their lives. Shakspeare, who had studied so closely all that pertains to man and his superstitions, makes Edmund in King Lear, say :—

> "Why brand they us with base?
> Who, in the lusty stealth of nature, take
> More composition and fierce quality,
> Than doth, within a dull, stale, tired bed,
> Go to the creating a whole tribe of fops,
> Got between sleep and wake?"

And proves by the atrocious villainy of the youth, and his utter want of natural affection, how false was the sentiment he expresses in these lines.

True, that a certain amount of passion is eminently desirable, and in all likelihood does beneficially affect the offspring; but here again, the judicious man will always remain master of himself.

The Avoidance and Limitation of Offspring.

He chooses the part of wisdom, which cannot be impugned, who attentively studies the laws of nature and obediently submits his life to her dictates. We have defined the only natural object of marriage to be to have and to rear a family of children. The question, How many children is it our duty to have? is one often asked by the married. The father feels his abilities to educate and provide for them limited; the mother, who travails in sorrow, and on whom the immediate care of them devolves, looks often with more dread than pleasure to another addition to her flock. Her health may be giving away and her spirits flagging.

If here, as elsewhere, we seek by observation to derive some reply to this inquiry from nature, we find that she has made certain provisions for the definite limitation of off-spring; and unmistakably warns us of the danger of too rapid child-bearing, not only by debilitating the mother, but by yielding imperfect, feeble, and deformed children.

This limit she sets may indeed be a distant one. The fecundity of some women is matter of astonishment. Italian history says that the noble lady Dianora Frescobaldi was the mother of fifty-two children. Brand, in his History of New-castle, mentions as a well-attested fact, that a weaver in Scotland had, by one wife, sixty-two children, all of whom lived to be baptized: and in Aberconway Church may still be seen a monument to the memory of Nicholas Hooker, who was himself a forty-first child, and the father of twenty-seven children by one wife.

Such examples are, we need not add, so rare that they belong to the curiosities of medical literature. We rarely meet a woman now-a-days who is the mother of more than ten living children. Even in such a family the youngest ones will usually be found puny, or rickety, or idiotic, or deformed. Dr. Matthews Duncan, a careful obstetric statistician, considers that that number, therefore, is too great.

The safeguard which nature has thrown out against over-production is by constituting certain periods of woman's life seasons of sterility. Before the age of nubility, during pregnancy, and after the change of life, they are always barren. During nursing most women are so, but not all. Some even continue their monthly change at this time. There is no absolute certainty that a woman will not conceive then, though the probability is against it.

A so-called *agenetic* or sterile period exists between each monthly change, during the continuance of which it is not possible for the female to conceive. This branch of our subject has attracted much attention of late years from its practical character, but the conclusions reached have so far not been as satisfactory as we could wish. The present views of the most expert physiologists are thus summed up by Dr. Dalton, of New York, in the last edition of his treatise on Human Physiology : " Intercourse is more liable to be followed by pregnancy when it occurs about the menstrual epoch than at other times. This fact was long since established as a matter of practical observation by practical obstetricians. The exact length of time, however, preceding and following the menses during which impregnation is still possible, has not been ascertained. The spermatic fluid, on the one hand, retains its vitality for an unknown period after coition, and the egg for an unknown period after its discharge. The precise extent of the limit of these occurrences is still uncertain, and is probably more or less variable in different individuals."

Those therefore who would take advantage of this natural law can do no better than confining themselves to a few days intervening about midway between the monthly epochs.

We are most decidedly of opinion that it is proper and right under some circumstances for married people to avail themselves of these provisions of our economy, and in this opinion we are supported by a large number of divines, philosophers, and physicians. For example, when the wife is distinctly suffering from over-much child bearing; when the children are coming so rapidly that they interfere with each other's nutrition ; when a destructive hereditary disease has broken out after marriage ; and when the wife cannot bear children without serious danger to her life.

Those who coincide with us here may urge the objection, and it is a partially valid one, that the observation of these natural periods of sterility does not answer the end in view ; that they are uncertain and inadequate. They are so to some degree, but we believe them to be much more reliable than they are generally supposed.

The next refuge is to renounce entirely the conjugal privilege. This is a perfectly allowable and proper course, if it be with mutual consent. St. John Chrysostom, the eminent father of the Greek Church, called Chrysostomos or the Golden Mouth for his eloquence, expressly states that the early Christians did not consider it amiss. The objection now-a-days urged against it is that it is too severe a prescription, and consequently valueless. This ought not to be. A man who loves his wife should, in order to save that wife overwork, and misery, and danger of death, and wretchedly constituted children, be able and willing to undergo as much self-denial as every one of his continent bachelor acquaintances does, not out of high devotion, but for motives of economy, or indifference, or love of liberty. The man who cannot do this, or does not care to do it, does not certainly deserve a very high position.

But while all this is granted, the question is still constantly put : Is this all ? Is there no means by which we can limit our families without either injuring the health, or undergoing a self-martyrdom which not one man in a thousand will submit to ?

There are dozens and scores of means if one might believe the indecent advertisements which are inserted by unscrupulous knaves in country newspapers. We warn against them as fraudulent and deceptive. Most of the artificial means proposed for this purpose, and we have reason to believe extensively vended, can none of them be used constantly without either failing to accomplish their purpose, or sowing the seeds of disease. Many of them are in the highest degree injurious and reprehensible, and are *certain* to destroy health.

The habit of uncompleted intercourse which many adopt must be disapproved on the same grounds. It does violence to nature, and is liable to bring about premature loss of virility, and serious injury to the nervous system.

It is a doubtful question whether any of the appliances of art recommended for this purpose, even if they are innocent in regard to health, are morally to be approved. Whether under some rare and exceptionable circumstances, as when women conceive during nursing, or are incapable of bearing children with safety to life, such means are permissible or not, must be left for the medical attendant to determine, and he alone must bear the responsibility of affirming or refusing to affirm the practice. But in the majority of marriages, where the avoidance of children is sought merely to save

expense or trouble, or to give greater room for freedom and
selfish pleasure, the resort to such means must be unequivocally condemned.

We may be criticized, as, indeed, we have been, for referring to this delicate and difficult subject at all. But, as the
Rev. John Todd pointedly remarks in an article on this very
topic: "If there be indelicacy, it is in the facts, not in calling
attention to them." "It has become the fashion," says that
distinguished clergyman, "for parents to be leading round a
solitary, lonely child, or possibly two, it being well understood,
talked about, and boasted of, that they are to have no more.
The means to prevent it are well understood instrumentalities
shamelessly sold and bought, and it is a glory that they are
to have no more children." This is sadly true, especially in
the cities and large towns of this country.

Its results are even more conspicuous in France. Dr.
Bergeret, a prominent physician in one of the provincial
towns of that country, draws a striking picture of the demoralization it has brought about. He shows how the bonds
of public morality have been loosened, the sacred institution
of marriage converted into legal prostitution, woman sunk in
respect, man yielding to unnatural debauches, losing his
better impulses to plunge into sensuality, diseases and debility
gaining ground, the number of births constantly decreasing,
and the nation itself incurring the danger of falling a prey to
its rivals through a want of effective soldiers. The picture
is a gloomy one, and is probably but little overdrawn.

If it is true that the native American population is actually
dying out, and that year by year the births from couples born
in this country are less in proportion than those from couples
one or both of whom are of European birth, as many have
asserted, then we must seek the explanation of this startling
fact either in a premature decay of virility, or a naturally

17

diminished virility in middle life in the husbands, or to an increased tendency to sterility in the wives, or else, and this has been the, perhaps, hasty conclusion of most writers, we must suppose there is a deliberate and wide-spread agreement between those who are in the bonds of matrimony, that American women shall be childless or the next thing to it.

Sometimes this is secured by the prevention of conception. This, when it is accomplished by any other means than the observation of the natural periods of sterility conjoined with abstinence, is not to be sanctioned as a rule.

But when resort is had, as it frequently is, to the practice of

Criminal Abortion,

then no language is too severe for its condemnation.

We need not here rehearse what others have said upon this topic, and what we ourselves have spoken concerning it with no uncertain sound. But there is one element in this crime which we wish here to bring prominently forward. It is the responsibility which the husband has in its commission.

It is useless to deny or to conceal the fact that in very many instances the husband's dislike of a large family, combined with his unwillingness to practise self-denial in regard to his appetites, is the motive which, beyond all others, induces the wife to visit the fashionable Aborter, and to destroy the fruit of her womb and imperil her own life and health. This cowardice and brutality on his part cannot anywhere find an excuse. As Dr. Horatio R. Storer observes in his *Is It I?*—

"In a very large proportion of cases, this shocking and atrocious act is advised and abetted, if not compelled, by the husband.

"For the woman, enfeebled perhaps by too excessive

child-bearing, for which her husband is generally wholly responsible, for few of our wives do not become, sooner or later, virtually apathetic; for the woman, timid, easily alarmed, prone to mental depression or other disturbance, and dreading the yet safe and preferable labor that awaits her, there is a certain measure of excuse. For her husband, none."

This flagrant abuse is not confined to immoral circles of society, nor to the corrupt atmosphere of our great commercial centres, but extends into remote country hamlets, and throughout all grades of social life. We call upon our readers by example and precept to do their utmost to stem its devastating tide, and at least in their own families, and among their friends, to mete its due reprobation.

Its worst effects are not seen in marriage, though no physician is ignorant how many women in the community suffer from the vile " French pills" and " female regulators" hawked about, as well as from rude instruments in awkward and unfeeling hands. But it is in the impunity which the vicious believe they enjoy, the temptation to indulge in lustful and illegitimate *liaisons*, the weakening of virtue, that its most serious consequences are manifest.

The laws in several ·of our States on this subject are severe. In New York it is a penitentiary offence to perform, or to obtain, or to aid in obtaining an abortion. But yet, such is the boldness of vice, that in the New York city papers scores of advertisements of professional abortionists may any day be seen !

On the Production of the Sexes at Will.

It is often a matter of the utmost interest in families to have a child of a particular sex. There is always a disappointment in having a number of children all either boys or girls. The father, as a rule, takes greater interest in his daughters, the mother in her sons. The ideal family is composed of some of each sex.

Now we believe that we are not asserting prematurely a scientific discovery, when we confidently say that the law which governs the production of the sexes has been ascertained; and that, with a due allowance for certain elements of uncertainty, and they few in number, persons can have either a daughter or a son as they prefer.

What is more, this law is not confined to the human race, but extends throughout all those species of animals technically known as oviparous, or which reproduce by means of an egg, whether this egg is deposited without the body or matured within it. And as stock-raisers, bird fanciers, bee merchants, and all engaged in the breeding of the various kinds of domestic animals, often would give a great deal to have it in their power to breed either sex at will, we shall give such details of the extent and workings of this law as to put it in their power, in the large majority of cases, to obtain either males or females as they prefer.

The discoverer of this law was a French veterinary surgeon, Prof. Thury, of the Academy of Geneva. He studied with particular care the sex of the offspring with reference to the date of conception. Of course, in mares, bitches, cows, and the other domesticated animals, this could be ascertained without any doubt. He found that when the male was given at the first signs of heat in the female, the result was a female; but when the male was given at the end of the heat, the result was male offspring. With hens the eggs first laid after the tread gave females, those laid subsequently, males. The eggs first laid by the queen bee yielded females, those laid later, males.

A certified report to the Agricultural Society of Canton de Vaud, Switzerland, made in 1867, reports the result of a careful testing of Professor Thury's law in the following words :—

"On twenty-two successive occasions I desired to have heifers. My cows were of the Schurtz breed, and my bull a pure Durham. I succeeded in these cases. Having bought me a pure Durham cow, it was very important to me to have a new bull, to supersede the one I had bought at great expense, without leaving to chance the production of a male. Accordingly I followed the advice of Prof. Thury, and the success has proven once more the correctness of his law. I have obtained from my Durham bull six more bulls for field-work ; and having chosen cows of the same color and height, I obtained perfect matches of oxen.

"In short, I have made in all twenty-nine experiments after the new method, and in every one I succeeded in the production of what I was looking for—male or female. I had not one single failure. All the experiments have been made by myself without any other person's intervention ; consequently I do declare the law discovered by Professor Thury to be real and accurate."

Much other evidence from recent writings on the rearing of domestic animals could be adduced to justify the opinion of this reporter. On a number of stock farms in France, England, and this country, experiments have been conducted which show that there is much that we can depend upon in Professor Thury's law. Certain exceptions and apparent contradictions have also been noted, and some objections on theoretical grounds have been urged. For instance, Dr. Waldeyer, of Breslau, in his recent able work on the "Ovary and Ovum," opposes Thury's hypothesis on the ground that the ovum, for some time after fecundation, is in a certain sense a hermaphrodite; in other words, the elements which go toward the formation of the sexual organs are alike in all. But as neither Waldeyer nor any one else has been able to say what mysterious something it is that finally decides the development of these elements into the peculiar organs of the one or the other sex, his objection falls to the ground. It is quite likely to be something in the ovum itself, dependent upon the length of time it has left the ovisac, as Thury asserts.

Some curious facts may be explained by this theory. We referred on an earlier page to the statistical observation that more male than female children are born. This would seem to be because the time when the ovum can produce a female is limited to a few days of its earlier independent existence; while all the rest of its life it can lead to a male. If we take a large number of observations, it will be seen that when the husband is from fifteen to twenty years older than his wife, most of the children will be boys. This again is because the conjugal rights are more rarely exercised by men of advanced years, and the limited time just referred to, when the ovum can become a female, is skipped more frequently.

Observations in the human subject on this point are of course vastly more uncertain and liable to error than in the lower animals. Nevertheless, a sufficient number have been recorded to remove any reasonable doubt that it holds good with man, as it does with the inferior animals.

Physicians constantly observe that if labor comes a few days before "full term," or just at term, the child is more likely to be a female ; but if labor is delayed beyond term, which is the same as saying if the conception took place quite a number of days after the cessation of menstruation, then it is more likely to be a boy.

Several physicians, interested in satisfying themselves on

this important topic, have noted the occurrences in their own families, and published the results in medical journals. So far as these have come to our notice, they are uniformly in support of Thury's law.

There remains an uncertainty as to the precise time at which the human ovum loses its power of producing the female sex in the fœtus. For reasons very readily under, stood, the study of this subject is surrounded with difficulties. Moreover, it may well be that a difference in this respect exists in ova and in individuals.

There is also a liability to error from a want of exact knowledge on our part as to how long the male element remains active after it is removed from the body and before it comes into contact with the ovum of the female. Should this indeterminate period extend over several days, as it is highly probable that it does, it will readily be understood that an error in the application of the rule might result.

A third possibility of error arises from some uncertainty as to whether the act of menstruation in the human female is strictly analogous to and coincident with the process of ovulation. While there is no question that the external sign, and the general congestion arise from the maturation of an ovum, it is not yet known whether this ovum is discharged from the sac in which it has been ripening, at the commencement, during the course, at the termination, or immediately subsequent to the presence of the monthly symptoms. Authorities differ on this, and it is most probable that their disagreement is to be explained by supposing that there is no fixed time for the discharge of the ovum. Consequently we are at a loss to estimate exactly the age of the ovum at any given period after menstruation.

We have been careful to note all these elements of error in adopting Thury's law, because we believe his discovery to be one of vast importance, and well established in the inferior species; and in its application to the human race, it were to be regretted if a few disappointments, which may readily be explained, should lead to its rejection. As a general rule, we consider ourselves perfectly safe in saying that the earlier conception takes place after the menstrual flow has ceased, the greater is the probability that the offspring will be female; and the further removed from that period (always omitting four or five days anterior to the following monthly illness), the more likely is it that the child will be a male.

Before leaving this subject we will glance at one obstacle which has stood in the way of its reception. Some have imagined that the theory of M. Thury is overthrown by the fact that twin children are sometimes of different sex. But this is an argument founded on our ignorance. We do not know at all positively that the conception of both these beings took place at the same time. It is not merely possible, but for various reasons highly probable, that days intervened between the commencement of life in the one and in the other. So this fact, too, fails to militate against the general law.

[AUTHORS AND WORKS REFERRED TO IN THIS SECTION.—Marshall, *Outlines of Physiology;* Dalton, *Human Physiology;* Dr. Seguin, *On the Causes of Idiocy,* N. Y. Medical Journal, 1870; Dr. Edward Smith, *Cyclical Changes in Health and Disease;* Acton, *Disorders of the Reproductive Organs,* p. 105; Hufeland, *Art of Prolonging Life;* De Brantome, *Vies des Dames Galantes,* Discours I. p. 35; Raciborski, *L'Age Critique chez la Femme,* p. 484; *Philadelphia Medical and Surgical Reporter,* vol. xix. p. 305; Rev. John Todd, *The Cloud with a Dark Lining;* Bergeret, *Les Fraudes dans l'Accomplissement de l'Acte Génératrice;* Dr. Hodge, *Criminal Abortion,* 1869; Storer, *Criminal Abortion;* Waldeyer, *Eierstock und Ei,* p. 152, etc.]

INHERITANCE.

What Fathers Bequeath Children.

" THE child is father to the man," it is said. We are not concerned with this adage, but with the seemingly self-evident axiom that "the man is father to the child," in a deeper sense than in being his immediate ancestor. The father has not merely transmitted life to his offspring, but he has fixed upon him, to a certain extent, his mental and physical peculiarities, and even his moral nature. The child does not, of course, always exactly resemble its father. Indeed, the father's influence is less potent than the mother's; but it is a constant ever-present force in the child's being which often writes with " pen of adamant on tablet of brass." Let us then study, briefly though it may be, the laws and limitations of that heritage which, in the language of a distinguished physiologist, " has, in reality, more power over our constitution and character than all the influence from without, whether moral or physical."

We will first consider

The Physical Qualities we Inherit,

particularly from our fathers. It is not difficult to prove that physical qualities are transmitted. We need not give instances of resemblances in form and feature between father and child, for they are matters of daily observation to every one. It is interesting to know that the male influence is noticeable even in plants, for through the pollen of flowers the tints and varieties may be modified at will.

The influence of the father is most marked in the exterior and extremities of the child, while the internal organs emanate from the mother. The father is most apt to determine the muscular organization, the mother the nervous system and temperament. This law is not an absolute one. The mule and hinny afford illustrations of its operation in the animal kingdom. The mule *brays*, while the hinny *neighs*. The mule derives its muscular structure from its sire, the ass, and, therefore, has his voice, for the voice is determined by the muscular organization of the part. The hinny, on the contrary, which has the muscular system of its sire, the horse, like him, neighs.

The influence of the father varies also with the *sex of the child*. The tendency seems to be for him to transmit to his daughters the conformation of the head and upper portions of the body. His sons are more prone to derive the form of these parts from the mother. Hence it happens, as we shall have occasion to remark presently in speaking of mental qualities which are inherited, that daughters partake more frequently than sons do of the intellectual peculiarities of the father.

Fathers not merely give the muscular organization to their offspring, but also the force and agility acquired by training. Thus, in ancient times, the *athletes* were found in families. In the case of animals celebrated racers are known as valuable breeders. Eclipse is said to have been the sire of 334 winners, who secured for their owners the amount of $800,000. King Herod, a descendant of Flying Childers, begot 497 winners. Unknown horses, which have unexpectedly won great races, have always been proved, upon examination, descendants, through many generations, of first-rate ancestors.

Stature is often hereditary. The giant Chang, who was, until recently, on exhibition in London, is eight feet six inches in height. His father was nine feet high. The tall guards of Frederick William of Prussia were for fifty years quartered at Potsdam. That place is now remarkable for the numerous gigantic figures met in its streets. They are the offspring of the guards and the women of the city.

Peculiarities of the sense of *taste* are in many cases the effects of inheritance. In this manner Montaigne accounted for his inveterate dislike for physic and physicians. One of his ancestors when dangerously ill and assured that if he did not suffer himself to be treated, he would die, replied " Je suis doncques mort." Montaigne asserts that his dislike for medicines was directly traceable to this ancestor. Louis XIV. was excessively fond of the pleasures of the table. All his children were markedly voracious and gluttonous.

Longevity is a family trait. Sobriety, and a regard for the principles of hygiene, will not necessarily insure long life. These may maintain a condition of health and vigor, but length of life is largely determined by inheritance. Longevity is a talent. It may be improved like any other talent, or it may be wasted, but no amount of cultivation will create it. In spite of intemperance and exposure, a man who has this talent for long life may become a centenarian. A saddler, aged 113, whose grandfather died at 112, and his father at 113, was asked by Louis XIV. what he had done to attain to such length of days, he replied : "Sire, since I was 50, I have acted upon two principles: I have shut my heart and opened my wine cellar." Again, Golombrewski, a Pole, notwithstanding the hardships of eighty years of service as a common soldier, the fatigues of thirty-five campaigns under Napoleon, the sufferings of the terrible Russian campaign, the effects of five wounds, and the reck- lessness of a soldier's life, survived, and in 1846 was still living at the age of 102. But, it is to be observed, his father attained the age of 121, and his grandfather 130. A well- known literary character, M. Quersonnières, was living in 1842 in the full possession of all his powers. He said: "My family descends from Methuselah; we must be killed to die ; my maternal grandfather was killed by accident at 125 years of age, and I," he added, smiling, "invite you to my burial in the next century." The experience of life insurance and annuity companies has made so apparent the influnce of heritage over longevity, that facts bearing upon this point in the family history have much weight in the calculations of the actuary.

Deformities are often transmitted from father to son through many generations. Edward Lambert, called the Porcupine man, is an illustration. He was first exhibited before the Royal Society, England, in the year 1731, at the age of fourteen. The whole surface of his body was covered with a peculiar horny or bristly growth, "looking and rus- tling like the bristles or quills of a hedgehog shorn off within an inch of the skin. When, twenty-six years after, he was again presented at the Royal Society, he was still covered by the same bristles. In the mean time he had had smallpox, followed by a temporary loss of his scaly covering, which was soon, however, renewed. He had been married, and had had six children, each of whom, at nine weeks of age, like himself, began to assume this rugged coat. Sub- sequently, it is on record that three grandsons of · the original porcupine man, Edward Lambert, were shown in Germany with the cutaneous incrustation above described.

In this connection an interesting question arises : *Are the results of accidents inheritable?* As a rule, they are not. Authentic instances are not wanting, which might readily be cited, showing that this rule has its exceptions. But the natural tendency is fortunately against the propagation of a physical injury. Thus, although the sins of the fathers are visited upon their children, their misfortunes are not.

For what purpose have we brought forward the above facts in regard to inheritance ? Merely because of their relation to the important question of prevention. It is this alone which concerns the father who reads these pages, influenced by one of the noblest of all human motives, the desire to benefit his offspring. Such a one wishes above all to know

How to avoid having Diseased and Deformed Children.

The father's care over the health of his child should begin before its birth, nay, before its conception. Proper attention then may avert taints of the system which, once implanted, no medical skill can eradicate. The truth of this statement is recognized by breeders of animals. Mr. Youatt, one of the best authorities upon the breeding of horses, observes, " The first axiom we would lay down is this, *like will produce like;* the progeny will inherit the qualities or the mingled qualities of the parents. We would refer to the subject of diseases, and state our perfect conviction that there is scarcely one by which either of the parents is affected that the foal will not inherit, or, at least, the predisposition to it; *even the consequences of ill-usage or hard work* will descend to the progeny. We have had proof upon proof that blindness, roaring, thick wind, broken wind, curbs, spavins, ring-bones, and founder have been bequeathed both by the sire and the dam to the offspring. It should likewise be

18

recollected that, although these blemishes may not appear in the immediate progeny, they frequently will in the next generation. Hence the necessity of some knowledge of the parentage both of the sire and dam."

The influence of one parent upon the other in counter-acting or intensifying the degree and the certainty with which the physical qualities of one or both are transmitted must be borne in mind. If the same defects be possessed by each parent they will be quite certain to appear in the children. If only one parent be affected, some or all of the children may escape the inheritance. Take, in illustration, that most common of all diseases, consumption. If husband and wife both have this affection, all of the offspring will be quite certain to be consumptive or scrofulous. If one of the parents be healthy, it is possible that only some of the children will be scrofulous, and even that none of them will inherit the disease. It is most fortunate that the tendency of a disease to propagate itself by inheritance is often over-powered by the stronger tendency of a vigorous constitution to impress itself upon the offspring. If it were possible to apply this principle to its fullest extent in every individual case, by never mating a feeble constitution excepting with one of that healthful vigor best calculated to counteract its trans-mission, the heritage of disease would, doubtless, soon be unknown. While it is impossible to lay down any absolute rule of conduct, and useless to hope that any such rule would be generally followed, even if enunciated, it behooves every man to know, be he strong or weak, that, for the reason just mentioned, he may marry a woman who will bear him healthy children, whereas his children by another woman may be doomed. The responsibility and risk are his own. We can only indicate them.

We have also words of cheer to utter in regard to the

descent of diseased conditions from generation to generation. It is a stern fact that " Our fathers have sinned, and are not; and we have borne their iniquities." But disease is not eternal. The offspring of sinning fathers are not without all hope. The counteracting influence of one parent over the other with transmission of life, of which we have just spoken, does much to maintain healthful vitality and beauty in spite of the degrading tendencies which may be present. In addition, however, there is a force resident in our nature by which the diseased organization tends to return to health. This benign healing force, this *vix medicatrix*,

> " Which hath an operation more divine
> Than breath or pen can give expression to,"

is ever influencing the effects of inheritance. Were it not for this beneficent law the human race would rapidly degenerate. The results of its operation can be seen in the faces of the children of squalor and vice who throng the narrow streets and wretched houses of our crowded cities. If, happily, time had not purified the debased organization and restored health, we should look in vain there for that comeliness of features, grace of figure, and strength of limb which are now frequently to be observed. As has been truly said, " the effects of disease may be for a third or fourth generation, but the laws of health are for a thousand."

The law of inheritance is a certain but not an invariable one. Its force must not be over-estimated. For if it were always true that the child of a father tainted with insanity or consumption is born with these affections, then moral law would imperatively forbid marriage. It is known that the offspring of a father who has too many or two few fingers sometimes escapes the transmission, when *both parents have not been similarly affected*. As the child inherits from the mother as well as the father, many or all the members of the family of a tainted father may be born with only a slight taint of the system, or none at all.

We shall now point out a few of those diseases which are especially liable to be transmitted from parent to child, with the view of indicating special means of preventing, before and after birth, the effects of inheritance.

The most cruel of all the maladies which afflict us, *pulmonary consumption*, is the one which is most constantly seen in its hereditary form. Dr. Theophilus Thompson, an English physician of very large hospital experience, states, in his " Clinical Lectures on Pulmonary Consumption," that " you will learn, amongst a thousand patients questioned on the subject, above one-fourth will mention having lost a parent by it."

Again, M. Herard and M. V. Cornil, two of the latest and most prominent of the French authorities on this subject, mention as the result of their investigations, both in hospital and private practice, that out of one hundred cases carefully questioned, they find the disease hereditary in thirty-eight instances. American statistics tell the same story of the large proportion of consumptives born with the taint.

The mother more frequently transmits this disease to the child than the father. Her daughters are also more apt to be affected by it, through her, than are her sons. Indeed, in regard to all diseases, the morbid constitution of the mother tends to impress itself upon her daughters rather than her sons, while that of the father has a reverse hereditary tendency. With reference to the inheritance of mental qualities and peculiarities, the opposite inclination seems to prevail, as we have seen, mothers most influencing their sons, fathers their daughters.

That terrible and invincible foe to human life, *cancer*, is a markedly hereditary affliction. Where the taint exists, medical art has few resources either to prevent its transmission or to antagonize its effects.

Gout, asthma, and *disease of the heart* are also transmissible. They are not, of course, exclusively the result of inheritance. They are often developed during the lifetime of individuals whose family record is a clear one. But once having made their appearance in a family, they have a greater or less proneness to recur.

Of all the affections which are transmitted by inheritance, the various *disorders of the nervous system* are the most common. *Hysteria, epilepsy, paralysis,* and *insanity* descend from the unhappy parents to the more unhappy offspring. Physicians who have devoted themselves to the study of that many-sided malady, insanity, are, of late, disposed to lay more stress than formerly upon the influence of inheritance in its causation. They allege that a vast number of the cases commonly attributed to physical or moral shocks are really instances of the breaking out of an inherited tendency, which has lurked unheeded in the system until aroused by some unusual excitement. According to the best authorities, from one-third to one-half of all attacks of insanity owe their origin to hereditary causes.

It is a noteworthy peculiarity of nervous ailments, that they are not always transmitted in the same form. The child of a person subject to epilepsy, for example, is as liable to be paralyzed or insane as it is to be epileptic. This change in the character of the nervous affection, in passing from the one generation to the other, is constantly met with.

Insanity furnishes another illustration of the greater disease-transmitting power of the mother. It is transmitted about one-third times oftener by her than by the father. Again, also, we have an illustration of the greater influence of the mother over the diseases of her daughters; for, when the mother is insane, it does not affect the sons any more than insanity in the father would, but, on the other hand, the danger of the daughters is double what it would be if the father, instead of the mother, were the affected parent.

The hereditary diseases of which we have been speaking do not always show themselves immediately after birth. It is more usual, in fact, for them to lie hidden until the period of adolescence or maturity is attained. Scrofulous complaints, however, manifest themselves in the offspring earlier. The time at which a disease will first make its appearance is frequently as much a matter of inheritance as its other characteristics. This is, above all, true of nervous disorders. For instance, that form of insanity which is developed only after a certain age is often inherited. A case is related of a noble family in Europe, all the male descendants of which became insane at forty years of age. Up to that epoch in their lives they all exhibited great military talent, and were entirely trustworthy in every respect. At last there remained but one son, a distinguished officer like his father. The critical age arrived, and he also lost his reason.

The immunity occasionally seen to the invasion of disease is capable of inheritance. Some individuals can never acquire, no matter how exposed, certain diseases, such, for example, as smallpox or intermittent fever. The happy security may be transmitted.

The Laws of Inheritance in Disease.

Undoubtedly, judicious marriages would eradicate all hereditary affections. Legislation upon this subject is, of course, impracticable. Yet its importance demands for it the closest attention from the philanthropist and the moralist. The moral and social responsibility incurred, by marrying into a family of which one or more members have suffered from constitutional disease, is great, and should not be lightly assumed. Some general rules for the guidance of those contemplating such a union may prove useful to a few at least of our readers. Dr. J. M. Winn, an English physician, who has elaborately studied the nature and treatment of hereditary disease, has drawn up an estimate of the amount of risk incurred under various circumstances, as follows :—

"1. If there is a constitutional taint in either father or mother, on *both* sides of the contracting parties, the risk is so great, as to amount almost to a certainty that their offspring would inherit some form of disease.

"2. If the constitutional disease is only on *one* side, either directly or collaterally through uncles or aunts, and the contracting parties are both in good bodily health, the risk is diminished one-half, and healthy offspring may be the issue of the marriage.

"3. If there have been no signs of constitutional disease for a whole generation, we can scarcely consider the risk materially lessened, as it so frequently reappears after being in abeyance for a whole generation.

"4. If two whole generations have escaped any symptoms of hereditary disease, we may fairly hope that the danger has passed, and that the morbific force has expended itself."

Hygienic Treatment of Hereditary Diseases.

As the precautionary rules which medical science has to offer are in many cases unknown, and in more numerous instances unheeded, injudicious marriages are constantly being formed. Children are therefore daily born into the world, with dispositions more or less marked towards heredi tary affection. Much may even yet be done to stay the mischief commenced. Efforts to maintain the health of such infants cannot be instituted too early. By intelligent care, continued through life, the appearance of the disease may be suppressed, and in some cases the predisposition eradicated.

The first attention should be directed to the nourishment of such an infant. It should not be brought up by hand. If it cannot be suckled by the mother, it must be placed at the breast of a healthy nurse. The child should be warmly clad, and carried daily in the open air, unless the weather be inclement. The use of the bath and other requisites to infantine health must not be lost sight of. This constant watchfulness over the well-being of the child should not be remitted during the whole period of youth. Great care ought also to be taken not to overexcite the brain by encouraging precocious exhibitions of talent. Active play in the open air with romping companions, will do more for the future of the child than any knowledge it can at an early age acquire with books. Much harm is done by competitive examinations about the period of puberty. This is especially the case in those inheriting a disposition to epilepsy or consumption. These diseases are at this age most liable to appear, and the intense application and undue anxiety which attend such examinations may develop them. Those disposed to hereditary afflictions should extend their care of themselves even to the choice of their avocation. Such pursuits as are sedentary and exposed to the debilitating influence of impure, in-door air are to be avoided. So also are those which require at times exhaustive mental or bodily exertion. Regular exercise in the open air, by walking or riding, is of the utmost moment every day. Where there is a tendency to consumption, epilepsy, or insanity, it is particularly valuable, and can do more than is generally supposed to avert them.

Dr. Winn speaks in strong terms of the value of cod-liver oil as a preventive remedy in inherited dispositions to disease. It is to be taken in small quantities (a teaspoonful three times a day is ordinarily sufficient). It must be continued for such a long period of time as to become a customary portion of daily food.

We might dwell much longer upon the nature, prevention, and treatment of hereditary disease, as we have not exhausted the subject. But have we not said enough to impress upon the reader the prominence which it ought to occupy in the hygiene of the marriage relation ?

As a rule, diseases are transmitted directly from the parents to the children, thence to the grandchildren, and so on uninterruptedly from generation to generation. In some cases the transmission takes place from the grandparents to the grandchildren, one generation escaping altogether. This resemblance of a child to its grandparents or great-grandparents, rather than its own father or mother, is known under the scientific name of *atavism*.

It is owing to this influence that diseases and deformity, as well as strength and beauty, pass by one generation to appear in another. A child resembles in form or feature its grandfather, or it inherits the epileptic fits or the consumption for which its grandfather is remembered, the father being entirely healthy. A remarkable instance, which, however, is not solitary, of the influence of *atavism* is related by the celebrated anthropologist, Dr. Pritchard. A black woman, the wife of a black man, had a white child. In great fear of her husband because of this, to her, unaccountable occurrence, she tried to conceal the child from him. When he saw it and noticed her trepidation, he said: " You are afraid of me because my child is white, but I love it the better for

that, for my own father was a white man, though my grandfather and grandmother were both as black as you and
myself; and although we came from a place where no white
people were ever seen, yet there was always a white child in
every family that was related to us."

Another manner in which disease may appear in the
children through parental influence has been well pointed
out by Dr. Elam. "The parents may be free from disease,
yet produce unhealthy children, owing probably to some
unfitness in the union; these affections stamp themselves as
hereditary, by affecting all, or nearly all, the members of
the family. Sir Henry Holland mentions a family consisting
of three sons and one daughter, all of whom had a paralytic
attack before the age of forty-five, though neither of the
parents had suffered from anything similar; and another of
a family where four children died in infancy from affections
of the brain, without any of the relations having been so
affected. I am acquainted with a large family, all of whom
suffered when young from enlarged tonsils, and almost all
of whom are short-sighted in the extreme, though neither
father nor mother have experienced either inconvenience.
At the Deaf and Dumb School in Manchester there were, in
1837, forty-eight children taken from seventeen families, of
which the whole number of children was one hundred and
six; amongst these, only one parent was known to have been
similarly affected."

The likeness of a child to its grandparents rather than to
its immediate parents is, although a noteworthy fact, one
which does not excite much comment from us. But when, as
is sometimes the case, the child partakes of the characteristics
of a very remote ancestor or of the traits of some far removed representative of a collateral line, descended from a
common progenitor, then a feeling of astonishment arises.

Such examples are, however, only illustrations of the law of atavism just mentioned.

The physical characteristics of the age of the parent at the time of conception are transmitted. Maturity reproduces itself. The stag, when born of mature parents, grows faster and stronger than when born of young parents. Old age is inherited. Breeders of animals are well aware of the inferior character of the progeny of old parents. The children of parents far advanced in years are peculiarly prone to senile affections, and from birth bear the marks of senility. Dr. Prosper Lucas, a French author who wrote a work of 1562 pages on the subject of inheritance, gives among others the following illustrations of the above remarks.

"The wife of one of the coachmen of Charles X. became, to the surprise of himself, her husband, and her children, who were thirty or forty years old, *enceinte* at sixty-five years of age. Her pregnancy followed the usual course, but the child presented all the marks of the senility of the parents.

"Marguerite Cribsowna, who died in 1763, aged one hundred and eight years, was married for the third time when aged ninety-four, to a man aged one hundred and five. From this union were born three children, who were living at the death of their mother; but they had gray hair and no teeth; they lived only upon bread and vegetables. They were sufficiently tall for their age but had the stoop, the withered complexion, and all the other signs of decrepitude."

While speaking of the physical effects of inheritance we cannot forbear to notice a form of bodily weakness impressed upon certain social classes by transmission. Mr. Whitehead, a writer upon "Hereditary Diseases," says :—

"The offspring of parents, both possessing great intellectual capacities, are liable to inherit such capacities in still greater proportion; but along with this refinement, so to speak, of the cerebral faculties, is usually conjoined a degree of physical delicacy, or of disproportionate development, which constantly endangers organic integrity; and the peril is further increased if education be urged, in early life, beyond a certain limit. The mind which seemed capable of comprehending intuitively the most abstract problem, is soon shaken and unbalanced, merging at length into insanity.

The Mental Qualities we Inherit.

We have hitherto been concerned merely with the transmission of physical qualities by inheritance. Are mental peculiarities, is talent, is genius itself, ever inherited ? We answer that there is undoubtedly a marked tendency to the transmission of not merely original but of acquired intellectual traits, the effects of education. No man of talent was ever born of an idiot. Mental imbecility is handed down from generation to generation. Haller, the physiologist, mentions two ladies of high birth, but nearly imbecile, who were married for their wealth. At the time he wrote, a century afterward, the same low grade of intellectual development was conspicuous in the fourth and fifth generations.

That talent is often the offspring of talent is shown by the two Herschels, the two Coleridges, the two Sheridans, the two Colemans, the two Montesquieus, the two Pitts, the two Foxes, the two Scalagers, the two Vossiuses, the two Mirabeaus, the three Adams, the Kemble family, the families of John Sebastian Bach' and Æschylus, etc. etc. But it may be said, the fact that talent is not the offspring of talent is shown by Shakspeare's children, and Milton's daughters; by the feeble son of the great Oliver Cromwell; by the only son of Addison, an idiot; by the unworthy Paralus and Xanthippus who sprung from Pericles the orator that "carried the weapons of Zeus upon his tongue;" by the idiotic Milesius and the stupid Stephanus, the only representatives of the weighty intellect of Thucydides; by the absence of inheritors of Henry IV. and Peter the Great, and by other instances which will readily occur to the reader. The explanation of such facts is to be found in the superior transmitting power of one parent over another. It has been clearly proved as a law of heritage that the father does transmit his mental powers to his children. The exceptions, such as we have quoted, do not invalidate this law. They only bring into prominence the great modifying influence of the mother. The persistency of the male power is apparent in the fact that a line of male parents may impress their peculiarities upon their male issue, notwithstanding the opposing influence of many mothers. Francis Galton, an English writer, who has given much attention to this subject, has accumulated an overwhelming array of facts in proof of the hereditary character of talent. In this connection Dr. Elam calls attention to "a circumstance worthy of note concerning the scale of intellectual development, viz., that the *extremes are solitary, i. e.,* do not transmit their characteristic. The lowest grade of intellect, the perfect idiot, is unfruitful; the highest genius is unfruitful, as regards its psychical character: true genius does not descend to posterity; there may be talent and ability in the ancestry and in the descendants, directed to the same pursuits even; but from the time that the development culminates in true genius, it begins to wane. I am acquainted with a family descended in the third generation from a true musical genius. Of the numerous branches, scarcely one is deficient in some amount of musical taste and ability, but none have a shadow of the genius of the grandfather."

Unsoundness of mind is markedly under the domain of

19

inheritance. Dr. Henry Maudsley, now probably the best authority upon this subject, states that the most careful researches fix the proportion of cases of insanity, in which positive hereditary taint is detectable, at not lower than one-fourth, if not so high as one-half. He thinks the proportion will be found to be greater as investigation in this direction becomes more searching and exact.

In order that a predisposition to insanity be inherited it is not necessary that the parents or ancestors be insane. Nervous diseases are not always transmitted in their identity to the offspring. Physical peculiarities are, as we have mentioned, so also are organic diseases. Consumption is transmitted to the child as consumption, not in the shape of a predisposition to cancer. But many of the affections of the nervous system, such as insanity, epilepsy, St. Vitus' dance, hysteria, neuralgia, and catalepsy, change their character in the descendant. Thus, the child of an epileptic may be insane, and the child of an hysterical woman have the like misfortune. We wish here, however, to draw a distinction which it is of hygienic moment to bear in mind. The inheritor of the predisposition to insanity may not become insane. He inherits merely the temperament. One of several fates may overtake him. Insanity may immediately result in consequence of the inherited taint. It may be postponed indefinitely by intelligent care of mind and body. It may be developed by injudicious training, by excessive mental application in early youth, by anxiety, by cruel treatment; or it may be awakened by the great changes which occur in the system at the period of puberty; or, in woman, at the time of child-bearing, or the change of life.

Intoxication is, all authorities agree, a great cause of mental degeneracy in the unfortunate offspring. This heritage of drunkenness is one of the most startling problems connected with intemperance. For, as has been truly said, " not only does it affect the health, morals, and intelligence of the offspring of its votaries, but *they also inherit the fatal tendency, and feel a craving for the very beverages which have acted as poisons on their system from the commencement of their being!*" It is known that drunkenness may be hereditary in a family for centuries. In spite of the influence of example and careful training, the children of drunkards become precocious inebriates. They say, "We can't help it; the love we inherit is too strong for us." One such bound himself to abstinence for months; then he could withhold no longer, avowing that the *craving was actual torture, and he could not help himself*. M. Morel, who has investigated this subject more profoundly than any living writer, says: "*I have never seen the patient cured of his propensity whose tendencies to drink were derived from the hereditary predisposition given to him by his parents.*"* The whole nature of the descendant of the drunkard is depraved under the influence of this fearful inheritance. The annals of vice teem with illustrations of the indecision and defective moral sense of those victims to the alcoholic abuse of their fathers; while the records of medicine are equally full of cases showing the

---

* The same experienced writer says elsewhere: "I constantly find the sad victims of the alcoholic intoxication of their parents in their favorite resorts (*milieux de predilection*), the asylums for the insane, prisons, and houses of correction. I as constantly observe amongst them deviations from the normal type of humanity, manifesting themselves, not only by arrests of development and anomalies of constitution, but also by those vicious dispositions of the intellectual order which seem to be deeply rooted in the organization of those unfortunates, and which are the unmistakable indices of their *double fecundation in respect of both physical and moral evil.*"

constitutional feebleness and the nervous disorders produced
in successive generations by the same influence. Dr. Hut-
cheson, in remarking upon the incradicable nature of an
inherited tendency to drink, says that "no sooner is the
patient liberated than he manifests all the symptoms of the
disease.   Paradoxical though the statement may be, such
individuals are sane only when confined in an asylum."
Additional testimony to the same effect is given by W.
Collins, who testified before a parliamentary commission, in
England, as the result of his large experience, and as a "*well-
established physical fact*," that this form of the drunken
appetite "never becomes completely extinct, but adheres to a
man through life."   All the writers upon the subject of inheritance, with a singular unanimity upon this point, no matter
how they may differ upon other topics, agree in imputing
to intoxication, in either parent, a potent agency in inducing
alcoholic mania, and moral and physical degradation in the
children.   These results are more marked among the poor,
who are deprived of the hygienic advantages which fall to
the lot of the rich, and who are also surrounded, ordinarily,
by fewer social and moral restraints.   None, however, escape
the disastrous influence, in some of its many protean forms,
upon mind and body.

Is our Moral Nature Inheritable?

This question brings us face to face with the consideration
of the *hereditary character of crime.*

Michel de Montaigne was a profound observer of man, as
well as a genial essayist.   One of his papers is entitled " Of
the Resemblance of Children to their Fathers."   In it he expresses his wonder at the mysterious nature of that heritage
which transmits to us not merely the bodily form, but even

the *thoughts and inclinations of our fathers.* A much older writer than he, Aristotle, also alludes to the transmission of moral qualities by inheritance. He tells of a man who excuses himself for beating his father by saying that, "my father beat his father, and my son will beat me, *for it is in our family.*" History is rich in illustrations of moral heritage. Alexander VI. and his children, the Borgias, will ever live upon its pages because of their atrocities. The crimes of the Farnese family are too infamous for mention. The same taint of wickedness runs through the cruel nature of the Medici and the Vicontes, the latter of whom are accredited with the invention of the "forty days torture." Sextus VI. and his children were notorious for their crimes, and to the Condé family have been attributed in addition to their courage and brilliant intellect, "odious vices of character, malignity, avarice, tyranny, and insolence."

Modern society furnishes us with an example and a proof of the hereditary nature of crime which touches us more nearly. There exists a distinctive criminal class in all our cities. This dangerous class is marked by certain physical and mental peculiarities. These so distinguish them that they can be readily pointed out in any promiscuous assembly. Even in Shakspeare's time this was possible. In Macbeth, one of the murderers, in defending his fellows, says:—

"We are men, my liege."

To which the king replies:—

"Ay, in the catalogue ye go for men ;
As hounds, and grayhounds, mongrels, spaniels, curs,
Shoughs, water-rugs, and demi-wolves, are classed
All by the name of dogs ; the valued file
Distinguishes the swift, the slow, the subtle,
The housekeeper, the hunter, every one

19*

According to the gift which bounteous nature
Hath in him clos'd ; whereby he does receive
Particular addition, from the bill
That writes them all alike ; and so of men."

Those who are born and live in crime are all marked by
the same traits of physical degeneration, as well as mental
and moral depravity. The truth in great measure, of the
assertion of Lemnius, that the "very affections follow the
seed, and the malice and bad conditions of children are
wholly to be imputed to their parents," is also shown by the
family histories of the criminal class. It would be easy to
fortify this statement by quotations from prison reports, for
which, however, we have not space.

There are some who, while they do not pretend to deny
the inheritance of physical infirmities and diseases, still
maintain that all men are born alike, intellectually and
morally, and that it is entirely due to circumstances and
education that they differ from each other. As well could
they uphold the doctrine that all men are born with equal
tenacity of life, and vigor of constitution. Such thinkers
hesitate to admit the heritage of immorality because they
fear that the admission would remove the check of individual
responsibility. They forget that it is merely the tendencies
which are inherited, not the acts themselves. As Dr. Elam
well observes, "man's freedom is not obliterated, but he is
destined to a life of more or less strife and temptation, according as his inherited dispositions are active and vicious,
or the contrary. Every sane man knows that, despite of
allurements or temptation, he can do or leave undone any
given act; he is therefore *free*, but his freedom is more or
less invaded, in accordance with the laws under consideration." How true then is it that "it is the greatest part of
our felicity to be well born ; and it were happy for human

kind if only such parents as are sound of body and mind should marry."

We have given instances of the inheritance of gluttony and intemperance, and of families remarkable for their crimes of violence. *Theft*, among other crimes, is hereditary. Dr. Steinase says, from personal observation, he has known it to be hereditary for three generations. A man, named P——, acquired in his native village the sobriquet of " *The thief.*" His son, although in prosperous business and beyond want, was remarkable for his propensity to steal small things. His son, the grandson of " *The thief,*" when only three years of age, would clandestinely take more food than he could eat; afterward he began to take small sums of money and soon ·larger amounts. Before he was fourteen years of age he had become an expert pickpocket and was confined in the House of Correction. *Pride* is passed down from father to son; the Stuart and Guise family afford illustrious examples. Of the latter it has been said that " all the line of the Guises were rash, factious, insolently proud, and of most seducing politeness of manner." Cowardice, jealousy, anger, envy, and libertinage are all met with as family traits. The passion of avarice is no exception to the others as is shown by the family of Charles IV., that emperor of Germany of whom it has been wittily recorded that he " vendait en detail l'empire qu'il avait acheté en gros.'" There is also such a thing as an hereditary passion for gambling. A lady, so strongly addicted to gambling that she passed all her nights at play, died of consumption, leaving a son and daughter, both of whom inherited from her alike her vice and her disease.

These facts, in regard to the inheritable nature of our mental and moral qualities which we have been considering, suggest to every thoughtful mind the inquiry

Does the Education of the Parents affect the Capacity and Morality of the Child?

We have elsewhere asked,* " Can virtuous habits be *transmitted?* Can we secure virtues in our children by possessing them ourselves?" And we have replied, that " we are scarcely more than passive transmitters of a nature we have received." Nevertheless, although this is true of the original nature, there are certain qualities capable of being superimposed upon that nature. We cannot by any course of virtue beget a child free from evil tendencies, but we can give him much to combat them through the virtuous qualities of civilization. The animal nature of man cannot be modified. It is invariably transmitted. It is always the same in the barbarian and the enlightened man. But moral and mental qualities can be added, which, although they can never crush out nor wholly obscure the animal nature, can improve upon it. Unless this were so, unless intellectual and moral culture did so influence not only the individual but the offspring, and thus through future generations the race, then the educator would have to say with Macbeth :—

> " Upon my head they placed a fruitless crown,
> And put a barren sceptre in my gripe."

Dr. Moore, a high authority, remarks : " Our education may be said to begin with our forefathers. The child of the morally instructed is most capable of instruction, and intellectual excellence is generally the result of ages of mental cultivation. From Mr. Kay Shuttleworth's examination of juvenile delinquents, at Parkhurst, it appears that the majority were deficient in physical organization, and this, no doubt, was traceable to the parent stock." Again, M.

* The Physical Life of Woman, p. 121.

Giran says that "acquired capacities are transmitted by generation, and this transmission is more certain and perfect in proportion as the cultivation has extended over more generations, and as that of one parent is less opposed by that of the other. Children receive from their parents, with the impress of their habits, all the shades of capacity aptitude, and taste which have been the fruit of such habits." The eminent physiologist, Burdach, also accords to the parent the power of transmitting to his offspring his intellectual development.

Inheritance of the *acquired* habits of life, the results of intellectual and moral training, or of daily vice, is more certain than the transmission of physical peculiarities. A course of vicious indulgence in the parent will corrupt the morals of the child. A life of virtue on the part of the parent will bear fruit in the stronger will and the increased power of conscience of his offspring. He, therefore, whose avocation it is to cultivate correct principles and habits of thought in his fellow men holds no "barren sceptre." His influence, above that of all others, is felt upon his race through many generations.

Before dismissing this subject of moral heritage, which we would like to pursue at much greater length if our space would permit, we wish to say a few more words in regard to its bearing upon the responsibility and accountability of every man for his own acts. No one has a right to urge inherited impulses in justification of his evil deeds. To do so would be to place himself on a level with the brute. Animals are swayed entirely by their instincts. Man is conscious of a higher, a moral law, the dictates of which he has it in his power to obey. In the language of the most recent writer upon this topic, "Every man is responsible for his voluntary acts, whatever the constitutional tendency. In the face of the facts before us, I see no reason to doubt or deny that one person is born with impulses and tendencies to particular forms of virtue or vice stronger than those of others, who, on the other hand, may be more prone to other forms of good or evil than the first. · The passions and appetites are doubtless much keener and more difficult of control in those who inherit them from a line of ancestry who have never checked them, but in whom vice has been accounted a glory and a virtue. It is much easier for some who inherit a placid, even temperament, with no strong emotions, to be outwardly virtuous and orderly, than for those just mentioned, but *all have it in their power*. Habitual selfishness, disregard of the rights or feelings of others, immorality, may reduce man *nearly* to the level of the brute; the vicious act may seem to be due to irresistible impulse, but the perpetrator is not the less culpable for that. He who wilfully intoxicates himself that he may commit a murder is still a murderer, and one of the deepest dye of crime. Life to all is a warfare, to some it is much more severe than to others; but all *may* fight the good fight, and all may attain the reward: none are born with a constitution *incapable* of virtue, though many have such a one as may well make life one long struggle against the power of temptations, so severe that it is well for man that he is not alone in the mortal conflict."

Why Children do not more closely Resemble Parents.

If there exists in nature, and that there does is abundantly proved, a law by which the offspring so strongly tend, as we have just been endeavoring to show, to inherit the physical, mental, and moral natures of their parent, how does it happen that there are so many exceptions to be noted? In other words, what are the causes of non-inheritance?

We have already mentioned a number, to which we need now only allude. One of these is *atavism, i. e.*, resemblance to remote instead of immediate ancestors. This agency we have sufficiently explained. Another is the neutralizing effect of the qualities of one parent over the other in their mutual transmission to the child. In this manner, a third being may be produced, unlike either parent. A third cause is the overpowering influence of hostile circumstances and unfavorable conditions of life. As is very aptly remarked by Mr. Darwin, in considering animals and plants under domestication, "no one would expect that our improved pigs, if forced during several generations to travel about and root in the ground for their own subsistence, would transmit, as truly as they now do, their tendency to fatten, and their short muzzles and legs. Dray horses assuredly would not long transmit their great size and massive limbs, if compelled to live in a cold, damp, mountainous region; we have, indeed evidence of such deterioration in the horses which have run wild in the Falkland Islands. European dogs in India often fail to transmit their character. Sheep in tropical countries lose their wool in a few generations."

A fourth check to inheritance is to be found in what is known as the " law of diversity." In obedience to this law children differ from their parents and from each other. This so-called law is, however, merely an illustration of the strength of inheritance, for its effects are due to the transmission of temporary and accidental conditions in the parents. There is always under such circumstances a strong inclination in future generations to depart from the modifications thus accidentally produced, and to return to the original type.

There are two potent influences affecting the character of the child to which we have made no allusion. We refer to the power of the mother's imagination over the physical and mental condition of her unborn infant, and to the influence of the mother's mind on the child at her breast. These subjects have been elsewhere discussed in treating of the physical life of woman.

We do not think it worth while to "point a moral" by applying the facts and principles we have now recorded about inheritance, to the life of the parents. Every intelligent reader can do this for himself.

Nor is it our purpose to prosecute the study of the formation of the child through the habits of the father beyond what we have already done.

From the first it has been our aim to impress upon our readers the momentous truth that the well-being of the generations to come, and consequently the destiny of races and nations, are closely dependent on the healthy condition of the male in his sexual relations. We have now traced these relations in the individual, and pointed out their hygienic laws, from the period when they are first manifested to their final effects on the offspring.

The Influence of Race.

Although somewhat foreign to the purpose of this work, which is concerned with the health of the individual rather than considerations of race, we cannot forbear to quote the thoughts of an eminent theologian, CANON KINGSLEY, in reference to the extent and power of hereditary influences.

" Physical science is proving more and more the immense importance of race; the importance of hereditary powers, hereditary organs, hereditary habits, in all organized beings, from the lowest plant to the highest animal. She is proving more and more the omnipresent action of the differences between races; how the more favored race (she cannot avoid using the epithet) exterminates the less favored, or at least expels it, and forces it, under penalty of death, to adapt itself to new circumstances; and, in a word, that competition between every race and every individual of that race, and reward according to deserts, is (as far as we can see) an universal law of living things. And she says—for the facts of history prove it—that as it is among the races of plants and animals, so it has been unto this day among the races of men.

" The natural theology of the future must take count of these tremendous and even painful facts; and she may take count of them. For Scripture has taken count of them already. It talks continually—it has been blamed for talking so much—of races, of families; of their wars, their struggles, their exterminations; of races favored, of races rejected; of remnants being saved to continue the race; of hereditary tendencies, hereditary excellencies, hereditary guilt. Its sense of the reality and importance of descent is so intense, that it speaks of a whole tribe or whole family by the name of its common ancestor, and the whole nation of the Jews is Israel to the end. And if I be told this is true of the Old Testament, but not of the New, I must answer, What? Does not St. Paul hold the identity of the whole Jewish race with Israel their forefather, as strongly as any prophet of the Old Testament? And what is the central historic fact, save one, of the New Testament, but

20

the conquest of Jerusalem—the dispersion, all but destruction of a race, not by miracle, but by invasion, because found wanting when weighed in the stern balances of natural and social law ?

"Gentlemen, think of this. I only suggest the thought; but I do not suggest it in haste. Think over it—by the light which our Lord's parables, His analogies between the physical and social constitution of the world afford—and consider whether those awful words, fulfilled then and fulfilled so often since—'The kingdom of God shall be taken from you, and given to a nation bringing forth the fruits hereof'—may not be the supreme instance, the most complex development, of a law which runs through all created things, down to the moss which struggles for existence on the rock ?

"Do I say that this is all ? That man is merely a part of nature, the puppet of circumstances and hereditary tendencies ? That brute competition is the one law of his life ? That he is doomed forever to be the slave of his own needs, enforced by an internecine struggle for existence ? God-forbid. I believe not only in nature, but in grace. I believe that this is man's fate only as long as he sows to the flesh, and of the flesh reaps corruption. I believe that if he will

> ' Strive upward, working out the beast,
> And let the ape and tiger die ;'

if he will be even as wise as the social animals; as the ant and the bee, who have risen, if not to the virtue of all-embracing charity, at least to the virtues of self-sacrifice and patriotism, then he will rise to a higher sphere; towards that kingdom of God of which it is written, 'He that dwelleth in love, dwelleth in God, and God in him.'"

[WORKS REFERRED TO IN THIS SECTION.—*The Variations of Animals and Plants under Domestication,* by Charles Darwin, vol. ii., p. 10 et seq. (Am. edition); J. B. Thompson, I.—R. C. S. Edin., *On the Hereditary Nature of Crime,* in the Journal of Mental Science for January, 1870, p. 487; Elam's *Physician's Problems* (Am. ed., 1869), article, *Natural Heritage;* Dr. Edward Seguin, *On Idiocy, as the Effect of Social Evils, and as the Creative Cause of Physiological Education,* in the Journal of Psychological Medicine for January, 1870, p. 1; Franois Galton, *On Hereditary Talent and Character,* in MacMillan's Magazine, vol. xii. ; Dr. Prosper Lucas, *Traité Philosophique et Physiologique l' Hérédité Naturelle dans les Etats de Santé et de Maladie du Système Nerveux;* Pritchard, *Researches into the Physical History of Mankind,* vol. ii. ; Flourens, *De la Longevité Humaine et de la Quantité de Vie sur la Globe,* (Paris, 1860) ; Hufeland, *Art of Prolonging Life* (Am. ed. 1870) ; Lewes, *Physiology of Common Life,* vol. ii. p. 314 (Am. ed., 1867) ; *The British Medical Journal,* January 11, 1868, p. 25 ; A. Debay, *Hygiène et Physiologie du Mariage,* p. 173 ; Carpenter, *Human Physiology,* p. 779 (Am. ed.) ; Mayer, *Des Rapports Conjugaux,* cinquième edition, Paris, 1868, p. 381 ; Sir Henry Holland, *Medical Notes and Reflections,* p. 30, et seq. *American Journal of Medical Sciences,* July, 1865.]

PART IV.

NERVOUS DISORDERS ORIGINATING IN THE MALE GENERATIVE SYSTEM.

This subject, singularly enough, has received little attention from medical writers. There have been no popular works of any merit on this important branch of medical science. Even in the text-books of surgery there is scarcely more than a brief allusion to those nervous disorders having their origin in man's generative system. Far otherwise has it been with the diseases peculiar to women. During the last quarter of a century the ablest minds in the profession have been occupied largely, some exclusively, in the study of their nature and treatment. Nor have there been wanting well-informed and popular writers to diffuse among wives and mothers a sound knowledge of the laws of their organization, and to point out to them the methods of avoiding the infirmities of their sex. Thousands have thus been benefited. Equal advantages would result to the male sex from a correct knowledge of the causes and results of those diseases to which they alone are liable.

We are glad to notice that attention has been awakened to the great need of popular enlightenment in this direction. One of the most prominent of the English medical journals, the London *Lancet*, in a recent series of editorials on this theme, asserts that a most important service would be ren-

dered to the community by lifting the discussion of the
consequences of derangements of the specific function of
mankind "out of the mire into which it has been cast by
ignorance, by shamefacedness, and by greed." On this side
the Atlantic, the Philadelphia Medical and Surgical Reporter expresses "the wish that some skilled writer would
dispel a little of the dense popular ignorance around these
subjects, an ignorance which, shared as it is by parents,
teachers, and professors, prevents them from giving instructions to their sons and pupils, by which the latter could be
saved from incalculable pain, mental agony, and vice."

It has been our purpose in the previous pages to dwell at
some length in treating of "The Celibate Life" upon three
of the principal affections to which the unmarried man is
more especially liable, viz., the consequences of the solitary
vice, spermatorrhœa, and contagious secret disease. But
there are many other disorders of the male reproductive
organs, and there are numerous obscure *nervous* diseases
which are set up and continued by irritation reflected from
these parts. Some of them we will briefly consider.

Every physician is acquainted with the host of strange
and seemingly remote consequences in women of uterine disease. In dealing with any affection in the weaker sex he
sees the necessity of inquiry in regard to the health of this
organ. Too often he overlooks the connection almost or
quite as intimate which exists between the nervous and generative systems in his male patients. As a result of this
neglect treatment is often nugatory.

Dr. Lewis A. Sayre, of New York, has recently recorded
several cases of *partial paralysis* due to the unsuspected
existence of generative malformations. When this able
surgeon remedied the local trouble the paralysis disappeared,
although it had previously resisted the most energetic and

best directed treatment. The doctor also relates, in the last volume of the *Transactions of the American Medical Association*, three cases of *hip-disease* in boys, for which he could at first find no cause in any injury, fall, blow, or wrench of the joint, but which he traced to the effect upon the hip-joint of frequent unnoticed falls to which the child was liable because of its muscular debility or partial paralysis caused by irritation of the genital organs. He is also satisfied, from recent experience, that to this same irritation may be traced many of the cases of excitable children with restless sleep and bad digestion, so often improperly attributed to worms.

It is the man of advanced years, however, whose nervous system is most susceptible to the influence of disorders of the reproductive organs. This topic occupied our attention to some extent while treating of the "decay of virility" and "the causes which hasten its decline." We again refer to it in this connection in order to emphasize the dangers to the nervous and vital forces of the aged from the slightest approach to excess. That prominent French surgeon, Dr. Parise, in pointing out these perils, utters the following words of warning : "One grand purpose pervades the creation, to live and to impart life. This last function ought to be considered the most important. If men will conform to the laws of nature—laws which, moreover, are immutable and eternal—they must submit themselves to conditions of existence and of organization, and learn how to limit their desires within the spheres of their real wants. If they will do. so, wisdom and health will bloom of themselves, and abide without effort; but all this is too often forgotten when the functions of generation are in question. This sublime gift of transmitting life—fatal prerogative which man continually forfeits—at once the mainstay of mora-

lity, by means of family ties, and the powerful cause of
depravity, the energetic spring of life and health, the ceaseless source of disease and infirmity, this faculty involves
almost all that man can attain of earthly happiness or misfortune, of earthly pleasure or of pain; and the tree of
knowledge of good and evil is the symbol of it, as true as it
is expressive. Thus, even love by its excesses hastens and
abets the inevitable doom for which, in the first instance by
the aid of passion, it had provided the victims. The greater
part of mankind, however, show excessive feebleness in with-
standing the abuse of the generative functions; and what
surprises us most is, that those advanced in life are not
always the least exposed to this reproach. It is certain that
in old age, at a time when the passions have given way to
reason, there are still many individuals who allow themselves to stray imprudently to the very precipitous edge of
these dangerous enjoyments. They applaud themselves for
postponing moderation till it is rather forced than voluntary;
till they stop from sheer want of vigor. What heroic wisdom! Nature, pitiless as she is, will cause them most
certainly to pay dearly for the transgression of her laws;
and the steady accumulation of diseases soon gives demon-
strative proof of it. This result is the more certain and
prompt, inasmuch as in these cases excesses are almost
always of old standing. The libertine in years has usually
been dissolute in youth and manhood, so that we may trace
the progress and calculate the extent of his organic deterioration."

It is principally by excessive indulgence that elder men
bring about nervous maladies. With them the strictest
moderation, often absolute continence, is necessary if they
would prolong their lives, and avoid numberless physical
miseries. The effects of undue indulgence at this period of

life, vary according to the temperament of the individual.
Men of a nervous temperament, are most liable to epileptic
or like seizures affecting the brain and nerves; those of a
sanguine temperament, run the risk of hemorrhage; those
of a bilious temperament, of some derangement of the digestive organs.

A latent predisposition to various diseases lurks in the
constitution of very many. This predisposition becomes
active under the influence of the depressing effect of venereal
excess. In this way we may account for many disorders of
the mind, of the heart, and of the lungs, which suddenly, as
it were, develop themselves. When there exists in the
economy, any organ or function which is diseased or feeble,
it is upon this that the evil results fix themselves.

Any part of the body may become disordered, as the
direct consequence of libidinous excess. Thus, an experienced physician, Prof. A. P. Dutcher, M. D., of Cleveland,
has found that even in the prime of life, immoderation in the
marital relation is a frequent cause of an obstinate form of
chronic bronchitis. He says in one of his lectures: "In
looking over a list of fifty cases of chronic bronchitis, which
have fallen under my care during the last six years, I find
that ten of them have been attributed to this cause. And
they were mostly individuals in middle life, the period when
the sexual propensities are the most vigorous, and prompt to
the most unlimited indulgence. You will occasionally treat
a patient for a long time, who is suffering from an ordinary
attack of chronic bronchitis, and after exhausting your stock
of therapeutics, you will wonder that he does not recover.
You are well-assured that the diagnosis is correct. He
assures you that his habits are all right, that your prescrip-
tions are faithfully attended to, and there is no improvement.
Indeed, you may treat him as long as you please, and he will

not be cured, until you expose the secret source of his malady, and compel him to abandon it. After treating a very intelligent patient for this disease a long time, I remarked to his wife one day, that it was exceedingly strange there was no improvement in his case, I could not see that he was any better than when he first came under my care, and I began to fear that there was something about his case I did not understand. 'Sir!' said she with great emphasis, 'my husband is a perfect animal. His sexual excesses I fear will be the death of him. If you could do something to make him more moderate in this particular, I think all would be well.' I took the hint, lectured him upon the evils of his habit, and ordered not only moderation but total abstinence. He followed my advice, and the lady's prediction was speedily verified."

Epilepsy, nervous tremblings, convulsions and various forms of paralysis are, as we have seen, sometimes the consequence of habits of excess, particularly in those who have passed the prime of life. Many diseases of the heart and brain, and numerous affections of the skin, are also often engendered and continued in the same way. It is only by recognizing these facts, that proper means of personal prevention and cure can be instituted.

At the same time it must be borne in mind, that a tendency to venereal excess and onanism is sometimes the *result* and not the cause of epilepsy, and other nervous tremblings. Inordinate desire may be the accompaniment, and the earliest sign of brain disease. At the outset of the disease, the unhappy patient may be conscious of, and capable of controlling, to a great extent, these morbid, and to him distressing promotings, which threaten to rule him. Dr. Echeverria, of New York city, in his recent work on epilepsy, records a striking illustration of these remarks, in the case of a patient

affected with this disease, "superinduced by mental overwork, who, pressed by my inquiry, wrote to me a history
of his case, with the following about his feelings : ' I would
not weary you with the vain confession of prayers and resolves of one sinning, knowing the while how he sins, but
yet, finding himself led to the act without any intention or
force to resist it. You may believe me or not ; as for myself,
I am unable to account for this venery that overcomes my
whole being, as anything but an evil result of my disease.
If this avowal offers no other moral, it presents that of which
you need not to be often reminded in the practice of your profession—how lightly we regard the blessings of health—and,
considering the self-abuse through which I pass, I think that
I may say with the Psalmist : "How fearfully and wonder-
fully are we made." '

"Nothing remains to be added to this description characteristic of an epileptic, and of the evil impulse and inability
of the patient, to carry out any course to repudiate it."

Among the nervous diseases originating in the reproductive organs *syphilis of the nervous system* calls for some
notice here. Many close observations on this subject have
been made within the last few years which leave no doubt
that the brain and the whole nervous organization are liable
to be affected by this subtle poison. Severe headache, epileptic convulsions, and even paralysis may be caused in
this way during any period of constitutional syphilis. Prof.
Van Buren, of New York, has recently published a series
of cases of the nervous forms of syphilis, which bring into
prominence many practical points hitherto not sufficiently
heeded. Paralysis, epilepsy, and mental derangement were
the symptoms presented by these cases. Enfeeblement of
the intelligence and loss of memory are common forms of
mental disturbance noticed. Whether insanity is ever of

syphilitic origin, is a question still mooted. The belief has been gaining ground among English and German physicians having charge of mental diseases, that such is the case. However it may be as to actual insanity, there are too many cases on record to permit of any scepticism as to the possibility of serious impairment of the intellect being the frequent effect of this animal poison. The question has recently been asked, " Does the presence of the syphilitic taint in the system ever so enfeeble the intellect as to render the subject less capable of mental exertion than he was before he acquired the disease, without at the same time giving rise to intellectual eccentricities or loss of memory sufficiently noticeable to disclose his mental condition to his associates ?" Prof. Van Buren, the propounder of this query, feels inclined to answer it himself in the affirmative.

A Cause of Wasting.

There is a disease which has recently attracted much attention in the medical profession. It is known under the learned name of *tabes dorsalis*, by which is meant an affection chiefly characterized by wasting of the body. Progressive emaciation is almost the only symptom present excepting slight hectic fever. The disease has its origin in the nervous system, and its generally assigned cause is too early or too frequent addition to venery.

There is a great difference of opinion in regard to what constitutes excess. It varies in different individuals and under different circumstances, as we have already explained in a previous part of our work. It is with this form of intemperance as it is with alcoholic intoxication, people's ideas vary as to what is undue indulgence, and different individuals are affected in diverse ways by the same amount

of indulgence. Venereal intemperance, whatever it may
be, is the most frequent cause of the sad disorder of which
we now speak. It is important, therefore, that the patient
should be candid with his medical adviser. Concealment is
too often practised, to the detriment of the sufferer, particularly when the indulgence has not only been vicious,
but criminal.

It is to be borne in mind that the evil results of excess
are not always immediately manifest. The effects do not
necessarily at once follow the cause. The connection between the two is, therefore, often overlooked, and a serious
medical error is thus committed.

Sexual excess is not the only cause of this disease, but
when present always favors its development. The celebrated Dr. Romberg, whose authority in nervous affections
none will call in question, says : " Two circumstances have
been shown with certainty to predispose to it, namely, the
male sex, and the period between the thirtieth and fiftieth
year of life. Scarcely one-eighth of the cases are females.
The loss of semen has always been looked upon as one of
the most fruitful sources of the complaint ; but this in itself
does not appear to be a matter of much consequence in
influencing the disease, as patients who have been laboring
under spermatorrhœa for a series of years are much more
liable to hypochondriasis and cerebral affections, than to
this. *But when combined with excessive stimulation of
the nerves, to which sensual abuses give rise,* it not unfrequently favors the origin and encourages the development
of the disease after it has commenced. When the strength
is much taxed by continued standing in a bent posture, by
forced marches and the catarrhal influences of wet bivouacs,
followed by drunkenness and debauchery, as is so often the
case in campaigns, the malady is rife."

21

Other writers speak still more positively of the intimate relation between this disease and sexual excesses. Every practising physician who has had experience with this fortunately comparatively rare malady must acknowledge that the history of the cases, when accurately obtained, has nearly always pointed to this causation.

A Cause of Convulsions.

There is a difference of opinion in the minds of the profession at the present time as to the *frequency* with which the solitary vice induces epileptic fits. All agree, however, that here is to be found one of the causes of epilepsy, some asserting that it is a prominent cause, others that it is far from being the usual one. We have just pointed out, on a previous page, that "a tendency to venereal excess and onanism is sometimes the *result* and not the cause of epilepsy." Bearing this truth in mind, and also the lamentable fact that there have been, and are, many ruthless alarmists who, some of them designedly, make exaggerated statements as to the connection between abuse of the masculine powers and epileptic disease, still it cannot be denied that an abundance of the best of medical evidence proves the existence of such a connection in a certain proportion of the cases. Thus Prof. Watson in his work on Practice, so familiar to every physician and medical student, says :—

"There are certain vices which are justly considered as influential in aggravating, and even in creating, a disposition to epilepsy: debauchery of all kinds; the habitual indulgence in intoxicating liquors; and, above all, the most powerful predisposing cause of any, not due to inheritance, is masturbation—a vice which it is painful and difficult even to allude to in this manner, and still more difficult to make the subject of inquiry with a patient. But there is too much reason to be certain that *many* cases of epilepsy owe their origin to this wretched and degrading habit, and more than one or two patients have voluntarily confessed to me their conviction that they had thus brought upon themselves the epileptic paroxysms for which they sought my advice."

Nervous Prostration.

The new circumstances and remarkable activity which characterize our modern civilization are so different from those which surrounded the monotonous lives of our forefathers, that we have not as yet become used to them. We are, as it were, in a new world of life, to which our systems are not yet acclimated. Hence it is that the annals of medicine chronicle a large increase in all varieties of nervous maladies within the last score or two of years, in both sexes and in all civilized lands.

What does this teach?

It teaches that the part of prudence is to avoid more sedulously than ever before the strains upon our systems which are unnecessary, for our nervous organizations cannot bear that which those of our fathers could.

Among the new diseases which have thus arisen is one which is peculiarly characteristic of crowded cities, of the great marts of trade and hives of busy life, where not only does the task of gaining subsistence demand the utmost exercise of the powers, but beyond this the temptations of vice are most shameless, most prominent, and most alluring.

In this disease, which has received the technical name of *paresis*, there is absolutely nothing present which we can put our finger upon and say, This is the weak point, here is the seat of the malady. Nor does the patient himself complain of any pain, and is hardly aware of his condition.

He feels languid, depressed, "out of sorts." His mind is not as clear as it was. It is an effort to produce anything original, or to undertake any unusual exertion; after a while even routine business is burdensome. Tired as he constitutionally feels, yet often he cannot sleep sound when in bed.

So the symptoms follow one after another—and it is not our intention to draw any harrowing picture of them to alarm the ignorant—until there is very visibly some definite enfeeblement of the functional power of the brain, showing itself in motion and in intellectual expression.

This is a disease which was certainly not recognized, even if it existed, before this age; it is the *maladie de la siècle*. And for what purpose have we introduced it here? It is to warn against a common, perhaps the most common cause of it; that is, excessive stimulation of the sexual passions.

Dr. Handfield Jones, of London, calls especial attention to the importance of this warning, and the frequency with which the vice referred to leads to a premature and seemingly unexplainable debility of the system, a want of energy, a *tedium vitæ*. He quotes the words of the celebrated Hufeland: "It is proved beyond all doubt that nothing renders the mind so incapable of noble and exalted sensations, destroys so much all its firmness and powers, and relaxes the system as this dissipation."

It is not easy to explain, even were it the place to do so, these effects, but the correctness of the observations is too well authenticated to be doubted, and of too much importance to the public welfare to be concealed. The men of our time are subjected to excitements such as none of their ancestors were, and they must be the more guarded therefore to avoid any needless exposure of their health. The same intelligence which has raised them from the depths of unlettered savagery, and enabled them to cultivate to such an extent the powers of the senses, must be their guide in using these new abilities as not abusing them, and in avoiding the perils with which a wider control over natural agencies is invariably associated.

Disorders of the Special Senses.

To illustrate still further the intimate relationship which exists between all parts of the nervous system, and how even remote functions are connected in their healthy activity, we shall speak of a few disorders of the special senses which occasionally take their rise from the same cause of which we have been speaking.

By the term "special senses" physicians mean the senses of sight, hearing, smell, taste, and feeling. They are at times all more or less affected in diseases such as we have mentioned, but the disorders of two of them—sight and hearing—are so important in themselves, and relatively so much more common and serious, that in the present connection we shall refer to them alone.

A greater or less debility of the sight, permanent or only occasionally present, is a well-known accompaniment of an abuse of the generative faculty. Sometimes this is merely a dimness, a tendency to confuse objects and to blur them. At others, it is associated with an appearance of specks and motes before the eyes, or a sensation of prickling and heat in the ball of the eye.

Of course all these and similar symptoms more frequently arise from other and more innocent causes than the one of which we are speaking, but it is well to know that they also arise from it, and well to be aware that often as long as such habits are continued and concealed from the physician, as is generally the case, medication may be useless, and the physician be blamed for want of skill, when no one but the sufferer himself is to blame.

It is gratifying to be assured that when the cause is removed, these disorders usually rapidly disappear, providing, of course, that they have not been in existence so long as to have impaired the organ. Dr. H. Müller, whose observations on these matters we have several times quoted, says : " The feebleness of the power of vision, which is so common among those suffering from disorders of the generative function, may increase to an actual loss of the power of sight. I have in many instances witnessed its gradual diminution. But I am pleased to say that in every instance in which the patient continued under treatment, I have witnessed its restoration; sometimes quite rapidly after an appropriate local application.

" It must not be supposed, however," continues Dr. Müller, " that this defect of the sight is always dependent in these cases on abuse, excess, or nocturnal emissions. On the contrary, there are various diseased conditions of the parts which, by some not well understood sympathy, lead to a disturbance of the powers of sight."

These he proceeds to mention, but as they could only be understood by the medical reader, we shall not recapitulate them. His observation. however, we deem it important to quote, for it is of utmost weight, in our opinion, that no hasty inference so damaging to the moral life of a person, or unfair suspicion of his conduct, should be drawn from anything we say. The facts are, that disturbance of the eyesight, even proceeding to actual blindness, may arise from irritation of the parts, and yet this be in no wise due to unusual practices.

The cases due to venereal excess, the same writer goes on to remark, the oculist is apt to treat in vain, for he rarely reflects on this distant sympathy, may not know it or believe in it, or feel a natural hesitancy in inquiring about it. Therefore it may be that cases which have been pronounced by the eye-surgeon incurable, will readily be relieved by attention to the precautions which we have given for preserving the function of sex in perfect health.

The HEARING is impaired in a less degree by such excesses, but it unquestionably is at times implicated.

The disorders to which it is subject from this cause are chiefly of that character which are termed subjective. The patient will be annoyed by imaginary noises, such as buzzing, ringing, and roaring sounds. Occasionally actual deafness has been observed, a peculiar character of which readily distinguishes it from that usually encountered, that is, its variable nature. One day it will be marked, and only a loud tone can be heard; the next it may entirely have disappeared, or be hardly observable.

So far from being deaf, an unusual sensitiveness of hearing may also proceed from the same cause.

In short, it is enough to say that most of these disturbances of this sense, which are found generally where the nervous system has been much shocked or prostrated, also make their appearance when it is suffering under a depression from injury from this source.

As these senses—sight and hearing—are the avenues through which the most that is good, and beautiful, and useful is conveyed to us, and as their integrity is essential to allow us to be of service to ourselves and our fellow-men, certainly no ephemeral or imaginary pleasure of a mere

ignoble and selfish sort should induce us for a moment to
imperil their perfect working and preservation.   Here,
again, drawn from the discussion of an obscure point of
medical practice, do we discover an argument and a powerful
one in favor of that golden moderation, that self-control, and
that temperate use of our powers, which in all times have
constituted the kernel of the maxims of sages and been the
aim of legislators.   Experience here is of accord with reason,
and proves by example that which the latter has long taught
by precept.

Disorders of Digestion.

The nourishment of the system depends, of course, very
directly upon the proper digestion of the food we eat, and
whatever interferes with the process, soon gives occasion for
the appearance of a number of other troubles, dependent
upon the starvation as it were of the separate organs.

Several authors have insisted that there is little or no
connection observable between the functions of sex in the
male and those of digestion; in the female, all agree that
they are intimately related, and that hardly ever is there a
disturbance of the former, but that it is reflected in the
action of the latter.

The analogy of conformation leads us to doubt, therefore,
their entire independence in the male, and we are inclined
to agree with that more numerous party in the profession
who maintain that many cases display a strong sympathy
between the parts in question.   Our own observation bears
this out.   Several striking cases have come before us where
dyspepsia of long standing disappeared when the disorder of
the lower organs was removed.

The fact that many who exhaust their systems by excess

are characterized by a voracious appetite, is not sufficient
to disprove this view. · The demand of the system for food is
urgent, but, when consumed, it is often productive of unpleasant sensations, eructation, water-brash, a sense of
weight and fulness, and the other familiar symptoms of
indigestion. While it is nearly always observed that such
persons, in spite of the amount of food they take, do not
increase proportionately in flesh, but are marked by a degree
of attenuation which has become proverbial.

Instances have come to our knowledge where attacks of
dyspepsia made their appearance only after dissipations of
the kind, and gave no trouble where the rules of health in
this respect were judiciously observed. In these the sufferers
themselves did not hesitate to attribute their complaints to
what they justly considered the real exciting cause.

Whatever doubt may exist in reference to the general
question of the sympathy of these parts, there can be none
concerning the relationship of certain complaints of the
lower bowels to disturbances of the masculine function.
Obstinate constipation may stand either in the relation of
a cause or a consequence to chronic irritation of the parts
from any cause, innocent or flagitious. So also the nearness
of position which they occupy in the human system leads
them to a participation in the same disturbances.

The Prospects of Cure.

The catalogue of nervous disorders which depend upon
disturbances of the generative functions is a somewhat long
and a formidable one, but we do not wish the reader to
carry away any false impressions of alarm. .

Our task here is difficult. We well know that we shall
fail of our purpose if, on the one hand, we create a terror

which may lead to melancholy and despair; and also if we give the idea that, after all, these various disorders are transient, rare, and of slight importance.

They are, in fact, frequent; they may be serious; and they may become incurable by leading to organic changes in the nervous system. But they are also generally readily curable, even after they have long been troublesome. While this does not hold good for all of them, it does for most.

There is no reason for despair, but the strongest for reformation. Continued indulgence will certainly end in wrecking the constitution irretrievably; but nature is slow to yield thus far. To the last there is hope; but from the first there is danger.

Let no young man, in the pride of his strength, flatter himself he can yield to dissipation with impunity. It may be that a single excess will ruin his bodily powers for life, and blight his every hope at the very outset of his career. Examples of this are not wanting, which may well give him pause, for who knows but their fate may be his.

The prospects for a complete restoration of the health are, in the large majority of instances, favorable, but only on one condition, the immediate and complete cessation of the wonted indulgence, whether this be solitary or sexual abuse. Without this imperative condition, we promise nothing.

Nor is this enough. The thought as well as the act must be put away. That is no reform which extends to the misdeed only, while the thoughts and wishes are as evil as ever. In no department of morals is this more true than here. "He who looketh upon a woman to lust after her, hath already committed adultery with her in his heart." And the evil consequences to his body as well as to his soul follow as surely in the one case as in the other.

If the sufferer will resolutely see to it that he is rigidly pure in heart, then we can conscientiously bid him take courage, for the victory will shortly be won.

The Means of Cure.

While here, as in the previous parts of our work, we disclaim the intention of pretending to qualify one unversed in the doctrines of medicine to manage successfully serious diseases, as are some we have mentioned, we shall attempt to put those who require it in possession of information which will enable them to escape from many of the ills they have brought upon themselves.

The treatment of nervous disorders in general has occupied prominently the attention of physicians since within the last score of years these complaints have become so much more numerous than formerly.

We may sum up the general principles of this treatment in a few words. The system must be relieved from the cause of its disorder at the earliest moment, and recourse be had to tonic and strengthening diet, and drugs to impart to it the vigor which it has forfeited.

The use of iron, as in the prescription given on an earlier page of this work, will be found of value. Change of air and scene, as by travelling, is an admirable tonic. Regulated exercise, always pushed short of the point of actual fatigue, is essential. The mineral waters which are rich in the salts of iron are of great service.

The free use of cold water is always advisable. To an ordinarily vigorous system it is singularly invigorating. It increases the nervous power and attracts the blood from the inner organs to the surface. The cold bath, whether as shower-bath or douche-bath, should be taken with regularity.

In feeble states of the system, cold water may be depressing, and there are some temperaments so sensitive to it that it almost throws them into convulsions. When this is the case, it is better to commence with tepid water, and gradually lower the temperature as the system becomes accustomed to it. The sponge-bath is often grateful and pleasant to those who cannot support without great discomfort the application of cold water in a more direct manner.

The wet sheet, though cold on its first application, soon becomes warm, and acts agreeably on those whose systems are feeble and irritable.

There is a strong desire in many of these cases of nervous trouble to quiet the irritability, and to cheer the depressed spirits with doses of alcoholic beverages; and there are physicians who do not hesitate to permit and even to recommend such stimulation. We must enter a decided protest against this advice and this habit. It " is not, cannot come to good." The fallacious sense of comfort temporarily imparted is followed by a reaction which requires a repetition of the dose, and soon a confirmed habit of tippling is formed. Bad at all times, this is unspeakably pernicious in cases like those we are discussing, where it is beyond everything important that the self-control be maintained, and the passions kept under.

But in spite of the rigid observance of the ordinary precepts for nervous disorders, there are some arising from this cause which will not be healed by these means, and yet are readily curable nevertheless. These are the cases which give themselves and their medical attendants the most trouble. They are weary loads to themselves and friends, and regard themselves as confirmed valetudinarians. Such require a special local treatment. Their general nervous troubles will disappear promptly when the irritation of the parts, the cause of all the symptoms, no matter how remote, is removed. Many striking cases to this effect are to be found in the various writers who have recorded their experience on these subjects.

Of course where, as in some of the cases alluded to in the earlier part of this article, the general symptoms depend upon some malformation, or upon some poison of contagion still lurking in the system, the special and appropriate means should be employed, either surgical, to reduce the malformation, or medical, to expel from the system, when possible, the morbid material.

The distinction between these various causes is often a matter of great difficulty, and no one can trust his own judgment in an obscure case. Even the expert at times is at fault, and is led to the adoption of methods of treatment which, if not injurious, are useless. This is often the fault of the patient himself. Either through ignorance, through a sense of guiltiness, or from a natural diffidence, facts which would throw light upon the cause are often withheld.

It need hardly be said that such reticence as this, however proper in general, is entirely misplaced between patient and physician. There should be no concealment when health and life are at stake. When sufficient confidence is not felt in a medical attendant to give him all the facts which are necessary for him to know, some other one should be sought.

That many fail to receive the proper treatment because they themselves are entirely unaware how closely their present troubles are related to their former vices, we well know. The hints we have given in the last few pages are for their benefit, and we hope they will lay them well to heart.

22

While pointing out, as we have done, a few of the nervous
disorders originating in the reproductive system, we have
carefully made our statements of even less strength than
our medical experience and knowledge would justify. We
desire to excite no unnecessary alarm in the mind of any one.
But the fact that various nervous maladies may be produced by different affections of the male organs should be
known to every man. Having learned how penetrating
and far reaching are the effects, may we not hope that some
of our readers, through the personal application of the
sanitary laws, which, in this volume, it has been our endeavor to make clear, will be led to avoid exposing themselves to the exciting causes of disease of the masculine
function?

[WORKS REFERRED TO IN THIS SECTION.—The Lancet, London,
July 16 and July 30, 1870; *Partial Paralysis from Reflex Irrita-
tion, caused by Congenital Phimosis and Adherent Prepuce*, by
Lewis A. Sayre, M. D.; Prof. A. P. Dutcher, M. D., *Lectures on
Chronic Bronchitis*, in the Philadelphia Medical and Surgical Re-
porter for October 12, 1867; M. Gonzales Echeverria, *on Epilepsy;
Anatomo-Pathological and Clinical Notes*, New York, 1870, p.
231; Prof. Wm. H. Van Buren, M. D., *on Syphilis of the Nervous
System*, in the New York Medical Journal, for November, 1870;
Traité Historique et Pratique de la Syphilis, par le docteur E.
Lancereaux, Paris, 1866, p. 441; *Les Passions dans leurs Rapports*

avec la Santé et les Maladies, par Xavier Bourgeois, p. 29; S. W. D.
Williams, M. D., on *A Case of Syphilitic Insanity,* in the Journal
of Mental Science for April, 1869; *A Case of Syphilitic Disease of
the Nervous System,* Journal of Psychological Medicine for April,
1869; *Lectures on the Principles and Practice of Physic,* by Thomas
Watson, M. D. (Am. ed.), p. 419.]

THE PHYSICAL TYPE OF MANHOOD.

In the foregoing section we have seen how the constitution is sometimes wrecked by the local diseases which we have treated of in the present work. We have traced these effects from their incipient stages until mind and body were involved. Let us now, in order to relieve this dark picture and dismal theme, turn our attention for a few paragraphs to the reverse of it, to man in the ideal perfection of his phy. sical frame, and learn whether there are any stable laws in that department of nature; and if so, what they are.

The artist who studies man not as he is, broken and debased by indulgence, but as he should be, in the enjoyment of all the powers which health and virtue can grant, will be our guide.

He discovers that in the perfect physical type of man there are certain definite proportions which constitute symmetry, and make up a harmony which reappears in every statue and painting of the highest class, and which the instinct of the artist appreciates more quickly than the tape-line of the anatomist.

The details of this harmony will be interesting to note.

The unit of the scale is *the length of the nose* measured from the inner corner of the eye downward.

Four times this unit equals the height of the head measured from the crown to a line horizontal with the point of the chin.

Eight times this unit equals the distance from the crown of the head to a line drawn around the chest at the level of the armpits.

Sixteen times the unit equals the distance from the crown to the junction of the lower limbs.

And thirty-one times the unit equals the total height from the sole of the foot to the crown of the head; and this again is equal to the distance from the extremity of the middle finger of one hand to that of the other when the arms are extended.

Very numerous and minuter measurements are given in works which treat of the rules of drawing and sculpture. The physician, with mind fixed on the attainment of life and health, naturally might expect this ideal physical type to coincide with that endowed with longest life and greatest strength.

Singular to say, he would be in the wrong.

"The graceful shape and form of perfect symmetry," remarks an eminent army surgeon of large experience, "are seldom connected with power, activity, and that inexhaustible fund of endurance which support toils and fatigues with constancy and firmness."

By what, then, can the capacity in a man for physical labor and endurance be judged?

This interesting question has recently been answered by a German physician, who has devoted much time to the study of the external conformation of the human body. He includes in his formula three factors, the *height*, the *weight*, and the *circumference of the chest on a line with the nipple;* and he decides that the greater the proportion of the latter to the former factors, the greater the physical capacity.

It was a familiar fact in our late war that neither very tall nor very short men supported the toils of field service as well as those of a medium stature. Nor is it common to observe either extreme in stature reach an advanced old age.

In one sense, the whole external form of a man is a commentary, and a disclosure of his nature, habits, and disposition. There is a physiognomy which is not confined to the face, but embraces the whole body. A gifted French surgeon, by close observation, became such an adept in this science, that he could, without fail, ascertain the profession to which a man belonged, by examining his body. As passion and indulgence leave their Cain-like brand upon the face, so occupation impresses its peculiarity on the muscles of the trunk and extremities.

The perfect physical type of manhood cannot be sought, therefore, amid the anxieties and toils of our marts and forums; it must not be expected in our gymnasia nor studios; it will not be found in struggling crowds; but we can expect it only where the wise ancients placed it, and where their works of art represent it—among the immortal gods.

MEDICAL VIEWS

ON

POPULAR MEDICAL INSTRUCTION.

Our belief in the necessity for a work similar to the one we have written has been abundantly justified, not only by the testimonials and warm recommendations which it has received from many eminent men and friends of education (as the reader will see at the close of the volume), but also by the sale in a singularly short space of time of three editions, and by the personal thanks of not a few who have read it and found profit and consolation in it.

While among those who have thus aided and countenanced our efforts in imparting instruction on an important and peculiarly difficult branch of hygiene, we are gratified to number not a few of our own profession who have achieved a deserved reputation by their studies in State Medicine, we have received from some others, whose opinions we value, expressed doubts as to the need for a work like this.

Desirous as we are to exonerate ourselves from the charge of having taken up weapons to conquer imaginary foes, or to have inaugurated a Quixotic crusade against sanitary windmills, it has occurred to us that we could, with propriety, at this stage of our labors, examine the objections to which we have referred. As far as they have been brought

(261)

to our notice, they are curiously diverse, and may be summed up separately as follows :—

1. There are no, or almost no evils to health which result from abuses of the masculine function. The terrors which accompany such abuses are purely imaginary, and works like this might increase them.

2. These evils are so real, so manifest, and so well known to the public already, that any further information upon them is superfluous.

3. Whether real or imaginary, such evils are so rare in moral communities like ours that the public mind ought not to be excited and alarmed by a description of them.

4. It is granted that these evils are both real and frightfully prevalent, but it is not wise to address the public concerning them, because it is best that the public be kept in ignorance of whatever concerns its physical being. In the words of a professor of obstetrics in a Massachusetts college, in a letter to us, " The reading of works on physiology makes men and women know just enough to be complete fools. It would be a lucky day for them should they forget that they have tongues, stomachs, and livers."

Nothing but our veneration for a number of those members of our profession who oppose popular information on physiology and hygiene, has prevented us from feeling some degree of amusement in comparing these various objections to the project which we have endeavored to carry out. It might not be becoming in us to meet them with opinions and arguments of our own, and, becoming or not, they would not have the same weight as those advanced by professional men of unquestioned superiority in medical science, of vast experience, and of world-wide reputation.

We add, therefore, some quotations from recent medical writers who have, with unbiased minds and with painstaking fidelity, studied this subject, and thought about the propriety of rendering it more familiar to the general public as an important department of hygiene.

ABBOTTS SMITH, M.D., M.R.C.P. Lond., M.R.C.S., Physician to the Finsbury Dispensary; late Physician to the North London Consumption Hospital; Physician to the Metropolitan Free Hospital, and to the City Dispensary, &c., says, in *The Medical Press and Circular*, of London, for December 21, 1870 :—

"For many years past, I have had extensive opportunities for observing, at the various institutions with which I have been connected, as well as in private practice, the frequency of cases of spermatorrhœa, and I have been especially struck by two facts, namely, 1. The remarkably helpless and dejected state of patients suffering from this affection; and 2. The relative facility of cure, as compared with numerous other disorders of the genito-urinary organs, if the patients remained under treatment for a reasonable period, and if they, at the same time, relinquished the bad habit which, in a certain proportion of the cases, had brought on or tended to perpetuate the ailment.

"A third feature presented itself with almost uniform regularity, and this was that in most of the cases (at any rate, in something like two-thirds of the whole number under observation) the patients had, before applying for hospital advice, foolishly placed themselves in the hands of ignorant, unscrupulous quacks, who, acting on the principle of the old highwayman's maxim, 'your money or your life,' had rapaciously extorted as much as they could of the former, while their victims ran no small risk of also losing the latter. To a certain extent, some of the sufferers could scarcely be blamed for their apparent want of discrimination in going to such men, as they had in the first instance resorted to medical practitioners, who had told them, either that their disorder was imaginary, or, rushing into the opposite extreme, that it was incurable, or only to be removed by the progress of time.

"It is not a little singular that the medical profession should have assumed such an apathetic or indifferent position as regards this disorder. There can be no doubt of the existence of spermatorrhœa in a large number of patients, and, in fact, it would be found to be much more common than it even appears to be, if it were more generally recognized as a distinct affection. Many of the cases which now fall into the hands of empirical pretenders, would then come within the range of observation of qualified practitioners. And this must, sooner or later, be the case when the false delicacy which is at present allowed to surround the subject of spermatorrhœa is removed. *It is the conscientious duty of medical men, standing as they do in the position of guardians of the public health, to grapple resolutely with this, as with every other phase of disease, instead of leaving unfortunate sufferers exposed to any charlatans who may happen to seize upon it as a fertile field for deception and extortion.* I write thus earnestly, because many instances have been published in the medical journals of patients—often of superior education, intelligence, and social position—who have suffered severely at the hands of quacks, partly through their complaint having been treated too lightly by medical practitioners, to whom they had previously applied for advice, partly through the *mauvaise honte* which induced them, misled by the specious promises held out, to fall into the traps set by quacks. '*Omne ignotum pro magnifico*' is an old and true axiom concerning the credulity of sick people, who, like drowning men, readily

snatch at any proffered assistance, without waiting to form
an opinion as to whether it is worthless or sound. With
regard to the almost culpable distaste for dealing fully with
the subject, I am of the same opinion with that which was
recently expressed to me by the editor of a medical journal,
that there can be no more real reason for ignoring the
functional disorders of the male, than those of the female
sex, upon which so much has been written and said of late
years.

"The general symptoms of spermatorrhœa need not be
dwelt upon, and I shall purposely pass over the minutely
detailed and grossly exaggerated symptoms, which the
quacks carefully and persistently parade before their victims' imaginations, such as 'involuntary blushings,' 'loss of
vigor,' 'gradual decay of nature,' and the like.

"Suffice it to say, that the general symptoms are similar
to those which are present in all cases of disease where the
patient is subjected to the effects of continuous exhaustion
of the system. He becomes languid, weak, and unfit for
any sustained physical or mental exertion, disposed rather
to brood in solitude over his misfortunes, than to join in
social conversation and amusements, thin, pale, and anæmic
in appearance.

"In the majority of cases, especially of those which are
connected with masturbation, the patient is unwilling to
speak of his ailment, and particularly reticent concerning
its causes and nature. To this peculiarity may be attributed,
in great measure, the uncertainty and difficulty of treatment. A physician may go on for a long time, treating a
case of this kind by general measures, but unless he should
eventually suspect its real character, and satisfy himself, by
closer questioning, of the accuracy of his suspicions, no improvement will be manifest in the condition of the patient.

23

In fact, the patient will be further off from a cure than ever; the physician, unconscious of the '*fons et origo mali*,' will get baffled and disheartened at the continuous want of success, while the patient, becoming more reticent, and it may be more addicted to the bad habit, will fall into an almost hopelessly chronic state of illness and despair. How much better would it be for the patient's health and happiness, if he could face the matter boldly, and at once disclose the nature of his case to his medical adviser. 'Half-confidences are bad,' remarked one of our most distinguished judges, Lord St. Leonards, with reference to legal consultations; what, then, must half-confidences be in a medical consultation where the real nature and origin of the case are known only to the patient himself?

"If the patient gives a fair history of his ailment, the physician will usually be enabled to mark out a definite course of successful treatment."

Dr. Storer, Vice-President of the American Medical Association, says, concerning the hygiene of the functions of sex:—

"The subject is one that concerns all, for it lies at the foundation of society—sexual health and disease, the need or advantage of marriage, the need or advantage of divorce, the chance of home being such or an empty name, an earthly heaven or a worse than purgatory—these are topics that affect each man, however careless or unconcerned he may think himself, or may appear to be.

"Is it asked, if these disclosures are not by their very publication subversive of good morals, and the calling attention to the true relation of the sexes suggestive to bad men of, and conducive towards, their false relations? I answer—

"First, that to ignore the existence of sin, error, misery, is in reality to encourage and to increase them. It is like walking upon thinly-crusted lava, or upon breaking ice, certain to prevent our saving others, ready indeed to ingulf even ourselves. We varnish over or seek to conceal vice, and it loses half its grossness—it becomes attractive perhaps, or fashionable; but if we strip it of its veil, any soul, not wholly smirched, will recoil with horror.

"Again, all of us learn the lessons of life by experience—sad experience, indeed, it too often is. Many a man would give even his own soul could his past life be restored to him, and its follies, its sins be effaced. Too often his soul is no longer his own to give: inextricably entangled in passion's web, wound about and about with its myriad threads, there remains but the dead and worthless semblance of himself, that can be restored by naught save the boundless grace of God. Who would not gladly escape such risk, and welcome every premonition of danger?

"Still again, many, claiming to be immaculate themselves, will ask, 'Am I my brother's keeper?' And yet, living together in communities, as we do, it must be confessed that we are responsible, every one of us, and to a very great extent, for the shortcomings and evil deeds of all the rest, and it must also be confessed that there does not exist, that there probably never existed, a perfectly immaculate man, who never once has erred in the very matter we are now considering, either in deed, or in word, or in thought. Consoling indeed for those of us who humbly confess our infirmities is this very fact. Take the very basest of us, and he at times is conscious of vain regrets of his own misdeeds, and a fond desire that those whom he loves, for every man has such, may be better than he. Take the very best of us, and he sees a height beyond any he has yet attained, that he prays he may yet reach and pass.

"And further: not merely are these researches, publications

for the general weal, perfectly legitimate and advisable in themselves; they have been sanctioned by precedents that have already been established. I do not refer to the attempts of unprincipled empirics to terrify the masses by overdrawn pictures of disease, nor of holy and well-meaning men to turn them to better ways by fervent descriptions of the wrath to come. We shall take neither the fear of things present nor future as our standard in this discussion, but appeal solely to each man's reason—and such appeals have been made before. They have been made in France by Ricord, by Lallemand, and others of the great medical philosophers of the day; by Parent-Duchatelet and by Diday. In England, there are men like Acton, who dare to sound the trumpet of alarm, bringing forward their facts from private practice, from the hospital, and from the dead-house, and drawing from these indisputable conclusions. In our own country there are men like those brave souls, now one of them at least translated to a better country, Blatchford, and Hodge, and Pope, and Barton, and Lopez, and Brisbane, physicians of the very highest rank in their profession, who were not ashamed, in the question of the frequency and the ill results of criminal abortion, to take stand beside me upon the platform of our personal knowledge, and knowing, they dared maintain. I will cite but one instance more. It is that of a good man now gone to his rest, and a very rock he was to the swelling tide of moral as well as physical evil— the late Professor John Ware, of Massachusetts. His little work has stayed many a headlong step and saved many a soul alive."

WILLIAM ACTON, M.R.C.S., Fellow of the Royal Med. and Chir., and statistical societies, etc. etc., in the preface and introduction to his work, addressed to the profession, on the

Functions and Disorders of the Reproductive Organs, says :—

"Should these pages accidentally fall into the hands of laymen of sense and information, many of the facts and opinions to be found therein will, I apprehend, prove at least suggestive. The continent student will find reasons for continuing to live according to the dictates of virtue. The dissolute will be taught, on positive and irrefragable grounds, the value of self-control. The married man will find advice and guidance ; and the bachelor, who is often placed in a trying social position, will glean consolation from observing that not only are his sexual sufferings appreciated and understood, but that rules are given him for their mitigation. The physiologist will see his principles reduced to practice. The comparative anatomist will judge how much light his investigations on the animal kingdom have thrown upon sexual relations in man. The surgeon will learn how to manage that difficult class, the hypochondriacal, and how to address himself to the audacious old libertine who, setting at naught religious principle and social customs, acts in open defiance of the laws of his country. Lastly, the advocate who practises in the ecclesiastical or criminal courts will here find the basis for many valuable arguments—nay more, he may learn how, in many cases of guilt, fair cause may be shown for a culprit's committal to a lunatic asylum instead of to a prison.

"Until lately, indeed, many standard writers on the generative system have practically ignored the functional aspect of their subject; dealing with the whole of the wonderful and complex machinery of which they treat as if the offices it fulfils, the thousand feelings it affects, the countless social, moral, and scientific interests with which it is so intimately connected, were of little or no moment. Others

23*

copy their predecessors, and perpetuate statements little in accordance with the advanced state of science at the present time.

"One reason of this reticence is obvious enough. The subject has been considered delicate—dangerous—unseemly —just as well let alone, even in scientific works.

"Of course there have been notable and honorable exceptions to this (as I cannot but think) rather cowardly, if not prudish, neglect of so large and important a branch of the boundless science of humanity. Foremost, perhaps, among these, I may be permitted to specify Dr. Carpenter. In the later editions of his 'Physiology,' that eminent author has boldly met the difficulties of the subject. Far, for instance, from ignoring the existence of sexual feelings, he has investigated them in the same calm and philosophic spirit with which he has approached all other inquiries. Popular prejudice he has quietly passed by; and has discussed a physical phenomenon, an intellectual faculty, or a sexual instinct, with equal simplicity and completeness. Indeed, every step in physiological science seems to reveal to us something more of that mysterious connection between the perishing frame and the imperishable part which at once rules, and is so largely influenced by its earthly companion. I conceive it to be of the greatest importance in no case to neglect or ignore their connection, and perhaps in none more than in the case of the generative functions. Those functions, and the feelings, instincts, and tendencies of which they are the exponents, are, perhaps, the most powerful social and moral agents in the world. They are fraught with happiness or misery to generations as well as individuals.

"Plain speaking is not of necessity impurity. It is not unfrequently its very opposite. I admit that matter so important as this should be treated gravely and by competent authority—not left to the scoffer and the quack. But I believe that in so doing, the truest wisdom and the best means of securing the results we desire will be found in a scientific candor."

From *The British and Foreign Medico-Chirurgical Quarterly Review :*—

"We doubt whether, among our human relations, there is one that exerts a greater influence upon most of us than that which draws its impulses from the sexual feelings. Indirectly, it governs the whole life of the female, from the time at which she dandles her first doll to the time when she teaches her grandchild " pattycake, pattycake ;" the vices and the virtues of the sterner sex—less confessedly, perhaps, but no less really—result from the vagaries and dreams of boyhood, or the waywardness or resolution of adult age, that are prompted by the sexual instincts. . . .

"Sexual excesses are the monster evil of the present, no less than of former times ; it is not, except in particular forms, a subject for legislation, because legislation cannot reach it; but it is essentially a subject for the clergyman and the schoolmaster to deal with. It is folly to ignore what every man who has been at school must know to prevail. It is wisdom to avail ourselves of the holiest aspirations of the youth to enable him to shun evil, not from fear —though from fear if need be—but from a just appreciation of the immutable laws, which may be traced equally in Holy Writ and in natural theology. We trust that those whose position as men of science and teachers enables them to speak with authority, will assist in combating and arresting the evils which it entails, and thus enable man to devote more enduring energies and more lofty aims to the advancement of his race, and to the service of his God."

From the London *Lancet* :—

" The only way by which some of the most important functional ailments and aberrant physiologic states affecting humanity can be rescued from the grasp of the most disgusting
and villainous quackery, and treated with benefit to the
patient, is by the scientific and conscientious practitioner
openly taking them under his own charge. . . .

" Now, however, that legitimate and able practitioners
permit themselves to be known as willing to bestow as much
consideration on the aberrations of the generative functions
as on those of any other, we trust that some stoppage will
be put to the basest system of plunder ever conducted under
the mask of ' medical advice.' "

The *Philadelphia Medical and Surgical Reporter* for
January 7, 1871, in an able editorial, entitled " The Realm
of the Quack," makes the following remarks :—

" Never anywhere in the field of human studies can we find
more striking illustrations of the dangers and the evils of
ignorance than in the history of that science whose votaries
we are. Nothing so touches the human heart, nothing so
puts to its utmost strain each faculty of our being, as the
love of life, the fear of death, the dread of pain. These are
the all-powerful and universal motives to which in every
age the true and the false physician appeal.

" The true physician seeks to allay unnecessary and un-
philosophical terror, to soothe with utmost promptness the
suffering he witnesses, to instil a calm resignation to the
universal law of death, to defer that inevitable close of the
career by wise and temperate precautions, and to defend the
public from the approach of pain. To accomplish this, the
master-minds of all ages are agreed that the most effective
means is the *diffusion of sound knowledge.* Socrates was

not the first to proclaim that the source of physical and moral evil is *ignorance*. And what he advanced and proved with such inexhaustible subtlety of logic and profuseness of illustration, has become the watchword of civilization and the hope of the race.

"The battle we have to fight is against the powers of intellectual darkness; and the history of each day adds another to the long register of facts that proves that in our science, as in all others, those who *know the most* are the leaders and the true benefactors of their race.

"A strong illustration of this axiom is found in the history of charlatanism. Within the last score of years we have seen it dispossessed of one after another of its strongholds by the careful study of them by able and conscientious observers. Hysterical phenomena, long the peculiar province of miracle vendors, are now too well known to allow them any further chance for their bold assumptions. The diseases of women, which twenty years ago was in its twilight period, is now a branch of medical science abounding in distinguished masters, and its most important facts, those which it is well for all to know, have been laid before the public in popular works of the highest order of merit, and which will prevent thousands from unwittingly violating the laws of their organization.

"There is still one department which remains far too largely in the hands of those who delight to play upon human suffering, and to foster it for their mercenary ends. Secret diseases have largely passed out of their hands, but they still thrive upon certain complaints which a native shame disinclines the patient to reveal to his family physician.

"The same is also true in England. In a recent number of one of the leading medical weeklies there, after remarking that 'quacks only thrive in that part of medicine which is

neglected by the faculty,' it adds, 'hence, since there have
been such able writers on syphilis in this country, that field
has been abandoned by these dangerous charlatans. The
only field left now for the quacks is that of spermatorrhœa
and the functional diseases of males. The Obstetrical
Society has attacked the diseases of our sisters in such a
positive spirit, that the outsider has no chance in that department. That there are plenty of diseases of the male
reproductive organs besides gonorrhœa and syphilis well-
educated medical men know, but there is a wonderful disinclination to taking up this question. We have a few honorable exceptions in the names of Curling, Erichsen, and more
recently Waring, Curran, and Teevan, but the exception
proves the rule that the subject is still in the twilight epoch,
and hence fit to be seized on by charlatans. Let us hope
that our best young men may soon clear away the silly
mysteries about this branch.'

" We echo that hope for this side of the Atlantic, and
extend to it the wish that some skilled writer would dispel
a little of the dense popular ignorance around these subjects,
an ignorance which, shared as it is by parents, teachers, and
professors, prevents them from giving instructions to their
sons and pupils, by which the latter could be saved from
incalculable pain, mental agony, and vice. Every physician
and most teachers must have witnessed repeated examples
of the need of just such information."

THE RELATION OF THE SEXES

IN

EARLY YOUTH.

A number of thoughts which occurred to us while writing the earlier pages of this work, related to our theme, yet not directly forming a part of it, seem to us of such interest and practical bearing, that it is well to group them together in the form of an appendix, under the above title.

Too often the student of nature, accustomed to the physiological aspect only of phenomena, and impressed with the importance of the function, regards reproduction as the only purpose of a difference of sex. He considers that the end is attained when the species is perpetuated, and may believe that could this be accomplished in any other mode, then sexuality would become a question of no moment.

The incorrectness of such a narrow view as this has been shown with extraordinary force of thought and beauty of language, by the eminent German philosopher and critic Wilhelm von Humboldt, in an essay on "The Difference of Sex and its Influence on Organic Nature."

We cannot enter here into the convincing and brilliant arguments which he adduces to prove the truth of his conclusions; we shall only repeat, in a brief and inadequate manner, what these conclusions are.

The distinction of sex, in his eyes, extends to the mental

(275)

and moral as well as the physical traits. "Without it, nature would no longer be nature, her mechanism would cease, and both the attraction which draws individuals together, and the struggle which forces each to put forth his best energies, would cease, and a tedious, debilitating monotony would ensue."

The male is everywhere, and in all his manifestations, characterized by peculiar traits, and the female by others quite as much her own. The predominance of these qualities in either sex, however, is no advantage, but a disadvantage. In the highest types of human physical beauty, the feminine and masculine traits are brought into intimate union and a perfect equilibrium. In the Apollo of the Belvidere, magnificent specimen of manhood that it is, there is yet something feminine, something lends the grace and softness of the other sex to the powerful muscles and manly frame.

On the other hand, in that most perfect model of the female figure, the Venus of Milo, exquisitely feminine as it is, there lurks constantly some line or vague expression which reminds us of a man. Instinctively the ancient artist, with the divination of genius, recognized and gave to his work that unity of the sexes which the philosopher reasons must belong to the perfect human creature.

Let us exemplify our meaning by another and a loftier example. The traditional face of our Saviour, which is so familiar to us in Christian art, ancient and modern, it is well known is not a likeness, but an imaginary portrait, developed by the inspiration of ardent piety, and perfected by a long series of monastic artists, until it expresses the ideal of their highest art-dreams. And who, on attentively examining any good copy of this traditional face, can fail to be struck with the feminine softness and sweetness which are present, and which, though present, do not in the least

weaken or deduct from the quiet decision, the unalterable
serenity, the unmeasured power, and the masterly dignity of
the countenance ?

What is in these lofty efforts of art portrayed in the
physical powers is not less true of the intellectual and moral
attributes. The remark has been made by some acute
analyst of human nature, we believe by Goethe, that there is
always something feminine in genius. Certainly that disposition is the most admirable, and that intellect most powerful,
which include in themselves what we are accustomed to define
as the masculine and feminine attributes, which temper the
rude force of man with the delicate sensibilities of woman,
which fortify her susceptible nature with his sterner strength.

These views, which we gather from the realms of art and
philosophy, are not idle reveries. They have an immediate
and most practical bearing on our own lives, on self-culture,
on the education of youth, and on the relation of the sexes
in early life.

An extended study of social life discloses to us two
diverse theories which have prevailed, and still obtain in
different nations, and in different families in the same nation,
with reference to this topic.

The one holds that as early as possible in life, and for as
long a time as possible, it is wise to separate the sexes and
keep them separated.

The second theory insists that any such action is most
inevitably calculated to defeat its objects, and to create and
foster the very evils it is designed to avoid.

Let us examine these opinions.

The Theory of Seclusion.

The Oriental nations from the dawn of history to the
present hour, as a rule, confine the females of the family to

24

separate apartments, restrict their knowledge of the world, and debar them from social intercourse. Young men grow to maturity without having any general female society.

In Italy, Spain, and many other of the European countries, unmarried girls of the better classes are sedulously secluded in seminaries or convents. If allowed to enter general society at all, it is under the strict surveillance of duennas, or other elderly female friends. Freedom of social intercourse among the young is not approved. Parents fear that the effect will be injurious.

In England there is much difference in this respect. From ancient times the women of Anglo-Saxon lineage enjoyed greater freedom than those of the South of Europe. They were never shut up in latticed boudoirs, and hidden from mankind by impervious *jalousies*. Their children grew up as playmates and companions.

The theory of seclusion is based on the belief that moral restraint applied to women is insufficient, that they cannot be trained to a virtuous self-control, and that the only efficacious means to guard them from social dangers are to keep them in profound ignorance and to deprive them of every opportunity of transgression. What the consequences of such a theory, deliberately carried out, are upon the woman we need not explain to those at all conversant with the social morals of Spain or Italy.

But the effects of this plan upon the male sex are even worse. The young man, with all his instincts drawing him toward the society of the opposite sex, finds none of it which suits his age and aspirations. He naturally turns to where it can be found, namely, to that class of society which spurns the restrictions of the social code, and, naturally enough, those also of the moral code.

This is why, in all the continental cities, there is an extensive and well-defined circle known as the *demi-monde*, an attractive, agreeable, and dangerous resort for the young. The polish and training which the votaries of this circle obtain may indeed satisfy the superficial demands of the world, but to the moralist, to the admirer of the sterner virtues, to the lover of his country, such a training is portentous in the extreme.

The nation which educates its youth in this school provides for itself an enervated and false civilization, and prepares for its own downfall.

The best physical training is not that which sedulously guards against every shock, and every breath of cold air, but which gives to the body endurance and vigor to enable it to bear with impunity the blasts of winter and the struggles of the arena. · So the best moral training is not that which diligently shuts out all knowledge of the world, and is based on an utter distrust of natural virtue, but that which teaches self-control, ability to resist evil and cleave to the good, to fight and overcome temptation, and to be actively virtuous.

This training is not to be had on the theory of seclusion. To attain it we must commence education from a different point, and wholly alter the relation of the sexes in early youth.

The Theory of Social Union.

In this country there is no excuse for the young man who seeks the society of the loose and the dissolute. There is at all times and everywhere open to him a society of persons of the opposite sex of his own age and of pure thoughts and lives, whose conversation will refine him, and drive from his bosom ignoble thoughts.

But our present intention is not to discuss this question as it pertains to general society, but to confine our remarks to the period of boyhood and girlhood.

As we remarked in the earlier pages of the present work, the sexual passion is developed long before the age of puberty. It is clearly visible in children of even tender years. As we there said, it is of the utmost importance that it shall be restrained and controlled to the utmost. Can this best be done by a rigid separation of the sexes, or by a free communion between them?

The common and ancient supposition is that the first mentioned is the best plan. Yet, as we have shown, this view is based upon a fallacy. The Latin proverb tells us we strive against that which is forbidden. The very rarity of an object excites curiosity, while familiarity breeds indifference.

Nowhere is this more true than in the history of the sexual passion, and there are numbers of evidences we could adduce.

That ingenious naturalist, Mr. Darwin, explains on this ground the abhorrence to the crime of incest. It is well known that, with widely different races in the most distant quarters of the world, marriages between relations, even distant relations, have been strictly prohibited. At first, Mr. Darwin thinks that a slight feeling arising from the natural indifference of familiarity and the sexual excitement of novelty, led to unions between members of different rather than of the same families. This feeling was augmented through "natural selection," and finally became instinctive. It seems more probable that degraded savages should thus unconsciously have acquired their dislike and even abhorrence of incestuous marriages, rather than that they should have discovered by reasoning and observation any evil results which might have followed on such unions.

It is this indifference which should be most assiduously cultivated in the young of both sexes, especially in males. Nature herself has provided for it to some extent in females. It is one of the acute observations of Wilhelm von Humboldt that such an indifference is the rule in the girl when just blossoming into womanhood. To quote his own admirable words: "The first emotions of her youthful heart wander,.like the glance of Diana, into the far distance. The earliest maidenly age is thus not unfrequently accompanied by a certain want of feeling, indeed, inasmuch as the feminine mildness depends upon the development of those emotions, we may say by a certain hardness. Some characters hasten over this period so rapidly that it is hardly perceived, but in most it is visible for some time."

There is strong reason to hold that one of the most effective means to bring about this indifference of familiarity is by

The Co-education of the Sexes.

We have spoken of this in a previous part of this work as an experiment, about the result of which we are not quite fully satisfied. The evidence which has been submitted to the public is nearly all in its favor. We are still, however, not yet inclined to give it our unreserved advocacy; there are many considerations of locality and custom which must "give us pause;" there are individual instances in which it cannot be approved, and there are limits to mixed classes which must be defined. But of such importance as a practical question do we consider it. that we venture to insert an extract of some length from the last Annual Report of the

24*

Board of St. Louis Public Schools, written by the efficient
superintendent, Professor William T. Harris.

He remarks :—

"It is in accordance with the spirit of our institutions to
treat women as self-determining beings, and as less in want
of those external artificial barriers that were built up in
such profusion in past times. We give to youth of both
sexes more privileges or opportunities for self-control than
are given in the old-world society. Each generation takes a
step in advance in this respect.

"Occasionally, as in San Francisco, there is a returning
eddy which may be caused by the unbalanced condition of
society found on frontiers. Old cities, like New York and
Boston, may move very slowly in this direction, because of
enormous expense required to change buildings and school-
yards so as to adapt them to the wants of "mixed schools."
In fact, the small size of school-yards in many cities renders
this change next to impossible. Western cities will take
the lead in this matter and outstrip the East. Within fifteen years the schools of St. Louis have been entirely
remodelled on this plan, and the results have proved so
admirable that a few remarks may be ventured on the experience which they furnish. I wish to speak of the effects on
the school system itself and of the effects upon the individual
pupils attending.

"I. *Economy* has been secured through the circumstance,
that the co-education of the sexes makes it possible to have
better classification and at the same time larger classes.
Unless proper grading is interfered with, and pupils of
widely different attainments brought together in the same
classes, the separation of the sexes requires twice as many
teachers to teach the same number of pupils. This remark
applies, of course, particularly to sparsely settled districts.

The item of economy is very considerable, but is not to be compared with the other and greater advantages arising.

" While it is conceded by the opponents of co-education that primary schools may be mixed to advantage, they with one accord oppose the system for schools of a higher grade. Now, what is singular in our experience is the fact that our high school was the first experiment on this plan for classes above the primary. Economy and better classification were the controlling reasons that initiated this experiment, and from the high school the system has crept down through all the intermediate grades. What had been found practicable and satisfactory in the highest grades could not long be kept away from the lower ones.

" II. *Discipline* has improved continually with the adoption of mixed schools. Our change in St. Louis has been so gradual that we have been able to weigh with the utmost exactness every point of comparison between the two systems.

" The mixing of the male and female departments of a school has always been followed by improvement in discipline ; not merely on the part of the boys, but on that of the girls as well. The rudeness and *abandon* which prevail among boys when separate, at once give place to self-restraint in the presence of girls. The prurient sentimentality engendered by educating girls apart from boys—it is manifested by a frivolous and silly bearing when such girls are brought into the society of the opposite sex—this disappears almost entirely in mixed schools. In its place a quiet self-possession reigns. The consequence of this is a general prevalence of milder forms of discipline. Boys and girls originating—according to nature's plan—in the same family as brothers and sisters, their culture should be together, so that the social instincts be saved from abnormal diseased action. The natural dependence of each individual upon all the rest in society should not be prevented by isolating one sex from another during the most formative stages of growth.

"III. *Instruction* is also greatly improved. Where the sexes are separate, methods of instruction are unbalanced and gravitate continually towards extremes that may be called masculine and feminine. The masculine extreme is mechanical formalizing in its lowest shape, and the merely intellectual training on its highest side. The feminine extreme is the learning-by-rote system on the lower side, and the superfluity of sentiment in the higher activities. Each needs the other as a counter-check, and it is only through their union that educational methods attain completeness and do not foster one-sidedness in the pupil. We find here that mixed schools are noted for the prevalence of a certain healthy tone which schools on the separate system lack. More rapid progress is the consequence, and we find girls making wonderful advances even in mathematical studies, while boys seem to take hold of literature far better for the influence of the female portion of the class.

"IV. *Individual development* is, as already indicated, far more sound and healthy. It has been found that schools kept exclusively for girls or boys require a much more strict surveillance on the part of the teachers. The girls confined by themselves develop the sexual tension much earlier, their imagination being the reigning faculty, and not bridled by intercourse with society in its normal form. So it is with boys, on the other hand. Daily association in the class-room prevents this tension, and supplies its place by indifference. Each sex testing its strength with the other on an intellectual plane in the presence of the teacher —each one seeing the weakness and strength of the other— learns to esteem what is essential at its true value. Sudden likes and dislikes, capricious fancies and romantic ideals give way for sober judgments not easily deceived by mere externals. This is the basis of that 'quiet self-possession' before alluded to, and it forms the most striking mark of difference between the girls or boys educated in mixed schools and those educated in schools exclusively for one sex.

"That the sexual tension be developed as late as possible, and that all early love affairs be avoided, is the desideratum, and experience has shown that association of the sexes on the plane of intellectual contest is the safest course to secure this end."

These judicious remarks, by one who has long and attentively studied the problem under advantageous circumstances, are so clear that we have few commentaries to make upon them. Of course there are certain branches of instruction to which they do not apply, but this is a question we do not enter upon in this connection.

The point to which we wish to draw especial attention is what Professor Harris calls the "late development of the sexual tension," in children of both sexes who are allowed freely to intermingle in the pursuits of education.

Furthermore, as we have shown at the outset of this appendix, that education itself is higher which develops the latent feminine instincts in boys, the inherent masculine traits in girls; which, in other words, tempers each sex with the best characteristics of the opposite sex.

Segregation and isolation do not improve the morality nor elevate the culture, but the contrary. From the earliest years it is better that the sexes should meet in an unrestricted manner, that diffidence, false modesty, and spurious sentiment should be avoided, and that much of the intellectual and social training should be in common.

While this is true, it by no means follows that the social

basis of children's society should be upon the same theories as that of adults.

No training is more objectionable and more caculated to bring about precocious maturity, in other words, to foster the very tension which it should be our aim to discourage, than to introduce into the thoughts and social life of children the sentiment of sexual love. Hence it was that we have said, on a previous page : "The growing custom of allowing very young people of both sexes to associate at parties, balls, dances, and similar amusements cannot be approved on the score of health. It is nearly certain to favor precocity."

Conversation about beaus and "girls," reference to the admiration of the opposite sex, teasing about early loves, and such subjects, on which too many parents delight to speak with their children, are thoroughly unwise.

While the ordinary intercourse of the family and the school is likely to bring about a condition of indifference, it is not to be trusted to alone. The minds of the young are too excitable and too eager for novelties to be left to their own discretion. It is essential that they be occupied with matters which will keep them away from seductive and insidious subjects.

The pursuit of the severer studies, such as mathematics, and the proper training of the physical powers, are what we must chiefly rely upon to accomplish this. With these precautions, we need not fear the result of the freedom which in this country is constantly extending in reference to the relations of the sexes in daily life.

While these associations should be looked upon with approval, they should not be unrestricted. Even in our country, in which we boast of liberty and equality, there are distinctions in society which we do, and which we ought to observe.

It is better that caildren find their playmates and companions among those of their own social position, than with others less carefully nurtured. Hence the impropriety of trusting them too largely, as is often done, to the care of domestics and to the companionship of their children.

THE RELATION OF SEX

TO

DISEASE.

———

It is an interesting inquiry to what extent the nature character, and frequency of disease in the human race are influenced by sex. The power of sex over disease exists to no inconsiderable degree. It is partly due to the difference in the physiological and partly to the diversity in the social life of man and woman. · The extent and practical bearing of this influence upon health and longevity deserve more attention at our hands than they have received in an incidental manner elsewhere in this volume.

First, we shall inquire into

Man's Liability to Disease as compared to Woman's.

In other words, which sex is the more subject to sickness, and what diseases show a partiality to the male rather than the female sex ? ·

The most natural reply to this question, and the one in accordance with popular notions on the subject, is that woman, with her feebler frame, more delicate nervous organization, and her host of affections peculiar to herself, is more frequently and dangerously sick than man; that she suffers

25   (289)

more, and dies earlier. This, however, is not the case. As
we have pointed out in speaking of "the physical traits of
the male," the average duration of life is greater with the
gentler sex, who more frequently attain extreme old age than
their sterner partners in the struggle for existence. Yet it
seems very like a paradox, that the race should not be to the
strong. Several explanations have been offered. It has
been asserted that man succumbs sooner because he is the
more exposed to danger and disease by his avocations and
the customs of society. War, which costs him his blood,
costs woman only her tears. For him, almost alone, are the
perils of the intoxicating cup, the exhaustions of the de-
bauch, the fearful anxiety of the stock-room, and the excitement of the political arena. The risks of maternity do not
equal these peculiar perils of manhood. Another explanation has been sought in the finer nervous organization of
woman, which enables her to endure more and react better.
Man, therefore, suffers less, but his powers of resistance are
less, and the tendency to death greater.

Both these explanations are doubtless just, and account
to a great extent for the singular disparity in the vitality of
the two sexes. The character of the diseases which are met
with in men more frequently than in women explain still
further the seeming anomaly.

We will pass in review some of the principal diseases
which our flesh is heir to, and note the sex they prefer.

Apoplexy.

Men are oftener assailed by this dangerous disease than
women. This may be accounted for, in part, by the well-
known fact that one of the most active causes of apoplexy
is the intemperate use of fermented liquors, which, in some
constitutions, produce a speedy impairment of the functions
of the brain. Alcohol also exerts a pernicious influence in

many instances upon the heart and arteries. The heart's action is not only increased under its influence, but positive alterations in the structure of the bloodvessels take place. In such instances, we find the movements of the heart permanently quickened, and the blood, therefore, driven more forcibly to the brain, while the coats of the arteries having lost their elasticity by a thickening or thinning (perhaps ulceration) of their substance are more readily ruptured by this forcible current, and hence the tendency to hemorrhage in the brain is vastly increased. The excessive use of tobacco is also supposed to predispose to congestion of the brain, and consequently to apoplectic attacks. As the excessive employment of alcohol and tobacco are essentially vices of the male sex, we may attribute to them, in part, the greater liability to apoplectic attacks to which men are the victims.

Epilepsy.

This disease also is more prone to attack the male sex. An exception, however, is to be made in this respect in regard to the French, particularly Parisians. All French authors agree that in Paris at least there are more women epileptics than men. Esquirol, the highest of the French authorities, states, after carefully comparing the number of patients at various asylums, that the number of women attacked was one-third greater than that of the men. English writers, however, are unanimous as to the greater proclivity to epilepsy being on the side of the male sex. An analysis of the returns of the Registrar-General of England with reference to the mortality from this disease in either sex, during the past seven years, shows that 6729 were males and 6149 females. Hence, " it would appear that the mortality of males at all ages from epilepsy is 52.26 per cent., of females 47.73 per cent., and that, therefore, 4.53 per cent. of male deaths occur from epilepsy in excess of female deaths from that cause; or, to put it in a different way, we find that the average male deaths in one year from epilepsy are 961.3, of females 878.1; so that annually in England and Wales 83.2 more males die epileptic than females." The census of the United States shows also that in America more men die epileptic than women.

Men when attacked by epilepsy are more apt to die o the disease than women. This greater liability to death on their part is not confined to epilepsy, but is true of all diseases of the nervous system, for whether in children, youth, or old age, death from these affections is more prevalent in the male than the female sex. Very extended statistics have shown that during the first five years of life the deaths among males from nervous diseases are greater by one-fifth than among females.

St. Vitus' Dance.

This disease, known to physicians under the name of *chorea*, unlike apoplexy and epilepsy, is both more frequent and more fatal with the female than the male sex. It is essentially a disease of children, being rarely met with after twenty. From ten to fifteen years of age is the favorite period of life for this affection, and, according to some of the most reliable statisticians, girls are three times more frequently the sufferers than boys.

Hysteria.

This nervous affection is almost monopolized by the female sex. It is nearly exclusively met with in women between the ages of fourteen and thirty. It is a mistake, however, to suppose that men are never hysterical. We have more than once seen attacks of veritable hysteria in the male sex. Under the influence of excitement and debility, men, of a certain temperament, are not unfrequently seized with hysterics. Shakspeare, the great master of the human passions, was aware of this. He puts into the mouth of Lear, upon hearing Kent's account of the cause of his being placed in the stocks, the words:—

> "O, how this mother swells up toward my heart!
> *Hysterica passio!* down, thou climbing sorrow,
> Thy elements below!"

A common name for hysteria in Shakspeare's time was the *mother*, by which term Lear therefore first designates his feeling before employing the more learned Latin synonyme.

Neuralgia.

This disease is more common, because probably of their greater exposure to the exciting causes, in men than in women. But that form of neuralgia which takes the shape of headache, is more of a feminine than a masculine affliction.

Headache.

There are few women who are not more or less sufferers from attacks of headache; many men are never troubled in this way. Women not only are more subject to this affection, but they also suffer more severely. Intensity of pain depends greatly upon the susceptibility, the capacity for suffering on the part of the individual. It is only by poetical license that it can be said, an insect crushed feels the pangs of a dying giant. The delicate sensibility of woman imposes upon her greater suffering from the same amount of pain.

The headaches peculiar to the female sex are very numerous. In men, late hours, improper food or habits of eating, dissipation, excessive or prolonged mental toil, business anxieties, and want of exercise, are the principal causes of headache. In women, exposure to the night air while thinly clad, tight lacing, a too sedentary, indoor life, imprudence at the monthly epochs, and family cares, are the main influences which induce it.

Insanity.

Males are more liable to insanity than females, in the proportion, according to the latest and most trustworthy tables, of fifty-three per cent. of males to forty-six per cent. of females. The period of life during which women are most subject to this disease, and most apt to die from its effects, is between the ages of twenty and forty. Most of the men, on the contrary, who die of this disease, are between the ages of forty and sixty, a time when strength and hope so often fail the anxious man of business.

Bronchitis.

Men are more liable to be assailed by inflammation of the bronchial tubes than women. This is probably due, to a great extent, to their greater exposure, in outdoor life, to the causes which induce bronchitis.

Asthma.

The male sex is much more predisposed to this troublesome affection than the female. According to the experience of some physicians of the widest practice in this disease, about eighty per cent. of all the patients are of the masculine gender.

Consumption.

This fatal disease numbers more victims among the female than the male sex. Sex influences, also, the time of development of the symptoms when the affection is hereditary. Thus in males the malady manifests itself about a year and a half later, on the average, than in females.

Dr. Edward Smith, F. R. S., etc., Physician to the Hospital of Consumption and Diseases of the Chest, Brompton, in a review of a large number of cases of consumption, and of the conditions of system and circumstance which had aggravated the disease, says:—

"One striking feature to which we must refer was the greater liability of the female over the male sex to many of the ills to which we have referred. Thus, in reference to the parents, more mothers than fathers had children early, had feeble general health, and had died early. Of the patients, more females than males had mothers who died early, had most relatives who had died of consumption, had parents with one child only, had experienced feeble health and defective appetite through life, had had delicacy of the lungs, were married when very young, had feeble children, had lost most children, had suffered from anxiety, had had measles, scarlet fever, and hooping-cough, had not worn flannel next the skin, had a very defective education, were of susceptible temperament, had brown eyes, florid complexion, and fleshy habit, and had suffered from coldness of the extremities. This is most striking evidence of the liability of females to conditions tending to constitutional disease."

Lung Fever.

Cases of inflammation of the lungs occur much more frequently among males than females. The influence of sex in the causation of the disease is probably, however, more apparent than real. Men are more generally exposed to changes of temperature, which are the principal exciting causes of the disorder.

Heart Disease.

Organic disease of the heart is more common in men than in women. The latter, however, are more liable to palpitation of the heart unconnected with disease of the structure of that organ.

Aneurism.

Males are more frequently affected with aneurism than females. According to the statements of some surgeons of the largest experience, more than seven-eighths of all cases occur in men. This greater liability of the male sex is due to the relative frequency in that sex of fatty and earthy degenerations of the coats of the arteries, and not, as has been well pointed out by Prof. Gross, to the difference in the occupation and habits of the two sexes. In the words of the professor of surgery at the Jefferson Medical College, "the opinion which ascribes the greater frequency of spontaneous aneurism in males than in females to their more laborious occupation, their more intemperate habits, and their greater exposure to all kinds of disease, is entirely untenable, and, therefore, unworthy of confidence. Women, it is true, are not sailors, carpenters, blacksmiths, or hod-carriers, but in many parts of the world they are tillers of the soil, and engaged in almost every variety of pursuit calculated to rupture the arterial tissues if they were in a serious state of disease, such as we so often meet with in the other sex."

Gout.

Women sometimes suffer from gout, but neither so frequently nor so severely as men. Hippocrates stated that women were not liable to gout at all until after the change of life. This is not strictly true, but it is quite certain that women are most subject to this disease before puberty and after the change of life, and but rarely affected by it during the intervening period.

Rheumatism.

The statistics of rheumatic affections show that, prior to the age of forty, more men than women die from rheumatic inflammations. After the age of forty, a curious change takes place in this respect. The female constitution is so altered that she becomes the one most readily affected with this malady. From forty to sixty more women die than men from the direct and indirect effects of rheumatic fever and inflammation of the joints. This much greater frequency of the disease in women after the change of life has been ascribed to the greater tendency of the skin to perspire, and hence the greater danger of checked perspiration.

Dropsy.

Men are more frequently afflicted with dropsical effusions than women. From forty to fifty years of age, the proportion of deaths from this malady is nine males to five females; from fifty to sixty, the still greater ratio of fourteen males to six females. Here again, as in the case of some of the other diseases we have mentioned, the cause of the disparity between the sexes may be in a measure accounted for by the more frequent instances of excesses in the use of intoxicating liquors with men than women. For, in the language of Prof. Dickson, "Intemperance in the use of ardent spirits is one of the most prolific sources of dropsy in its worst forms. Whether this fatal habit be carried to the extreme of sottish debauchery and drunkenness, or limited to such indulgence as may be allowed without actual exposure and ruin to the reputation, the effect is ultimately the same; the vitality of the system is exhausted by the incessant application of inordinate stimuli; the powers of the stomach are worn out by the repetition of excesses, each more debilitating than the former, or its tissues thickened and inflamed by being so constantly bathed in a heating and almost caustic fluid; the viscera concerned in digestion become universally obstructed and indurated, and disease and death must at length ensue."

Enlargement of the Liver.

Increase in the size of the liver occurs more frequently in females. The highest living authority upon diseases of this organ, Dr. Murchison, of England, attributes this to the practice of tight-lacing, so much in vogue among fashionable women. Occasionally also the same effect is produced by the habitual wearing of a tight belt by a man.

Constipation.

There is a greater tendency to costiveness, and consequently a greater liability to the many evil results it brings, among females than males. The reasons commonly assigned for this are the more sedentary habits and over-confinement to the house of women.

Cancer.

Cancerous disease is of more frequent occurrence among women than men. Thus, it has been found that of the 11,662 persons who, during a period of five years, died from it in England (exclusive of the city of London), there were 8746 women and 2916 men. That is to say, three times as many women as men lost their lives through this terrible malady. The womb and the breasts are the favorite sites of malignant tumors in women. It is owing to this extraordinary predilection of malignant disease for these parts, that women suffer so much more than those of the other sex.

Stone in the Bladder.

This affection, so common in certain districts of the country with males, is very rarely met with in women. This is owing largely to anatomical reasons.

Typhoid Fever.

To this affection women are less subject than men. There is also a greater mortality among male patients than female.

The influence of sex over disease is apparent, as we have seen, in many of the most common and serious maladies, in reference to the liability to attack, the character of the invasion, and its mortality. Each sex is also subject to its peculiar disorders. A few words upon those peculiar to men will not, we trust, be without practical value.

A Disease peculiar to Old Men.

In a previous chapter we called attention to the nervous disorders originating in the male generative system, their causes, and the prospects and means of cure. To these, therefore, we need not recur. But there are certain local troubles to which the male sex is liable as years advance which have not yet been more than alluded to by us; one of these is an affection known as *enlargement of the prostate gland*. This gland, situated immediately in front of the neck of the bladder, when it increases in size causes much inconvenience and suffering.

The causes of this enlargement are, according to Prof. Gross, always those "which act in a slow and permanent manner. Whatever, therefore, has a tendency to keep up habitual engorgement in the organ may be considered as being capable of producing the affection. Augmented action necessarily occasions an augmented afflux of blood and a corresponding increase of nutrition. Diminished action has a reverse effect. Amongst the more frequently enumerated causes of the malady are excessive venery, stricture of the urethra, disease of the bladder, horseback exercise, gonorrhœa, and the employment of stimulating diuretics; but, in general, the influence of these causes is apparent rather than real. They are, no doubt, all capable of inducing the disease; but, on the other hand, it is equally certain that they are often accused when they are entirely innocent. Some of the very worst cases of hypertrophy of the prostate occur in old men who have led the chastest of lives, who have not ridden on horseback for forty or fifty years, and who have never had the slightest disease of any kind of the urethra."

The symptoms which first attract attention are mainly those which are connected with the voiding of water—irritation, a frequent desire, difficulty in passing it, and slight pain. The lower bowel "never feels empty, even after the most thorough purgation." These symptoms gradually increase and bring others in their train. When noticed at the age of fifty or over, they should lead the individual to seek at once medical counsel in order that aid may be extended him at the outset of the trouble. He should, also, scrupulously avoid all irritating and stimulating foods and drinks, and never take any griping purgatives. Salts, citrate of magnesia, and cream of tartar are innocent and beneficial laxatives to employ. All these causes which we have just enumerated as liable to excite the disease must be avoided—hence horseback exercise and sexual intercourse are eminently improper. Rest in a recumbent position is of very great service. Of course, this should not be carried to the extent of the avoidance of all gentle exercise in the open air during pleasant weather.

Few men in advanced life escape altogether some trouble with the bladder and contiguous organs. It is important, therefore, for every individual to avoid everything which experience has taught him will excite even temporary discomfort of these parts. That moderation in the gratification of all desires, which is so conducive to health in early and middle life, becomes imperative now, when there is no surplus vitality to be drawn upon to repair the ravages of imprudence.

26

THE MORAL RELATIONS

OF THE

SEXUAL LIFE.

WE have confined ourselves so far in our considerations
on the relations of the sexes to the physiological aspects of
the question, its physical and, to some extent, its intellectual
bearings. It seemed more appropriate to the nature of our
studies and to the character of our researches. Now, however, that we have brought our labors so nearly to a close,
and have examined the peculiarities of sex in their various
bearings upon the temporal welfare of the individual and the
race, we may be permitted to step aside from our path and
explain the influence which these powerful instincts have
exerted and continue to exert on his actions and destiny as
a moral being.

The historian or theologian who does not carefully estimate the strength and power of the sexual impulses will
often fail to interpret the actions and the creed of past generations. He will attribute to motiveless caprice and to un-
meaning malignity many actions which were merely the
expression of an uncontrolled instinct.

So also in the lives of individuals, it is a matter of daily
observation that in these respects it is next to impossible to

(303)

understand the vagaries which govern otherwise prudent and cautious men.

The Sexual Relations in Heathendom.

Did we desire to magnify the importance of our theme, we could readily illustrate from history how in all times it has so fastened itself upon the minds of men that it has shaped their destiny and even formed the basis of their hopes beyond this life.

Every student of mythology is aware that the rites of many primitive religions are but the complex symbols which represent the power of transmitting life, and that the myths which have been devised to perpetuate the signification of these rites are but veiled descriptions of the same fact. The East Indian God appears under his triple form of the Creator, the Preserver, and the Destroyer; and in his form as the creator, he is represented by and worshipped under the image of the *membrum virile*. The bull Mithra in Persian story, and the god Bel who was worshipped on the plains of Euphrates, are repetitions of the same idea.

As might be expected, such distorted conceptions of divinity, this confusion of ideas which confounded together the creation and the transmission of the vital principle, led to licentious ceremonies and a general abasement of the moral sense. The scenes recorded by the Hebrew prophets which transpired in ancient Babylon, and which were parts of the religious observances of that city, necessarily laid the foundation for that disintegration of society and destruction of individual powers which finally resulted in the ruin of the state.

When the antique austerity of the classical republic of Greece and Rome became tainted with the corruption of Oriental communications, the most glorious traits of these commonwealths disappeared, and in their place came Cæsarism and profligacy. So clearly was this introduction of foreign religious rites the commencement of the state's deterioration, that the ancient heathen historians, Tacitus for example, directly attribute it to this cause.

We refer to these degraded misconceptions of physical truths, and this apotheosis of the animal instincts, so that we may bring into stronger contrast with them the just and beautiful estimate which was given them by Christianity.

Sexual Relations in the Mosaic Law.

The Old Testament by its clear and sublime teachings preserved the Israelites from the contamination by which they were surrounded. Situated in the midst of nations by whom an unlicensed debauchery was regarded as a part and parcel of religious life, the chosen people successfully maintained its purity, and even in the darkest hour of its history there were found four hundred men who had never bowed the knee to Baal.

The doctrines of the Mosaic law are most explicit in what relates to individual purity. Far from passing by in silence these delicate relations as indifferent, or of doubtful utility, or as possibly harmful if discussed openly—as the modern fashion widely prevails—the sacred word enters with singular minuteness into the admonitions for chastity, for temperance in the marital relation, and for sanitary precautions connected therewith.

We do not think it necessary to quote all the many texts which are at hand to support this assertion. Any one who will take the pains to examine the various chapters in Leviticus and Deuteronomy, which contain the directions to single and married men, will there find an explicitness and a minuteness which writers of the present day cannot attempt to imitate.

26*

· It will be of interest and value, however, to recall and clothe in modern language the directions given on some of the points to which we have referred in the preceding chapters, both for the purpose of substantiating what we have just said and to admire again the accuracy and wisdom of the inspired word, even in its minutest portions.

In regard to *nocturnal and involuntary emissions* the law distinctly recognizes them as an "uncleanness." The man was ordered to bathe himself thoroughly in water, and his garments likewise The cold bath, the value of which to control such discharges we have several times emphasized, was thus early enjoined for the same affection. A soldier who was so disturbed during war was to wander about outside the camp during the whole of the next day, and at night, when fatigued with the exercise, was to bathe himself and return. The exercise and the cold affusion were quite certain to prevent any immediate return. (Leviticus xv. 16; Deuteronomy xxiii. 10, 11.)

The intimate connection which we have shown to exist between the health of the parts and the general mental and physical soundness is recognized in the Mosaic law in a variety of references. Any one wounded or maimed there was forbidden to enter into the congregation of the Lord, and still less could he become a priest. Even during a struggle it was positively forbidden for a wife to interfere in such a manner that she might cause an injury to functions of the man; and if she did so, the penalty was to be carried out without mercy; "thou shalt cut off her hand, *thine eye shall not pity her.*" (Deuteronomy xxiii. 1; xxv. 11.)

The diseases peculiar to the organs, those which in the former pages we have designated as "secret diseases," were clearly by no means uncommon, and, whatever a spurious modern diffidence may say about it, were most indubitably considered by the publisher of that great law and admirable hygienic code, as most proper subjects for public instruction. For it must not be forgotten that the Mosaic law was no series of esoteric maxims for the behoof of a limited few, but was regularly read aloud to all the assembled people, without omission and without reserve. They were nurtured from childhood in its precepts, and no one arose to proclaim that it contained perilous and insidious information.

Considered in this aspect, the very full and detailed descriptions it gives of sexual diseases have additional importance. Some inaccuracies, or, perhaps, hesitations, in the rendering considerably obscure to the ordinary reader the real purport of the advice. For instance, there can be no reasonable doubt but that in the earlier verses of the fifteenth chapter of Leviticus the disease referred to is gonorrhœa. The words in the second verse, "a running issue out of the flesh," is rendered in the margin of the English version "a running of the reins." Saint Jerome, the translator of the Latin vulgate, thought that the disease intended was spérmatorrhœa, and therefore rendered the original by: "*Vir, qui patitur fluxum seminis.*" The third verse, which contains what physicians call the diagnosis, is in the English version wholly unintelligible; but in the vulgate the test is clearly given which we now recognize as distinguishing a slight and innocent discharge from one which is specific and contagious:—

"Et tunc judicabitur huic vitio subjacere, cum per singula momenta adhæserit carni ejus, atque concreverit, fœdus humor."

The contagious nature of the disease was impressed on the people by the most stringent regulations. The saddle that the victim rode on, the cup that he drank from, the bed he slept in, and the bench he sat upon were all to be considered unclean and not to be touched by a healthy person. In part explanation of the minuteness of these directions, it is to be remembered that the clothing in ancient times did not provide the concealment and protection which our modern fashions afford. Even after a complete cure had been obtained, the man must hold aloof for seven days and wash himself and his clothes in fresh *running* water.

The thirteenth chapter of Leviticus has been subjected to several most critical examinations of late years by physicians who were also skilled Hebraists. One of the most recent of these studies is before us, written by a learned teacher in Vienna. He gives an exhaustive commentary on the original text, and adduces strong evidence that the word in the second verse and elsewhere, rendered in the English version "flesh," has reference solely to the virile member; and that the disease designated as leprosy, and which as described does not exist at present either in Palestine or Europe, was *syphilis*. He supports this view by pointing out with a large array of evidence that the description given does apply to this loathsome and dangerous complaint, and that the injunctions of complete seclusion and periodical examinations of a suspected sore are precisely those which, were it in our power, ought to be carried out to-day. We do not pretend to judge on so difficult a question in linguistic and Biblical lore as is here presented; but so far as the medical aspect of the discussion is concerned, we have been strongly impressed by the arguments used. And certainly, after what we have already said of the subtle and disastrous character of this scourge, we may well believe that special precautions would have been given by the Divine Voice to guard the chosen people from its contamination.

Passing to another part of the law, we find the vice of masturbation in the form in which it was then commonly practised by the heathen nations as a religious rite, condemned and punished with death. (Leviticus xviii. 21; xx. 2.)

That other and more heinous sin, which brought down the wrath of God upon, and derived its name from the city of Sodom, was repeatedly condemned as an "abomination" (Leviticus xviii. 22; Deuteronomy xxiii. 17); and an equally vile crime against nature is solemnly cursed in more than one passage. (Exodus xxii. 19; Leviticus xviii. 23; xx. 15.)

The relations of the sexes were defined with an accuracy which left no pretext for unrighteousness. In spite of all that modern political economists have written about the uselessness of sumptuary laws, we perceive a deep wisdom in the prohibition of either sex using clothing which pertains to the other. (Deuteronomy xxii. 5.) Prostitution was absolutely prohibited; incest, adultery, rape, and fornication punished with severe penalties.

In marriage the relations of the sexes were defined distinctly. A newly married man was not to be called upon to go to war, nor to be charged with any onerous business for the space of one year. (Deuteronomy xxiv. 5.) Husbands were not to deny their wives "the duty of marriage," but were forbidden to demand from them this duty during the monthly illness, and not until after the cleansing from it, which took place on the eighth day after its cessation. (Leviticus xviii. 19, and xv. 28.)

As the reproduction of the species was considered one of the chief ends of marriage, any action by which this was permanently avoided, as in the case of Onan, who refused to be instrumental in raising up an heir to his deceased brother's estate, was regarded as criminal, and punished accordingly.

We have by no means exhausted this interesting Biblical study. We might exemplify by many copious quotations from different parts of both Old and New Testaments, the importance which the Word of God attributes to a proper understanding of our duties as parents of future generations. And why, let us ask, was it deemed of such importance? The reason given is both a fact in history and a warning for all time.

"Ye shall not commit any of these abominations.

"That the land spue not you out, when ye defile it, as it spued out the nations which were before you.

"For whosoever shall commit any of these abominations, even the souls that commit them shall be cast off from among their people."

Terrible words, true at all times, and of all people! The curse of uncleanness, of sexual vice, is sure finally to destroy the individual, the family, society, the nation, and extend its blighting power to unborn generations.

The Meaning of these Warnings.

Would these instructions have been given with this solemnity and with this care were they of small moment? We cannot for an instant entertain the idea. Can we suppose that their intention was *merely* sanitary in character, that they had no reference to the moral relations of the individual? Such a view were inconsistent with the known objects of revelation. Finally, if instruction on these relations was deemed so important in the infancy of the world, long before civilization with its new crimes and its new vices had multiplied temptations and penalties, can it be possible that they are now no longer needed? Or if needed, that it is no longer right to give them.

If, as we believe, there is a profound moral significance in these apparently hygienic admonitions, has that significance departed from them now?

The answer to this question is too palpably given by the enormous amount of vice and misery which results from

sexual vice in this day and generation, for there to be any
need of a reply from us. A keen student of human nature
has bitterly said : "When modesty departs from the heart
she takes up her residence in the lips ;" and we fear that the
prudishness which would leave unsaid the warnings to youth
and men concerning the dangers to which their sex exposes
them is, in reality, far more to be suspected than the candor
which sounds aloud those warnings, even at the risk of shocking some sensitive minds.

We know from multitudinous examples that there is no
one vicious tendency which more surely saps the strength of
the state, destroys the happiness of the domestic circle, con-
taminates social life, and leads the individual to destructive
habits, than that which regards the sexual relations. Where
the mothers are virtuous, the sires will be brave, and the
sons will be dutiful. Where libertinism is winked at, where
soiled reputations are excused, where statutes protect traffic
in human sin, we may surely look for lack of courage, lack
of patriotism, lack of prosperity ; and though such a plague
spot may appear fair and flourishing enough for a time,
sooner or later a swift destruction will overcome it. And
even since the time at which we penned the line where we
characterized a certain city as the "*lupanar* of Europe,"
the curse has gone forth upon that city, and she is now in
blood and ashes doing penance for her sins.

In the New Testament.

Too frequently there are those who in their natural inclinations allow themselves whatever liberties are not specifi-
cally prohibited by the moral code, just as there are in
business matters too many who do not hesitate at any trans-
action which is " o' the windy side of the law," and construe,
like the lawyer Mr. Vholes in Dickens' novel, everything to
be moral which is legal. One such it was our chance to

meet, one who professed to live according to the highest
religious life, and yet who defended the propriety of an occasional indulgence in solitary licentiousness on the ground
that it was nowhere prohibited in the New Testament.

This defence, urged as it was by one decidedly above the
average in talents and acquirements, impressed us strongly
with the need of a more definite expression of opinion on the
part of teachers, both medical and religious, in reference to
the duties of man in relation to his sexual nature.

All readers are familiar with the cardinal difference that
exists between the manner of teaching of the Old and the
New Testament, that the former lays down a defined ethical
code chiefly in the method of prohibition, while the latter
inculcates principles and motives of a positive character,
which, followed out, necessarily carry with them all and
more than all the force of the older law.

While, therefore, in the older books we found a minuteness of detail not surpassed even in special sanitary works,
we must not expect a reiteration of these in the Evangelists
and Apostles. But what we may expect, and what we do
find in abundance, are numberless exhortations to purity,
chastity, and cleanliness, warnings against lewdness, uncleanness, the lusts of the flesh, and the abominations which were
in vogue in the corrupt cities of the Roman Empire, at that
time rapidly declining toward the pit of effeminacy and ruin
into which it finally fell. The prevailing licentiousness of
the times is over and over again referred to, and the
strictest injunctions given to the early Christians to keep
themselves aloof from the pitch which defiled the social life
of the heathen.

Paul was too well aware of the destructive consequences
of sexual vice either to omit the mention of it, or to pass it
by with a timid delicacy. He refers to it with distinct
emphasis, and sounds his warnings in no ambiguous words.

The precise view taken of the marital relation by our Saviour and his disciples, has always been and continues to be an unsettled point between rival schools of theologians. Even in the second century there arose a Syrian sect under the leadership of Saturninus, who declared, somewhat as do the Shakers of to-day, that sexual intercourse at all times and under all circumstances is a sin of the darkest dye, and that marriage is an invention of the devil. As Mosheim well remarks in his Ecclesiastical History, it is gratifying to consider that any such extreme view brings with it its own correction, for as it prevents the birth of children, it must look for recruits solely to the adult population, and must consequently-be of limited duration.

Certain it is, however, that the expressions used by the Great Teacher led to a much higher estimate of the sacredness of the marriage tie, and produced a loftier respect for woman than had been usual either in the Israelitish or the European nations.

The law of divorce which was then promulgated, was based upon a view of marriage very different from that previously existent. Under the Mosaic law, as well as under the Greek and Roman codes, the husband and wife were united by a tie previously civil in its character. The deeper unity which binds them, which makes them one, which sinks the duality of person in the oneness of life and aims, and which is now recognized as a physiological truth, was not so much as suspected by the most contemplative philosopher of classical days.

Then again, the duty of fidelity to one wife, and to the marriage vow, was never before impressed upon either Jew or Gentile. Polygamy was practised and authorized among the Jews, while the Greeks, though approving of only one wife, did not consider it obligatory upon the husband to be faithful to her. On the contrary, we read frequently in the

27

Greek classics of married men visiting the houses of the *hetaeræ*, and passing their time in this company, without any general denunciation of the act, and almost without comment.

Only when we compare the social life of that day with that which Christianity introduced, can we appreciate the immense superiority of its morality, and the enormous vices it had to combat and to conquer. All social life is based upon family life; and this, in its inception, history, and character, depends directly upon the moral relations of the sexes. Social reforms must commence here, and here is where Christianity did commence.

Sexual Relations in Christianity.

Thus Christianity, which came not to do away with the Mosaic law, still less to do away with the evils that law was given to correct, reiterates and defines the warnings and the instructions of the Old Testament on the relations of the sexes. It elevated the bond of marriage, increased the stringency of the lien, lessened the causes of divorce, and ordained the principle of monogamy, which previously had been an approved custom but not an obligatory enactment.

The precepts inculcated by the Apostles on these points, and on the sins of uncleanness, were required at a time when the weight of the examples of men high in station and eminent in intellect was thrown in favor of vicious indulgence.

The rigidity of the early Christians on these points, maintained as it was amid the temptations of a lascivious pagan state enormously wealthy and incredibly dissolute, naturally passed into austerity, and from austerity to asceticism.

They reversed the example of the Oriental nations, and instead of regarding the instincts of procreation as natural and proper when controlled and enlightened, they looked

upon it as the sure proof and sign of man's moral degradation, the one greatest foe to his spiritual advancement, the
peculiar stronghold of Apollyon and his imps, and that
which beyond all else it behooved the seeker after righteous-
ness to utterly crush and stamp out of his nature.

These false and exaggerated notions, the product of an
ignorance of the physical nature of man, gave rise to sad
results. A morbid fear of sexual excitement, a constant
turning of the thoughts to dangers from this source, are
precisely calculated in some temperaments to weaken and
not to strengthen the resolution. There is a fatal attraction
to some constitutions in the forbidden. ˙*Nititur in vetitum*,
nature seeks what is not allowed, and the result of over-
strained terrors manifests itself occasionally in fearful scenes
of violence.

Mr. Lecky, in his "History of European Morals," gives
some striking illustrations of the dangers of this code of
morals. He remarks:—

"Most terrible at times were the struggles of young and ˙
ardent men through whose veins the hot blood of passion
flowed, who were borne on the wave of enthusiasm to the life
of the anchorite in the desert. In the arms of Syrian or
African brides, whose soft eyes answered love with love, they
might have sunk to rest; but in the lonely desert no peace
could ever visit their souls. Multiplying with frantic energy
the macerations of the body, beating their breasts with
anguish, the tears forever streaming from their eyes, ima-
gining themselves continually haunted by forms of deadly
beauty. their struggles not unfrequently ended in insanity
and suicide. When St. Pachomius and St. Palaemon were
once conversing together in the desert, a young monk rushed
into their presence in a distracted manner, and, convulsed
with sobs, poured out his tale. A woman had entered his

cell, and had seduced him, and then vanished, leaving him half dead upon the ground; then, with a wild shriek, the monk broke away, rushed across the desert till he arrived at the next village, and then leaping into the open furnace of the public baths, he perished in the flames."

This narrative is but one of numbers which could be brought forward illustrating the dangers of ignorance and prejudice on the important topics we have discussed in the present volume, and the close relations they bear to the moral part of man's nature. Here was a misguided young man crazed and driven to self-murder by the phantom which his own imagination, diseased by long dwelling upon one function of his system, had conjured up.

During the Middle Ages.

The same unfortunate interpretation of the Christian doctrines produced similar violations of natural laws throughout the Middle Ages. The violence done to the natural impulses by an enforced and unwilling celibacy showed itself in prevailing dissoluteness of life, and too often those who should have been the models and exemplars of holy life, were the leaders in profligate ways.

The struggle by which others attempted to maintain a formal continence, while their imaginations were uncontrolled, remained, and ever will remain, bitter and hopeless. The unavoidable continence of the monasteries was not slow to foster vices of a more deleterious character than licentiousness itself, and consequently to injure rather than to benefit the general weal. Of course, we do not mean that this was commonly or even frequently the case, but there is too much evidence from original records to deny that much moral turpitude arose from this misunderstood position of the procreative instinct in the economy.

Matrimonial life itself felt the effects of this erroneous view. It was looked upon as an allowable, but not the most holy condition of life. That there was real chastity in marriage, though perhaps conceded in words, was not in act and belief, for the condition of virginity was constantly upheld as the only really pure state of living. "To cut down by the axe of virginity the wood of marriage is the true object of the saint," is the energetic metaphor of Saint Jerome. The consequence of this belief that the marriage state was inconsistent with pure holiness was that when a strong religious fervor fell upon a husband or wife, its first effect was to make any continuation of happy married life out of the question. The more religious partner at once desired and attempted to lead a solitary life, or to join some monastery or sisterhood.

In other words, it came to be generally understood that married people, by the very act of marriage, put themselves upon a lower plane of morality.

The inevitable consequence was a loss of self-respect, a diminished esteem for marital purity, and a visible tendency to infidelity in the marriage relation. It is not too much to say that an impartial student of national traits can still distinguish the fruits of these views in the southern nations of the European continent.

In Modern Times.

In more modern times the inconsistencies and the incorrectness of these views of the relations of the sexes became apparent, and able men rose who maintained that neither continence nor virginity was more pleasing in the sight of God than married chastity and fidelity, and that any doctrine to the contrary, so far from elevating a national standard of morality, did exactly the reverse. These teachers further maintained that the sexual impulse is not in itself

27*

evil, nor is it any more liable to result in evil than any other passion or appetite appertaining to man ; and that, in reference to its temperate indulgence under proper and legal restrictions, it is entirely in accordance both with the laws of natural science and the maxims of pure Christianity.

This was, indeed, a step in advance, and it has redounded to the well-being of those who have appreciated and recognized it. But in its full bearings in social and individual life, it is still too superficially understood by the masses.

This is, in a measure, owing to a general hesitation in stating distinctly to the public the nature and laws which govern the more recondite functions of the human frame. As far as this has been done, it has been by those very insufficiently qualified to act as the interpreters of scientific results, and much more for selfish and immediate ends than from any abstract desire to promote the comfort and the happiness of their fellows.

Yet the various facts which we have adduced, not from remote or limited fields, but from the general history of the race, prove conclusively how intimately associated with man's moral nature, and consequently with his life hereafter, are these questions concerning his peculiar powers.

In a double sense is there a perpetuity connected with the exercise of this function. In our article on Inheritance we have told how distant generations will certainly be moulded in their moral, mental, and physical natures by the actions of their ancestors now living. Now, we call attention to the individual destiny of each as dependent, to no small extent, upon the same actions. Impressed, as we hope our readers will be by this double responsibility, they should seek to learn how to perform these important duties intelligently.

The practical deductions which we could make from such facts are that we should not supinely fold our hands and sit

contented with indolence and ignorance in the face of these
demands upon our attention.

No one denies that almost the greatest scourges of modern
societies are still the products of a want of regulation in the
sexual relations. Hitherto, renouncing as unsuited to the
refinement and purity (!) of our social life the plain and
direct admonitions which God saw fit to impart to His
chosen people that they might be kept unspotted from the
evils which surrounded them, we have tried the plan of saying nothing and doing nothing. We have hoped that by a
well-bred silence on the subject of carnal abominations, they
would presently disappear and be forgotten.

The result has unfortunately not yet justified this agreeable expectation. If anything, it seems that these vices are
increasing at quite as fast a rate as population, wealth, and
luxury increase. The simplicity of the Society of Friends,
the severity of the Pilgrim Fathers, or the heroism of the
Huguenot refugees which marked the early history of our
country, were hard to discover now in any corner of our
wide domain.

At the Present Day.

These topics, we well know, lie without the field of medical inquiry, and we feel that we may be criticized for having
spoken on matters which other and abler pens could treat
with greater power. Nor would we thus have ventured
beyond the legitimate limits of our sphere, had we not been
persuaded that for reasons heretofore urged, there has been
and is an injurious reticence about the subject.

We have had placed at our disposal a library of recent
theological works tolerably comprehensive, and we have
spent a number of hours in examining the works of recent
divines and religious instructors. But in not one of them
have we found as definite and positive warnings on the

dangers of a misunderstood relation of the sexes as we have already referred to in the Bible itself. We may, and hope we have overlooked some works which do contain them. But that there is no longer any need of such warnings, or that it would be of doubtful utility to give them, or that it would be unadvisable on the score of propriety, are excuses for their absence which we cannot admit.

There is far greater latitude customary in social relations in this country than in the old world; there is a precocity of intellect and a susceptibility of the nervous system which is scarcely met elsewhere. Unless these traits are guided by morality and intelligence, they will soon bring forth a corruption unsurpased in our times. Concealment and attempts to enforce ignorance will not succeed. These instruments of crafty despots and a bigoted priesthood are inconsistent with our institutions.

What then, to sum up, are the questions concerning the moral relations of the sexual life, which remain open to-day, and which it is our duty, without hesitation, to confront?

They are the duty which each man owes himself not to sin against the ordinances of his own life by violating his functions; the duty which he owes the other sex to rescue them from the gulf of prostitution, and to withhold the temptations which attract them there; the duty he owes his children in keeping himself free from the taint which will render them miserable invalids. Marriage is to be rescued from the views which are degrading it once more to a mere civil contract, a legalized concubinage. The lax sentiments about divorce are not to pass unchallenged. The relations of husband and wife are to be redeemed from the estimate which places them upon a plane with a business partnership or with those of employer and employed.

There is also the prohibitory part of the moral statute to be enforced. If there is one sign more portentous than another concerning the tendency of American civilization, it is the remarkable activity of the press, and even of the pulpit (in some of its forms), in disseminating a false view of sexual morality.

On the one hand, we see on every news-stand illustrated books and papers familiarizing the public mind to indecency —the periodicals of widest circulation are filled with tales of morbid sentimentality; and not a few through their advertisements offer concealment and aid to debauchery.

On the other hand, a populous State is sunk in polygamy; another dissolves the marriage tie as readily as a copartnership; and at many points over the land communities are found who dispense with marriage altogether, and live in a condition of miscellaneous fornication.

A talented English traveller who visited this country a few years ago, and who chose to study the tendencies rather than the statistics of our people, considered these aberrations of the healthy sexual instinct as at once the most remarkable and the most ominous features of our civilization. As a nation, we were not well pleased with Mr. Dixon when we read what he had to say about us, and sought rather to discover the motes which exist in the eyes of his own countrymen than to remove the beams he had so clearly pointed out in ourselves.

But the facts he recorded are undeniable, and nothing but their familiarity prevents them from impressing us as unpleasantly as they did him. The remedy for them is not remote nor difficult. It is to insist upon better understanding of the ethical bearings of the reproductive function, upon the purity and permanency of marriage, and upon those sounder views of duty which we have already explained.

CONCLUSION.

As we reach the conclusion of our subject we cannot but feel the inadequacy with which we have treated the theme which has occupied us. The portion of man's nature whose laws and liabilities we have with great brevity rehearsed, is at once the most mysterious and the most momentous of all. This alone it is which allies him with an earthly future beyond the limit of his own existence; this it is which in its use or abuse controls not solely his own life and welfare, but in ways and to an extent wholly beyond our power to estimate, the welfare of generations to come.

Whether we regard the subject from a purely ethical or a purely physiological point of view, its importance cannot but impress us profoundly. What impulse of man's physical nature most potently governs his actions, his aspirations, and the moral complexion of his life? Precisely this on which we have been engaged. On what do some of the most difficult questions of modern social morality turn? Once more, on the control of this impulse. How can we as individuals most certainly secure the moral progress of posterity? By endowing them with a physical constitution free from the taint of hereditary disease, and a mental constitution devoid of inherited tendencies to crime. To accomplish this, science warns us again and again that no subtle compound of chemicals will suffice, and no future reformation and late adopted purity of life, but only early, unalterable, permanent fidelity to principle.

The hesitancy which has so long, and so naturally kept silent the voice of the medical profession upon these points, should now be laid aside, for the immense collection of statistics leave no doubt as to their accuracy, and their bearing on the future of the race. Many of the best minds in the world of practical and statistical medicine have been earnestly turned in this direction, and, as a consequence, during the last decade great advances in knowledge have been secured, and numerous suggestions have been presented looking to the preservation of the general health. It is not possible for the profession alone unsupported by the public, to carry out those measures of repression and protection, which we have referred to as necessary to effect any reform. And the public, in order to be induced to take any action, must be made acquainted in no uncertain manner with the necessities of the measures asked of it.

Finally, the private individual who is suffering or who only thinks he is suffering, (which is often quite as sad a condition,) from his own misdeeds, and is deprived by the nature of these misdeeds from the sympathy and attention he would otherwise have, should be put in possession of a sufficiency of facts, to enable him to judge whether his fears are groundless, or whether it be not wiser to lay aside all reticence, and seek by prompt means a recovery.

Such have been our aims in composing the foregoing chapters. Whether or not we have succeeded in expressing ourselves regarding them lucidly, instructively, and satisfactorily, the reader who has accompanied us thus far, is better able to judge than ourselves.

28

INDEX.

A.

C.

28*

D.

G.

H.

I:

N.

O.

P.

Q.

R.

S

U.

V.

W.

Y

TESTIMONIALS.

THE publishers take pleasure in presenting the following testimonials to the practical value and the moral tone of this work:—

FROM THE REV. JOHN TODD, D. D.,
Author of " The Student's Manual," " Index Rerum," etc.

GEO. H. NAPHEYS, M. D.—

DEAR SIR: I am surprised at the extent and accuracy of your reading; the judiciousness of your positions and results; the clear, unequivocal, and yet delicate and appropriate language used; and the amount of valuable information conveyed. It is comparatively a new, but very important field, and you have done well. The book cannot fail, I think, to do good—great good—if rightly heeded.

Yours truly,

JNO. TODD.

PITTSFIELD, MASS., Dec. 26, 1870.

FROM BISHOP LEVI SCOTT, D. D.,

Methodist Episcopal Church.

"I partake largely of the favorable opinion of Dr. Todd, and wish your work great success."

FROM THE REV. H. CLAY TRUMBULL,

Missionary Secretary for New England of the American S. S. Union.

DR. NAPHEYS—

MY DEAR FRIEND: You certainly have a very rare power of writing from a scientific stand-

point, with extreme plainness and entire purity,
of the most delicate matters that concern us all.
I, who know you, accept this as added evidence
that "to the pure all things are pure;" and I am
indeed glad that *you* were called to the mission
you have performed so well.

Your new work, on "THE TRANSMISSION OF
LIFE," is one that every boy, and every man,
every bachelor, parent, or teacher, should have
and read, and be grateful for. I have given
sufficient study to the ways and needs of boys
and young men, to appreciate perhaps more
fully than most, the importance of your theme.
I have been much instructed by your writings,
and I desire others to be benefited thereby.

Your teachings are based on the word of God,
and the nature of man; they tend to build
up man into the lost image of God, and to restore his body to its primitive beauty and purity,
as the temple of the Holy Ghost. I wish I could
say what would give your work the very widest

30

circulation, and secure to your views the most
general adoption.

Yours sincerely,
H. CLAY TRUMBULL.

HARTFORD, CT., Feb. 8, 1871.

FROM THE RT. REV. THOMAS MARCH CLARK, D. D., LL.D.,

Protestant Episcopal Bishop of Rhode Island.

GEO. H. NAPHEYS, M. D.—

DEAR SIR: I have read your work entitled
"THE TRANSMISSION OF LIFE," and I do not
hesitate to say that I regard it as a most timely
and valuable treatise on an important and delicate subject. I do not see a line to which the
most fastidious could object, and I believe that
its general circulation among the young would
avert a vast amount of misery and sin.

Very truly yours,
THOMAS M. CLARK.

PROVIDENCE, R. I., March 16, 1871.

FROM BISHOP T. A. MORRIS, D.D.,

Methodist Episcopal Church.

"The subject of this work is one of intense interest, and the manner of treating it is very proper. Both will command public attention and approval. May the book find a hearty welcome among all the wise and good."

——

FROM THE REV. HORACE BUSHNELL, D.D.,

Hartford, Connecticut.

DR. NAPHEYS—

DEAR SIR: I have read your book with great satisfaction. I see it to be a work immensely wanted, and think it will do much good. The subject, as related to family life and the condition of posterity, is a really awful one, and ought to be just as much more awful to young men, as it more deeply concerns their welfare. Give it as great circulation as you can.

Very respectfully yours,

HORACE BUSHNELL.

FROM THE REV. LEONARD BACON, D.D.

New Haven, Connecticut.

" I think you have treated very judiciously a difficult subject. My belief that some such work may be useful is derived from the fact that the newspapers in all parts of the country overflow with advertisements addressed to the ignorance, the fears, and the guilt of transgressors. If your book can diminish the sale of the nostrums offered in those advertisements— still more, if it can put any on their guard against the vices which make such advertisements worth paying for, you will have done a good work."

FROM THE REV. HENRY A. NELSON, D. D.,

Professor of Systematic and Pastoral Theology,
Lane Seminary, Cincinnati, Ohio.

"You have treated an important subject with great wisdom and fidelity. I could wish every young person to receive *early* the valuable—shall I not say necessary?—instruction which it contains."

———

FROM PROF. WILLIAM G. WILLIAMS,

Leavenworth, Kansas.

"The spirit of candor and delicacy as well as the high moral tone and profound reverence for the sacred mysteries both of our physical organization and of the teachings of the Bible, everywhere apparent in the work, are worthy of all praise. Not less remarkable are the ability, learning, and professional skill of the author displayed in the treatment of the various topics discussed."

———

FROM THE REV. C. P. SHELDON, D. D.,

President of the New York Baptist Convention,

Pastor of the Fifth Baptist Church,

Troy, N. Y.

"I have read attentively the advance sheets of the work by DR. NAPHEYS, entitled 'THE TRANSMISSION OF LIFE.' The subjects of which it treats are of great importance; and I am much pleased with the careful, candid, and able manner in which DR. NAPHEYS discusses them. The public need just such information, and in this work it is so imparted, that it cannot but be healthful and salutary. In moral and religious tone it is unexceptionable. I earnestly recommend its publication and circulation."

FROM NOAH PORTER, D.D., LL.D.,
President of Yale College.

DR. GEO. H. NAPHEYS—

DEAR SIR: I thank you for a copy of your work on "THE TRANSMISSION OF LIFE." There is in it much valuable information, carefully considered and industriously collected. The topics —of greatest delicacy—are treated with all possible refinement, while the much-needed warnings concerning the offences against nature, which are practised in ignorance by many, and with shamelessness by others, are faithfully administered. Very respectfully,

N. PORTER.

FROM DR. S. AUSTIN ALLIBONE,
Author of the "Dictionary of Authors."

GEO. H. NAPHEYS, M. D.— •

DEAR SIR: I have read through your work on "THE TRANSMISSION OF LIFE," and think it calculated to be extensively useful. The subjects discussed are of great importance; the literary style is excellent—terse, vigorous, and perspicuous; the philanthropic zeal evinced is highly creditable to your heart; and the moral and religious spirit of the work is such as to give me a profound respect for the writer. The tendency of the book is good, and good only. It makes vice abhorrent, and virtue cheaply purchased by all the wholesome restraints which it imposes.

I am, dear sir, very faithfully yours,

S. AUSTIN ALLIBONE.

PHILADELPHIA, March 10, 1871.

FROM THE REV. ABNER JACKSON, D.D., LL.D.,

President of Trinity College, Hartford, Ct.

"I have found your volume both interesting and instructive. It contains a large amount of useful information and suggestion in regard to human welfare and duty. Matters of great delicacy, but of great importance in their bearings on health and happiness, are here treated of in a manner to instruct and guide, without shocking, or giving offence. The wide circulation of this work cannot fail to do good."

FROM REV. GEORGE W. SAMSON, D.D.,

President of Columbian College, Washington, D. C.

DR. GEORGE H. NAPHEYS—

MY DEAR SIR: I have read your work, "THE TRANSMISSION OF LIFE," with care, as has my son, who is a practising physician. I regard it as scholarly in its discussion, chaste in its expression, and unobjectionable in every respect. I cannot but commend your worthy effort in this field, where faithful instruction is so needed.

I am, truly,

Your friend and serv't,

GEO. W. SAMSON.

FROM REV. WM. A. STEARNS, D. D., LL. D.,

President of Amherst College, Amherst, Mass.

DR. GEORGE H. NAPHEYS—

. MY DEAR SIR: I have read the advanced sheets of your work entitled "THE TRANSMISSION OF LIFE." It is a difficult subject, which you have treated with propriety and success. The information which you give is of the greatest importance to the community, and especially to young men; and it is a thousand times better that they receive it from a work like yours, than be left to obtain it from sources of doubtful influence, or from bitter experience.

Very respectfully,

Your ob't serv't,

W. A. STEARNS.

FROM THE REV. SANSOM TALBOT, D.D.,
President of Denison University, Granville, Ohio.

"I have read carefully the advance sheets of 'THE TRANSMISSION OF LIFE,' and most heartily join in recommending its publication. The candor and learning of the author are very manifest; the information imparted is just that which the public most need, and the moral tone of the work is altogether pure and elevating."

————

FROM THE REV. W. T. STOTT,
Acting President of Franklin College, Franklin,
Indiana.

"Having examined DR. NAPHEYS' 'TRANSMISSION OF LIFE,' I cheerfully recommend it. There is certainly great need of such information on the subjects treated, and I know no author who has succeeded so well in combining information with safe advice."

FROM THE REV. J. AVERY SHEPHERD, D.D.,

Head Master of St. Clement's Hall, Ellicott City, Md.

"I have examined DR. NAPHEYS' 'TRANSMISSION OF LIFE' with a good deal of care. The subjects treated of are not merely of great interest, they are of *vital importance*. But the misfortune is that many books, in discussing these things, are calculated to do harm, rather than good. My decided impression is that this work *will do good.*"

FROM THE REV. CYRUS NUTT, D.D.,

President of Indiana State University.

"I know of no work, recently issued from the press, calculated to do so much good as 'THE TRANSMISSION OF LIFE.' It contains information of the utmost importance to the individual and the race, and should have a wide circulation."

FROM ANDREW D. WHITE, LL.D.,
President of Cornell University.

GEO. H. NAPHEYS, M. D.—

DEAR SIR: Accept my thanks for the copy of your work, "THE TRANSMISSION OF LIFE."

Your thoughtful and delicate presentation of the subject seems to me to merit great praise. That your discussion will do much good I firmly believe.

I am, sir, very truly yours,

AND. D. WHITE.

PRESIDENT'S ROOMS, ITHACA, N. Y.,
April 20, 1871.

FROM PROF. JOHN S. HART, LL.D.,
Trenton, N. J.

GEO. H. NAPHEYS, M. D.—

DEAR SIR: The examination I have given "THE TRANSMISSION OF LIFE" has impressed me with the care and discretion that you have shown in the treatment of a very difficult subject.

I am very truly yours,

JOHN S. HART.

31

FROM PROF. J. ORDRONAUX, LL. D., M. D.

*Professor of Physiology, Pathology, and Medical
Jurisprudence, Columbian College,
Washington, D. C.*

"The subject treated of in 'THE TRANSMIS-
SION OF LIFE' is certainly one of increasing importance at this day, from the popular degradation it has undergone at the hands of unprincipled writers. It was due, therefore, to the cause
of science, no less than morality, that some competent and honorable physician should reclaim
it from the slough of pollution into which it
had been dragged.

"Your work bears the impress of religious
and scientific truth."

FROM PROF. HARVEY L. BYRD, M. D.,

*Professor of Obstetrics in the Medical Department
of Washington University, Baltimore, Maryland.*

MY DEAR DOCTOR: You have done your work
well. I am one of those who believe the lay-

members of every intelligent community should be educated in a general knowledge of the laws of life, not only for the good of the race, but, if you please, for the good of our profession also. Hence I indorse your efforts in this direction.

I am, with high esteem,

Very truly yours,

HARVEY L. BYRD.

FROM JOHN H. GRISCOM, M. D.,
New York City.

"I have devoted considerable time to the perusal of 'THE TRANSMISSION OF LIFE.' Its numerous and important subjects have been nowhere, to my knowledge, as intelligently and effectively treated. The sanitary advice, so well inculcated, should be learned by every individual, especially by parents for the safety of their children."

FROM THE PHILADELPHIA MEDICAL AND SURGICAL REPORTER, Feb. 4, 1871.

"This book is intended to meet a want which, during the last year, has been urgently expressed by several medical and literary journals in this country and England, namely, to place before the public, in popular yet irreproachable language, what information regarding the hygiene, nature, uses, and abuses of the procreative function in the male, is necessary to protect the individual from the evil consequences of his own folly or ignorance. It will readily be conceived that to discuss such topics clearly, positively, and with benefit to the lay reader, requires no ordinary tact; and we must say that the author has succeeded beyond all our expectations. No one can possibly be harmed by perusing his pages, and none but will be instructed and benefited.

"The work is characterized throughout by sound scientific views, and indicates extensive and careful reading."

FROM THE AMERICAN LITERARY GAZETTE,

Philadelphia, March 15, 1871.

" We feared on taking up this work to find it another of those productions of which there have been enough, either too technical to be intelligible to the general reader, or filled with vague platitudes. Such, however, is far from being the case. It treats in popular and forcible language the medical aspects of some of the most flagrant vices of modern life, born of ignorance of physiological laws. As a work on the preservation of individual health by the special prevention of those disorders peculiar to the male sex, it is filled with most valuable suggestions. Many eminent educators testify to its usefulness and elevated moral tone. Those who are acquainted with the author's 'Physical Life of Woman' will find this new book fully equal to that very popular and extraordinarily successful work, to which it may be said to form a sequel, being addressed to the other sex. We are glad to see that able physicians are coming forward to give to the public information on subjects of such interest to every reading man.

"The appearance of this work, by a physician and writer so well and favorably known as Dr. Napheys, and indorsed by eminent members of the regular profession, educators, and divines, is a sign of the decadence of the exclusive reign of quackery in an important branch of personal hygiene."

FROM THE NEW YORK INDEPENDENT,
March 30, 1871.

"'THE TRANSMISSION OF LIFE' treats of an important and difficult subject with perfect delicacy of thought and expression, and its counsels are eminently sound and judicious. It is, we believe, calculated to do great good."

FROM THE CHRISTIAN SECRETARY,
Hartford, March 15, 1871.

"Dr. Napheys, author of 'The Physical Life of Woman,' has written a book on 'the nature and hygiene of the masculine function.' It is a delicate topic, but one upon which information, properly communicated, is immensely needed by multitudes. Dr. Napheys has treated it with excellent discretion, and his book comes highly recommended by some of the best and wisest men among us. Its perusal may save thousand of persons from untold evils."

FROM THE COLLEGE COURANT,
New Haven, Conn., April 8, 1871.

"The author of 'The Physical Life of Wo-man' has even surpassed that splendid treatise by the masterpiece before us. He was led to commence the work through the belief, formed after an extensive practice in a large city, that

the present amount of suffering and misery
would be greatly lessened if young men and
those having the care of boys understood clearly
the nature and hygiene of their sex. The
papers of to-day are full of the advertisements
of quack doctors and quack medicines, so
worded as to excite the fears and gain the confidence of the hundreds of sufferers, who endure
untold misery in secret rather than consult a
physician by whom they are known. Once in
the hands of these impostors, they may rest
assured that they will not escape until their
money or their lives are gone. The evils which
result to one and all from the violation of the
laws of this function, which are sometimes referred to by parents or teachers, but generally
in a vague and blind manner, Dr. Napheys has
endeavored to treat of in language which can be
readily understood, and to which the most refined cannot object.

"This work ought to be in every one's library,

in every family throughout the country. No young man should be without a copy of it. *It has no equal.*"

————

FROM THE AGE,

Philadelphia, April 24, 1871.

"These are topics of vast importance, which are better suited for private reading than for public discussion on the platform, or in the columns of the newspaper. A knowledge of them, however, is essential to health and happiness. This knowledge a physician of our city, of high character and standing, has put within every one's reach. It is a book for all who are of age to understand it. Parents will find in it wise cautions, and men, young and old, may acquire from it precise knowledge of the physiology of the most important natural functions. In language, moral tone, and purpose, the book is unexceptionable."

FROM THE CHRISTIAN RADICAL,

Pittsburg and New York, May 13, 1871.

"This eminently practical work supplies a want hitherto felt by the major part of the human family. Ignorance in regard to the care and use of the physical functions in man has resulted in untold sufferings, deranging and perverting the system. Formerly there was no alternative but to submit; now, with the aid of this excellent manual, every man of ordinary intelligence will know how to take care of himself; and the hygienic advice imparted in its pages, if put into practical use, will be of the greatest benefit to the race. It is a book that should be read. Every man and woman, too, will be the better for it."

FROM THE LUTHERAN OBSERVER,

Philadelphia, May 5, 1871.

"The subject of this book is at once difficult, delicate, and dangerous; and Dr. Napheys has been singularly successful in treating it in a way to subserve the public health and public morals. It is both scientific and practical. Its style is clear and plain, but does not offend the most refined taste. The information it contains is of vital importance to all, but especially to young men, who too often obtain what information they have on the subject from the demoralizing and licentious publications of charlatans. The fearful and increasing prevalence of certain vices among the young, to which all physicians bear witness, requires that parents and teachers should possess the knowledge which Dr. Napheys' book imparts, and should conscientiously consider their duties in view of the perils which are therein revealed."

FROM THE METHODIST,

New York, May 27, 1871.

"'THE TRANSMISSION OF LIFE,' by Dr. George H. Napheys, is a thorough treatise on the most important physical function. It furnishes information on a subject on which correct information is much needed, which deeply concerns all men and women and their children."

FROM THE CHRISTIAN ADVOCATE,

Nashville, June 3, 1871.

"The delicate and difficult subject is handled with great skill, prudence, and fidelity. The appalling prevalence of licentiousness in all its forms in our country shows that the question must no longer be allowed to rest. The reticence and fastidiousness which have characterized the pulpit, the press, the lecture-room, etc., must give way to earnest, well-directed efforts to stop the plague, which is sapping the foundations of society.

"We call earnestly upon parents, pastors, and teachers to watch over the youth committed to their care with the utmost vigilance, so as to save them from the first transgression—and in order to this, you would do well to procure this volume and give it a serious and careful perusal."

FROM THE PACIFIC CHURCHMAN,

. *San Francisco, May* 18, 1871.

"This is a book for honest, God-fearing men and women. Its subject is one of the most important and sacred in the world, and is treated with the highest scientific and professional ability; and, what is more important, is written from a Christian stand-point. It is one of the good signs of the times that such matters are written upon by honest, able hands, and the field not abandoned to quacks. Every young married couple should possess and read it."

32

www.ingramcontent.com/pod-product-compliance
Lightning Source LLC
Chambersburg PA
CBHW030915270326
41929CB00008B/707